BRAIN-
—————— Compatible
Science
second edition

Margaret Angermeyer Mangan

Skyhorse Publishing

Skyhorse Publishing books may be purchased in bulk at special discounts for sales promotion, corporate gifts, fund-raising, or educational purposes. Special editions can also be created to specifications. For details, contact the Special Sales Department, Skyhorse Publishing, 307 West 36th Street, 11th Floor, New York, NY 10018 or info@skyhorsepublishing.com.

Skyhorse® and Skyhorse Publishing® are registered trademarks of Skyhorse Publishing, Inc.®, a Delaware corporation.

Visit our website at www.skyhorsepublishing.com.

10 9 8 7 6 5 4 3 2 1

Library of Congress Cataloging-in-Publication Data is available on file.

Print ISBN: 978-1-63220-548-3
Ebook ISBN: 978-1-63220-965-8

Printed in the United States of America

Contents

Preface   vi
   A Need for Change   vi
   Metaphors for Reform in Science Education   vii
   Putting Brain-Based Learning to Work in the Science Classroom   vii
   A Paradigm Shift   ix

Acknowledgments   x

Publisher's Acknowledgments   xi

About the Author   xiii

Introduction: Envisioning a New Paradigm for Science Education   xiv
   The Old and the New Science   xiv
   A Change in Metaphors   xv
   Chaos Theory and the New Sciences   xv
   Reform in Science Education   xvi
      Recurring Themes in Science Reform   xvi
      Science Education Reform Initiatives   xvii
   Brain-Based Learning Theory   xviii
      Mind/Brain Principles   xviii
      Nine Essential Classroom Strategies   xix
      Brain-Based Science Classrooms   xx
   Implications of Chaos Theory Principles for Science Education   xxi
   Implications of New Science Principles for Science Education   xxii

SECTION 1   CHAOS THEORY   1

1. Fractals: A Metaphor for Constructivism, Patterns, and Perspective   3
   Background: What Is a Fractal?   3
   Implications of Fractals for Brain-Compatible Science   6
      Wait for Simple Truths to Reveal Greater Complexities   6
      Construct New Meaning From the Old   7
      Search for Repeating Patterns and Different Perspectives   11
   Application for Brain-Compatible Science   12

   Lesson: Changing Perspectives   13

**2. Iteration: A Metaphor for Change in Science Curriculum
   and Information Management**   24
   Background: What Is Iteration?   24
   Implications of Iteration for Brain-Compatible Science   25
      Emphasize Dynamic Process and Flexibility   25
      Look for Similarities in Systems   28
      Feed New Information Into the System   34
   Application for Brain-Compatible Science   35

   Lesson: Magma Mix   35

3. **Sensitive Dependence on Initial Conditions: A Metaphor for Change in Gender Equity and Diversity**   **43**
Background: What Is Sensitive Dependence on Initial Conditions?   44
Implications of Sensitive Dependence on Initial Conditions for
    Brain-Compatible Science   45
        Pay Attention to Details   45
        Show Sensitivity to Unique Dynamics   49
        Accept the Impact of Changing Demographics   51
    Application for Brain-Compatible Science   53
Lesson: A Closer Look at Crystals   **53**

4. **Strange Attractors, Phase Space, and Phase Portraits: A Metaphor for Change in Learning Environments and Habits of Mind**   **60**
Background: What Are Strange Attractors, Phase
    Space, and Phase Portraits?   60
Implications of Strange Attractors, Phase Space, and
    Phase Portraits for Brain-Compatible Science   62
        Trust in the Inherent Order   62
        Set Invisible Boundaries With Freedom to Expand   66
        Offer Greater Freedom and Flexibility   67
        Believe in the Power of Guiding Principles and Values   68
    Application for Brain-Compatible Science   69
Lesson: Dancing Raisins   **70**

5. **Bifurcations and Period Doubling: A Metaphor Featuring Choices, Joy, and Surprise**   **77**
Background: What Are Bifurcations and Period Doubling?   77
Implications of Bifurcation and Period Doubling for
    Brain-Compatible Science   78
        Recognize More Than One Right Way by Providing Choices   79
        Seek Out Turmoil and Surprise   88
        Provide a Joyful Classroom Atmosphere   99
    Application for Brain-Compatible Science   100
Lesson: Invention Bifurcations   **100**

6. **Turbulence: A Changing Perspective of Discipline and Classroom Management**   **107**
Background: What Is Turbulence?   107
Implications of Turbulence for Brain-Compatible Science   108
        Expect the Order to Reemerge   108
        Loosen Up and Have Some Fun   109
        Let Go of the Control to Keep It   113
    Application for Brain-Compatible Science   114
Lesson: Magical Milk Colors   **116**

SECTION 2   NEW SCIENCE PRINCIPLES   **123**
Implications of New Science Principles for Science Education   123

7. **A New Look at Evolutionary Biology: A Metaphor for Change in Curriculum Integration and Localization**   **125**
Background: What Is Evolutionary Biology?   125
Implications of Evolutionary Biology for Brain-Compatible Science   127
        Be Adaptable and Expect to Change   128

Teach in the Boundary Between Steadiness and Oscillation 128
Integrate Curriculum for a Holistic View 131
Think Globally, Act Locally 132
Application for Brain-Compatible Science 133
Lessons: Sand Patterns **133**

8. **A New Look at Self-Organization: A Metaphor for Change in Knowledge Construction** **152**
Background: What Is Self-Organization? 152
Implications of Self-Organization for Brain-Compatible Science 153
Make Connections 153
Focus on Thinking Scientifically Rather Than on
Accumulating Facts and Definitions 155
Look for New Forms 156
Allow for Self-Organization 161
Application for Brain-Compatible Science 162
Lesson: Jabberwocky: Webs and Transformations **162**

9. **Dissipative Structures: A Metaphor to Emphasize the Significance of Community and Values** **173**
Background: What Are Dissipative Structures? 173
Implications of Dissipative Structures for Brain-Compatible Science 175
Stay Open to the Environment 175
Affirm the Power of Community in Learning 176
Commit to a Compassionate Concern for Morality and Humanity 177
Sustain Order Through Growth and Change 178
Application for Brain-Compatible Science 183
Lesson: Endangered Species Boxes **183**

10. **Quantum Mechanics: A Metaphor for Change in the Power of Relationships, Energy, and Paradox** **191**
Background: What Are Quantum Mechanics? 191
Implications of Quantum Mechanics for Brain-Compatible Science 192
Develop and Nurture Relationships 193
Learn to Accept Uncertainty 197
Focus on Energy, Not Things 199
Welcome the Tension of Paradox 200
Application for Brain-Compatible Science 201
Lesson: Quantum Alternatives **201**

SECTION 3 CHAOS THEORY AND NEW SCIENCE PRINCIPLES SUMMARY **207**
A New Approach to Science Education 207
Implications for Teaching 208
Implications for Learning 210
Implications for Assessing 211
Implications for Designing Curricula 211
A Final Glimpse of Chaos 212

Glossary **214**

References **217**

Index **221**

Preface

A NEED FOR CHANGE

Although a challenging, exciting, and relevant science education for all American students is a national goal, quality science programs are missing in many classrooms. Something is very wrong when Americans consult tarot cards and astrologers, believe far-fetched tabloid stories of aliens abducting earthlings, and do not understand how the Earth revolves around the Sun (Hampton & Gallegos, 1994). Sadly, votes cast by these same Americans affect major environmental policies and technological decisions. With society becoming increasingly more dependent on scientific and technological skills, Americans lacking these skills will be severely handicapped for living and working in the twenty-first century.

Science is a creative pursuit that has changed the way teachers view the universe and inspired a need to explore that continually alters the process and quality of human life. Science is an ever-changing process, not simply a collection of facts. Science allows us to experience the excitement and richness of the natural world. In *Science for All Americans,* F. James Rutherford and Andrew Ahlgren (1989) discussed the need for a standard set of recommendations on what understandings and ways of thinking are essential for all citizens in a world shaped by science and technology:

> Education has no higher purpose than preparing people to lead personally fulfilling and responsible lives. For its part, science education—meaning education in science, mathematics, and technology—should help students to develop the understandings and habits of mind they need to become compassionate human beings able to think for themselves and to face life head on. It should equip them also to participate thoughtfully with fellow citizens in building and protecting a society that is open, decent, and vital. America's future—its ability to create a truly just society, to sustain its economic vitality, and to remain secure in a world torn by hostilities—depends more than ever on the character and quality of the education that the nation provides for all of its children. (Rutherford & Ahlgren, 1989, p. v)

Today's children will rely on science and technology more than people do today for jobs, communication, food, health care, energy, and the protection of the environment. The future of the world will someday be in the hands of the children.

METAPHORS FOR REFORM
IN SCIENCE EDUCATION

Students need constant and rigorous exposure to new ideas and methods of think-ing as society continues to move toward a new educational paradigm. Many teach-ing, learning, and assessing strategies and curriculum frameworks are still rooted in the seventeenth century, the Newtonian Age of machines and precision. Newtonian strategies in schools may need to be reassessed, and perhaps replaced, with more modern strategies, reflecting an infinitely more complicated and nonlinear world-view. This is not to imply the elimination of Newton's teachings from science cur-ricula. On the contrary, Newtonian physics still provides the groundwork for much of modern science, and it will always remain central to the scientific knowledge base. While science educators continue to embrace Newton's scientific contributions, the research in this book suggests that educators need to move beyond the Newtonian paradigm to discover a new paradigm more in keeping with the twenty-first century.

With reform in science education a major goal for educators, *Brain-Compatible Science* is intended to offer a glimpse of where that reform could be headed. The appli-cation of chaos theory and new science concepts to construct metaphors of change in science education just might motivate teachers to discover new ways of thinking about teaching, learning, assessing, and designing science curriculum. Chaos theory with its incredible metaphors of order emerging out of chaos brings new vigor into science education, creating a new way of viewing old problems. Looking deeply into the unpredictable randomness of these contemporary theories, science educators may find new patterns, meaning, and direction to revitalize their teaching. A redirected vision for the future, a holistic new framework for brain-compatible science, and a more productive way of viewing the earth and the universe could emerge.

PUTTING BRAIN-BASED LEARNING
TO WORK IN THE SCIENCE CLASSROOM

Brain-Compatible Science defines and summarizes essential principles of chaos and new science theory, using them to organize a review of the most recent reform in science education and brain-based learning research. Six chaos and four new science principles are explored to discover their implications for teaching, learning, assess-ing, and designing curriculum for brain-compatible science education. The book is most appropriate for teachers of grades 3–8, although many of the lesson plans and assessment ideas can be easily adapted for younger or older students.

Also included in the book are numerous lesson plans, science labs, reproducible student handouts, a lesson plan guide, assessment rubrics, checklists, lab reports, and even cooperative group roles for the science classroom. Everything that a science teacher needs to be effective and current can be found within the pages of this book. Best practices in science education are discussed, with topics including:

- Brain-based learning theory
- Gender equity
- Cultural diversity and changing classroom demographics
- Classroom management

- Multiple intelligences theory
- Constructivist learning
- Science inquiry
- Higher-level thinking strategies
- Alternative forms of assessment
- Curriculum integration
- Cooperative learning
- Community in learning
- Guiding principles and values

The Introduction provides an overview of the old and the new science, which creates the impetus for reform in science education. The Introduction also introduces chaos theory and the new sciences, the major reform initiatives in science education, and brain-based learning theory. Following the Introduction, the book is divided into two major sections, Chaos Theory and New Science Principles, and the third section summarizes the implications of chaos theory and new science principles for teaching, learning, assessing, and designing curriculum. At the back of the book is a glossary to define the chaos theory and new science terminology.

Although much of the current thinking in chaos theory and the new sciences, as well as the latest knowledge of brain-based learning, parallels the recurrent themes found in the science education reform literature, no scientific evidence and very few studies exist to date to determine if there is a one-to-one correlation between the dynamics at an atomic level and human dynamics. Many of the images and metaphors discussed in *Brain-Compatible Science* are based on complicated, nonlinear equations and scientific principles that are beyond the scope of the research purpose.

Each chapter in the first two sections includes the following:

- Background information to introduce, define, and discuss the chaos or new science principle
- Implications of chaos or new science principle for brain-compatible science featuring best practices in science education
- A detailed science lesson featuring chaos and new science theory
- Additional lessons, assessments, and surprises
- Concept Web, which includes a summary of the implications for science education and additional lesson ideas
- Navigating the Road to Change in Science Education chart comparing three paradigms for science education:
  – Too Much Order: a traditional, conservative view
  – On the Edge: the preferred view fostering creativity, growth, and renewal
  – Too Much Chaos: an unstructured, liberal view

The 10 featured lessons include the following components:

- Grade level appropriateness (grades 3–8, adaptable for others)
- Chaos or New Science Connection providing background
- Curriculum Connection
- Targeted National Science Education Standards
- Objectives
- Materials needed for the activity
- Preactivity discussion to prepare students for the activity

- Procedure providing step-by-step instructions for the teacher
- Closure to appropriately wrap up the lesson
- Questions and extensions to pursue the topic in greater depth
- Technology Connection suggesting possible Web sites to visit

The 10 featured lesson plans, along with other ideas presented in this book, are designed to incite a paradigm shift in science education. The lesson plans are suitable for integration into existing science curricula, and although they contain references to chaos theory and the new sciences, the intent is not to teach chaos theory directly or to imply that chaos theory principles belong in science curricula. Certain elements of the principles may be appropriate, however, and certainly could be offered as enrichment alternatives for interested students, or the principles could simply be viewed metaphorically as a means of motivating educators to embrace changes in their vision of what embodies quality science education.

A PARADIGM SHIFT

The paradigm shift from a textbook-driven program to a process-oriented science curriculum has been a gradual evolution, disquieting for some, energizing for others, and not without the usual frustrations that accompany change. During my years in the science classroom, a growing number of teachers have plunged whole-heartedly into the new science education paradigm. Although I see a significant change overall, many teachers, especially those in elementary classrooms, still prefer the old way.

Too little preparation and collaboration time, difficulties obtaining supplies, lack of confidence, not enough ongoing staff development in science, and the school structure itself hinder many teachers' ability to initiate a more expeditious change. Pulled in many directions, teachers must compact lessons for gifted students; individualize instruction for learning disabled (LD) students; integrate technology into their teaching; and work around gym, art, and music schedules. Add in their regular correcting, planning, grading, disciplining, and conferencing, and today's teachers never have enough time! As teachers continue to learn and evolve together, I hope that new ideas for science teaching, learning, assessing, and designing curriculum will emerge, and that somehow the process will simplify.

Moving into the twenty-first century, the wondrous images of chaos theory may provide science educators with fresh insights and offer a new sense of direction for science education. As we search for contemporary strategies to rejuvenate curriculum and inspire learning, and as we invent new ways of teaching and assessing our children, I believe that we have much to learn from chaos theory principles. The haunting metaphors and computer-generated fractals have already changed the way I think about the world and my role as a science educator. I hope that my insights, serving as a "strange attractor," will inspire others to do the same.

Acknowledgments

Many people have inspired me throughout the research and writing stages of both editions of my book. I wish to acknowledge all the authors who appear in my references, especially Renate Caine, Geoffrey Caine, Stephanie Pace Marshall, John Cleveland, Margaret Wheatley, Myron Kellner-Rogers, Robert Garmston, and Bruce Wellman. Their research and works strengthened my resolve to look to chaos theory and the new sciences as metaphors for reform in science education and gave me confidence to trust in my own thinking. I am indebted to Stephen Hawking, James Gleick, John Briggs, David Peat, Ian Prigogine, Isabelle Stengers, Rosemary Grant, Peter Grant, and Leonard Shlain for their inspired research; to Loren Eiseley for his insightful metaphors; and to Benoit Mandelbrot for his beautiful fractal images.

I am also grateful for Project 2061's *Benchmarks for Science Literacy,* developed by the American Association for the Advancement of Science, and the National Research Council's *National Science Education Standards.* I thank Robert Marzano, Myra Sadker, David Sadker, Howard Gardner, Robin Fogarty, Jonathan Weiner, Alfie Kohn, Eric Jensen, Lawrence Lowrey, Ian Jukes, Ted McCain, Ken O'Connor, Robert Slavin, William Parrett, Robert Barr, Linda Elder, Richard Paul, and again Geoffrey and Renate Caine for providing the conceptual framework for my book.

I extend a special thanks to Dr. Robert Pavlik, previously from Cardinal Stritch University and currently associated with Marquette University's Institute for the Transformation of Learning. His outstanding insight and leadership allowed me the freedom to define my own "phase space" within which to understand my work. I also acknowledge my friends and colleagues in the Whitefish Bay School District who, until I retired in 2005, provided me with wonderfully chaotic situations every day.

I especially wish to thank my friends and family; my husband for his patience, kindness, love, and encouragement throughout the research and writing process of both editions; and my parents who instilled me with productive habits of mind, and my students who have taught me more than they will ever know.

Publisher's Acknowledgments

Skyhorse Publishing gratefully acknowledges the contributions of the following reviewers:

George Bodner
Professor of Science Education
Purdue University, West Lafayette, IN

Barry Farris
Dean of Science and Mathematics
Columbia Academy, Columbia, TN

Mandy Frantti
Science and Mathematics Teacher
Munising High School, Munising, MI

Susan Goins
Gifted Education Teacher
Howard Middle School, Macon, GA

Debra Greenstone
Science Teacher
Mount Pleasant High School, Wilmington, DE

Susan Leeds
Science and Gifted Curriculum Leader
Howard Middle School, Orlando, FL

Wendy Skaggs
Fifth Grade Teacher
Beech Hill Elementary School, Summerville, SC

With love for my husband, Richard Mangan

About the Author

Margaret Mangan is an award-winning educator whose teaching experience spans 36 years in Grades 1 through 8 in Wisconsin schools. Most recently, Margaret taught science at Whitefish Bay Middle School, and prior to that she was a science specialist for elementary schools in Whitefish Bay. Operating from a cart, Margaret traveled to 41 classrooms a week to teach hands-on science to first through fifth graders. Drawing from inquiry, constructivist, and brain-based learning models, Margaret uses a variety of teaching strategies that address diverse learning styles. In addition, she has written and presented numerous hands-on science workshops for teachers. Margaret has a Master's of Education degree in professional development with an emphasis in science education from Cardinal Stritch University in Milwaukee. Recently retired, she resides in Whitefish Bay, Wisconsin, with her husband, Richard.

Introduction

Envisioning a New Paradigm for Science Education

We do not throw out everything we learned about quantification; we simply extend our picture of reality, which has suddenly become larger. Nor does the new paradigm mean that the new sciences are in some way fully formed and fully understood, or that different theorists and practitioners even fully understand and agree with each other. Rather, we are finding immensely powerful and all-embracing new ways to perceive and describe trends and patterns over time. With that come new ways of acting and interacting with our world.

Geoffrey & Renate Nummela Caine (1997a, p. 55)

THE OLD AND THE NEW SCIENCE

Searching for meaning in the universe, scientists and philosophers throughout history have sought after simple laws and truths to explain the mysteries of the world. Newton's seventeenth-century view of the universe was ordered, predictable, and measurable, like the mechanical pendulum motion of a clock. Simple cause-and-effect laws governed Newton's deterministic outlook that things were more important than relationships and that parts could be put back together again. Time had no real significance because of the precise nature of the universe. Matter and energy were thought of as separate entities in a step-by-step, sequential world. The accepted view in Newton's day was highly rational, logical, and linear, with little parts in the great machine of life working together in factory-like precision to achieve perfection and order. Finding solutions to problems was more important than the problem-solving process.

With a more connected view of space and time, Albert Einstein's theory of relativity challenged Newton's linear perspective and set the stage for the development of quantum mechanics. In the randomness of a quantum universe, different outcomes arise from identical physical situations. A paradigm shift began with a movement from the industrial Newtonian outlook toward nonlinear, complex, and dynamical systems, which are open to and readily exchange information with the environment.

A CHANGE IN METAPHORS

Stephanie Pace Marshall (1995) asserted that as a society people have used the science of the times for grounding institutions, including schools. Explaining how school design has paralleled Newtonian thought, Marshall maintained that the time has come to adopt a paradigm more in keeping with current scientific thinking. She replaced the Newtonian clock metaphor with a kaleidoscope metaphor, more appropriate for a continually changing, quantum universe. The factory paradigm schools contradict everything that Marshall wrote about human potential and capability and what the neurosciences teach about how the brain functions and learns. Learners search for meaning, exploration and discovery, adventure, integration, and connection. Therefore, a current paradigm would emphasize meaningful, risk-free learning opportunities, compatible with current brain research.

In another work Marshall (in Hesselbein, Goldsmith, & Beckhard, 1997) summarized her vision of organizational reform, including the redefinition of schools for the twenty-first century. Marshall averred that the Newtonian mechanistic model has changed into a much more fluid, organic, and biological metaphor as new understandings about adaptive systems and brain-based learning theory have surfaced. Building on discoveries in fields as diverse as quantum physics, systems theory, chaos mathematics, evolutionary biology, neuroscience, and cognitive science, revolutionary insights about the universe, the natural world, and human learning have all converged into a new understanding of how human systems continue to grow, evolve, and learn (or change). Marshall envisioned an integrated holistic learning community, emphasizing connection, purposeful meaning, dynamic relationships, and "the evolutionary nature of the human experience itself."

Geoffrey and Renate Nummela Caine (1997a, 1997b) also found inspiration from chaos theory and the new sciences. They agreed that the time has come to change metaphors from the mechanistic worldview to an unpredictable living systems paradigm. Believing that education is poised on "the edge of chaos," which they prefer to call the "edge of possibility," the Caines described how nonlinear, highly complex systems actually thrive when they are in a state of disequilibrium. The Caines' two outstanding books, *Education on the Edge of Possibility* (1997a) and *Unleashing the Power of Perceptual Change* (1997b), describe their work with schools to implement brain-based teaching and learning, as well as their perceptions about the process of educational change. Organizing teachers into process groups that provided them with both support and freedom to question their deepest assumptions about teaching and learning, the Caines expected that this deep questioning would shift teachers' mental models and lead to changes in education (see Chapter 2).

CHAOS THEORY AND THE NEW SCIENCES

A major challenge to Newtonian thinking came from chaos theory, a significant mathematical development of the twentieth century. James Gleick (1987) described how gifted mathematicians, physicists, and biologists dared to look at the world differently, and in the process discovered the science of chaos. Randomness and unpredictability manifest this new science, describing the way systems change over time. Chaos theory reveals how many constantly changing systems are extremely sensitive to their initial state. Through simple nonlinear equations, people may arrive at very complex and unpredictable results.

With the world evolving in cycles as energy transforms matter into self-similar patterns, systems that look chaotic have a deeper order within. Chaos is found within dynamical systems, or processes in motion, in every discipline (e.g., astronomy, biology, economics, population dynamics, and engineering). Gleick (1987) explained how simple, deterministic systems breed complexity and how systems too complex for traditional mathematics obey simple laws. Systems may be as large as the universe or as small as an atom. Examples include the motion of stars and galaxies, changing weather systems, chemical changes, pendulum motion, and the rise and fall of populations (Devaney, 1992). Additional examples include the human brain and schools undergoing change.

Generally speaking, a dynamical system is an evolving, self-organizing network. Moving away from the either/or Newtonian paradigm to a new worldview of both/and, people need not choose between the two. Order and chaos exist simultaneously. Structures of order are embedded within chaotic and unpredictable systems. Cause and effect, space and time appear unrelated as people proceed nonsequentially, creating order out of chaos in a world of many paradoxes.

Marshall (1995) wrote about a nonlinear, adaptive, dynamic, and pattern-seeking world of inherent order, interconnections, and potentials. Increasingly complex behaviors arise from very simple rules that govern the relationships of individuals to each other. Deep inner creativity and coherence weave the fabric of nature. Chaos theory and the new sciences tell educators that to reinvent schools (and science education), they must look at teaching, learning, assessing, and designing curriculum from different perspectives, viewing them as dynamic, adaptive, self-organizing systems inherently designed to transform and renew themselves through growth and change.

REFORM IN SCIENCE EDUCATION

Also paralleling the movement from Newtonian thinking to a more holistic worldview, current reform in science education centers around a movement from the traditional textbook and test, direct-instruction, and learning-alone-through-competition approach, to a process-driven curriculum, featuring constructivist, hands-on, inquiry-based activities.

An advocate for changing the metaphor to define the design of science curricula, Lawrence Lowery (1996a) explained how new programs were being developed to change the way that science is taught in our schools. Lowery wrote about "engaging the learner in the process of actively constructing and restructuring knowledge . . . within developmentally appropriate complex networks that progressively increase in conceptual depth and consistency as students advance through the grades" (p. 8). When change occurs in science education, new metaphors will emerge.

Recurring Themes in Science Reform

Strong themes recur throughout the science reform literature (American Association for the Advancement of Science (AAAS) Project 2061, 1993; Holloway, 2000; Lowery, 1996a, 1996b, 1997; National Research Council, 1996; National Science Teachers Association, 1998; Willis, 1995; Zemelman, Daniels, & Hyde, 2005). Recurring themes include the following:

- Feature a process-oriented, hands-on, inquiry approach.
- Incorporate brain-based learning research.
- Emphasize higher-level thinking skills.
- Provide a more in-depth approach to fewer topics.
- Encourage students to construct meaning, making connections to everyday life.
- Teachers guide and facilitate.
- Integrate science with other subject areas.
- Integrate science with technology.
- Emphasize learning science concepts over memorizing terms and facts.
- Consider multiple intelligences and alternative ways of learning.
- Insist that science is equal for all students regardless of gender, race, culture, or differences in educational needs.
- Feature cooperative and collaborative learning.
- Offer alternative forms of assessment.
- Value student questions, strengths, interests, and needs.
- Provide opportunities for discussion and debate.
- Support a respectful classroom community.

Designed to help students view science in a more connected way, the new science education paradigm focuses on relevant topics integrated into other curricular areas, emphasizes brain-based learning, and promotes collaboration and teamwork in flexibly structured classrooms with many things happening at the same time.

Science Education Reform Initiatives

Two key science education reform initiatives include Project 2061, developed by the American Association for the Advancement of Science (1993), and the *National Science Education Standards,* developed by the National Research Council (1996).

Project 2061

In 1985 the American Association for the Advancement of Science (AAAS) founded Project 2061 to encourage all Americans to become literate in science, mathematics, and technology. Two major publications, focusing on science curriculum, assured the AAAS a place in United States science education reform history, *Science for All Americans* (Rutherford & Ahlgren, 1989) and *Benchmarks for Science Literacy* (AAAS, 1993) are the foundation for Project 2061's continuing efforts to make a significant contribution to science education reform. More recent publications, *Atlas of Science Literacy* (AAAS, 2001a) and *Designs for Science Literacy* (AAAS, 2001b) are examples of how Project 2061 continues to facilitate change.

Science for All Americans (Rutherford & Ahlgren, 1989), emphasizing that science is for everyone, defines a set of literacy goals in science, mathematics, and technology that all students should know and be able to do by the time they finish high school. *Benchmarks for Science Literacy* (AAAS, 1993), prepared as a tool to be used to transform learning in science, mathematics, and technology, translates the scientific literacy goals in *Science for All Americans* into K–12 benchmarks. *Benchmarks for Science Literacy* identifies thresholds rather than average or advanced performance, concentrates on the common core of learning, and focuses on extending content to explain how students arrive at scientific conclusions. *Benchmarks for Science Literacy* states that although goals for knowing and doing can be described separately, they should be learned together in many different contexts so that they may also be used together in life outside of school to make science relevant.

National Science Education Standards Project

Developed by the National Research Council (1996), the *National Science Education Standards* were designed as a vision to enable the nation to meet the goal that all students should achieve scientific literacy, and with the assumption that "lifelong scientific literacy begins with attitudes and values established in the earliest years" (p. 18). The standards aim to prepare students for living in a technical and information-rich world after high school graduation. Besides clarifying important content standards, the national goals feature teaching, professional development, and assessment standards for science educators; program standards that describe the conditions necessary for quality science programs; and system standards that address resources and coordination at the state and federal level.

The content standards focus on fundamental concepts, going beyond the traditional life sciences and the physical and earth sciences. Science is inquiry. Science is an active process. "Learning science is something students do, not something that is done to them" (National Research Council, 1996, p. 20). Shifting the emphasis from teachers presenting information and covering science topics to students learning science through active involvement, the standards emphasize the teaching and learning of basic concepts in the context of investigations.

The assessment standards state that science educators should assess with a variety of methods for a variety of purposes, not just assigning a grade. Useful for decision making and as a catalyst for improvement, the standards were not written to be followed exactly but to be seriously considered in the development of science curriculum. Included with the *National Science Education Standards* are changing emphasis charts, envisioning change throughout the science educational system. Major points that should receive less emphasis or more emphasis are listed and compared. Included are charts on standards for teaching, professional development, assessment, content, program, and system. Representing thousands of hours of dedicated work by science educators, scientists, business people, and government officials, these charts may help to guide educators toward a new science education paradigm.

BRAIN-BASED LEARNING THEORY

Mind/Brain Principles

As the human brain searches for order in the patterns of the world, and knowledge and skills are acquired through experience, learning naturally occurs. Brain-based learning recognizes the need for constructing knowledge by reorganizing complex, prior conceptions into new knowledge through questioning and readjusting knowledge to fit with real-life experiences (Gardner, 1991). Renate and Geoffrey Caines' mind/brain principles (2006) provide a theoretical justification for brain-based learning, including the learning of science. Each principle will be explored in greater depth throughout *Brain-Compatible Science*.

Principle 1. The brain is a complex adaptive system.

Principle 2. The brain is a social brain.

Principle 3. The search for meaning is innate.

Principle 4. The search for meaning occurs through "patterning."

Principle 5. Emotions are critical to patterning.

Principle 6. Every brain simultaneously perceives and creates parts and wholes.

Principle 7. Learning involves both focused attention and peripheral perception.

Principle 8. Learning always involves conscious and unconscious processes.

Principle 9. We have at least two ways of organizing memory.

Principle 10. Learning is developmental.

Principle 11. Complex learning is enhanced by challenge and inhibited by threat.

Principle 12. Every brain is uniquely organized.

Brain-based learning is an approach to education which, when integrated throughout educational systems, will most certainly redefine current practices of teaching, learning, assessing, and designing curriculum.

In one of his numerous books, *Brain-Based Learning* (2000a), Eric Jensen integrated what is known about the human brain with educational practices. Jensen included success strategies to increase motivation, meaning and recall. He defined a brain-based approach as "learning in accordance with the way the brain is naturally designed to learn" (p. 6). A brain-based approach encourages educators to consider the way the brain works when making educational decisions. "By using what we know about the brain, . . . we can reach more learners, more often and with less misses. Quite simply it is learning with the brain in mind" (Jensen, 2000a, p. 6). Although Jensen cautioned educators not to base a school on brain-based learning research alone, to ignore the findings would be irresponsible (Jensen, 2000b).

Nine Essential Classroom Strategies

Mid-continent Research for Education and Learning (McREL) researchers have identified nine brain-compatible, instructional strategies that are most likely to improve student achievement across all content areas and grade levels. Many of these strategies featured in the book *Classroom Instruction That Works* by Robert Marzano, Debra Pickering, and Jane Pollock (2001), will be explained more thoroughly throughout the book *Brain-Compatible Science, Second Edition*. The nine strategies are:

- Identifying similarities and differences
- Summarizing and note taking
- Reinforcing effort and providing recognition
- Homework and practice
- Nonlinguistic representations
- Cooperative learning
- Setting objectives and providing feedback

- Generating and testing hypothesis
- Cues, questions, and advance organizers

Brain-Based Science Classrooms

"How does the brain learn science?" asked John Holloway (2000), and "Can we improve student achievement in science by using new knowledge about learning?" Holloway continued with a review of research advocating a constructivist approach to enhance conceptual growth and a positive classroom atmosphere providing an environment conducive to brain-compatible science learning. Holloway presented the research of Anderson and Stewart (1997), who concluded that teachers in brain-based science classrooms encourage students to articulate theories; elaborate on responses; ask thoughtful, open-ended questions; reflect on experiences; and predict future outcomes. These teachers tune into student misconceptions and provide wait time during class discussions. They empower students by encouraging student autonomy, leadership, and interaction. They encourage student initiative by allowing student thinking to alter the course of a lesson. Holloway also reviewed the research of Pinkerton (1994), who experimented with teaching techniques to make his science classroom more brain compatible. Pinkerton discovered that his students learned better when they were actively engaged in long-term, thematic projects featuring enriched language and alternative forms of assessment.

Lawrence Lowery (1998) stated that "although the individual constructs basic knowledge through experience, the quality of the construction depends on how well the brain organizes and stores the relationships between and among aspects in the event" (p. 27). The brain constructs knowledge by taking in data through the body's five senses. Interest, prior knowledge, and richness of the environment determine how constructions develop in a student's brain. Hands-on science activities activate student interests and stimulate connections in the brain to promote new scientific understandings.

> Today, thoughtful schools and school systems are engaged in systemic changes whereby new curriculums, especially in mathematics and science, are a fundamental component of those changes. And the array of quality, research-based curriculums is continuing to grow as scientists, mathematicians, and educators work together to study learning and improve the ways by which important ideas are taught. (Lowery, 1998, p. 30)

Entering the twenty-first century, changes in science are imminent. Growth and change in science education must follow suit to ensure a healthy future for our world.

Implications of Chaos Theory Principles for Science Education

Fractals

Wait for simple truths to reveal greater complexities.
Construct new meaning from the old.
Search for repeating patterns and different perspectives.

Iteration

Emphasize dynamic process and flexibility.
Look for similarities in systems.
Feed new information into the system.

Sensitive Dependence on Initial Conditions

Pay attention to details.
Show sensitivity to unique dynamics.
Accept the impact of changing demographics.

Strange Attractors, Phase Space, and Phase Portraits

Trust in the inherent order.
Set invisible boundaries with freedom to expand.
Offer greater freedom and flexibility.
Believe in the power of guiding principles and values.

Bifurcation and Period Doubling

Recognize more than one right way by providing choices.
Seek out turmoil and surprise.
Provide a joyful classroom atmosphere.

Turbulence

Expect the order to reemerge.
Loosen up and have some fun.
Let go of the control to keep it.

Implications of New Science Principles for Science Education

Evolutionary Biology

Be adaptable and expect to change.
Teach in the boundary between steadiness and oscillation.
Integrate curriculum for a holistic view.
Think globally, act locally.

Self-Organization

Make connections.
Look for new forms.
Focus on thinking scientifically rather than on
accumulating facts and definitions.
Allow for self-organization.

Dissipative Structures

Stay open to the environment.
Affirm the power of community in learning.
Commit to a compassionate concern for morality and humanity.
Sustain order through growth and change.

Quantum Mechanics

Develop and nurture relationships.
Learn to accept uncertainty.
Focus on energy, not things.
Welcome the tension of paradox.

SECTION 1

Chaos Theory

Section 1 presents six chaos theory principles and their implications for reform in science education. *Chaos* means order without predictability or persistent instability. The science of chaos, a significant mathematical development of the twentieth century, presents a random and unpredictable world with systems that change over time. The world evolves in cycles as energy transforms matter into self-similar patterns. Systems that look chaotic have a deeper order within. Metaphors from chaos theory, the science reform initiatives, and the brain-based learning research, including the mind/brain principles proposed by Geoffrey and Renate Caine (2006), aid teachers in reconceptualizing science education by removing teachers from their traditional paradigms and guiding them to redefine science education for a nonlinear and much more complicated future world.

1

Fractals

A Metaphor for Constructivism, Patterns, and Perspective

Why is geometry often described as cold and dry? One reason lies in its inability to describe the shape of a cloud, a mountain, a coastline, or a tree. Clouds are not spheres, mountains are not cones, coastlines are not circles, and bark is not smooth, nor does lightning travel in a straight line.

Benoit Mandelbrot (1983, p. 1)

BACKGROUND: WHAT IS A FRACTAL?

Perhaps the most frequently studied and visually appealing principle of chaos theory is the spectacular, computer-generated set of fractals, first conceived by modern mathematician Benoit Mandelbrot (1983). Frustrated with the perfectly regular shapes of Euclidean geometry, Mandelbrot developed a whole new geometry more in tune with the natural world. He called the irregular shapes *fractals*, meaning fragmented and irregular. Trees exhibit a chaotic growth plan. Clouds change constantly. Mountains result from a combination of tectonic forces and erosion processes. Nature evolves in irregular patterns: Bird beaks, canyons, sand, and waves are intricately fashioned by the dynamic forces of growth, evolution, and erosion.

Whether viewed from afar or from a closer perspective, natural irregularities repeat on smaller and smaller scales until they are no longer discernible to the human eye. The delicate shape of a fern or a feather does not behave in straight lines and perfect curves. Viewing patterns within patterns, Mandelbrot (1983) explained:

Nature exhibits not simply a higher degree but an altogether different level of complexity. The number of distinct scales of length of natural patterns is for all practical purposes infinite. (p. 1)

3

Nature's patterns are never exact.

The Koch snowflake, well-known to mathematicians, is a fractal shape that was first constructed in 1904 by Helge von Koch, a Swedish mathematician. (To construct a Koch snowflake, see Figure 1.1.) When magnified and rotated, exactly four pieces of the snowflake's edge, known as the Koch curve, yield the entire edge of the snowflake (Figure 1.2). Congruent circles may be drawn around the original triangle and each transformed view of the snowflake as it progresses from simple to complex. Although the snowflake always fits within a finite area, the perimeter of the snowflake is infinite. No piece of string could ever be long enough to fit completely around the snowflake's edge (Devaney, 1992).

The Koch snowflake may be compared to a lake or ocean shoreline when viewed from a variety of different perspectives. Coastlines become increasingly longer as more and more detail is included in the measure. When viewed from an airplane, much of the shoreline detail is smoothed over and lost; however, when viewed from a closer perspective, more details appear, and the perimeter increases. Unless a scale is agreed on, all coastlines are infinite in length (Briggs & Peat, 1989). No wonder reference books give conflicting mileage for the same shoreline. A snail traveling around each tiny sand pebble would crawl farther than a deer would leap! Imagine following the shoreline journey of a microscopic organism.

Mandelbrot (1983) retold a story in which young children are asked how long they think the coastline of the eastern United States is. Children understand immediately that the coastline is as long as they want to make it, and that the perimeter increases as each bay and inlet is measured with increasingly smaller scales. Margaret Wheatley (1994) discussed the futility of searching for precise measures for fractal systems:

> Since there can be no definite measurement, what is important in a fractal landscape is to note the quality of the system—its complexity and distinguishing shapes, and how it differs from other fractals. (p. 129)

Mandelbrot's coastline question has no final answer.

Mandelbrot (1983) discovered a surprising paradox emerging from chaos theory and fractal geometry. Complex fractals may be generated from a simple mathematical process. In the 1980s, using computer technology, Mandelbrot first viewed the fractal set that has been described as the most beautiful image of modern mathematics (Figure 1.3). A voyage through the Mandelbrot Set reveals finer and finer scales of increasing complexity, sea-horse tails, pinecone spirals, and island molecules all resembling the whole set (Gleick, 1987). The beautiful jewel-like shapes are symbolic of the nonlinear, modern world so full of complexities and seemingly insolvable problems.

If simple leads to complex, could not the reverse be true? Margaret Wheatley and Myron Kellner-Rogers (1996) believed so when they discussed how people seek organization and order in the world, even when chaos is present at the start. "Life is attracted to order—order gained through wandering explorations into new relationships and new possibilities" (p. 6). Perhaps complex problems have simple solutions that remain hidden from view until the time is right for their simple truths to come forth.

Paradoxes such as simple to complex often appear in today's world. Paradoxes enrich people's thinking by providing them with more choices, allowing them to view things differently, and opening up the world for them to generate and create

Directions for Koch Snowflake

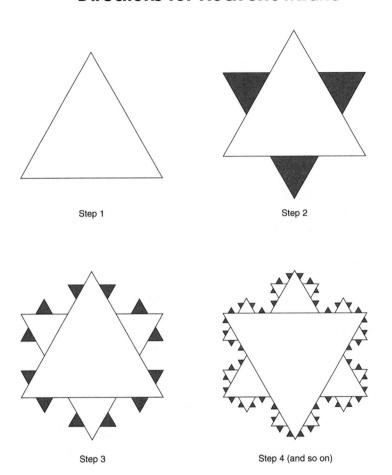

Take the middle one-third of each side of an equilateral triangle and attach a new triangle one-third the size. Continue attaching smaller-scale triangles onto the middle third of each new triangle side, resulting in a self-similar and increasingly more intricate snowflake pattern (Gleick, 1987).

Figure 1.1

Koch Curve

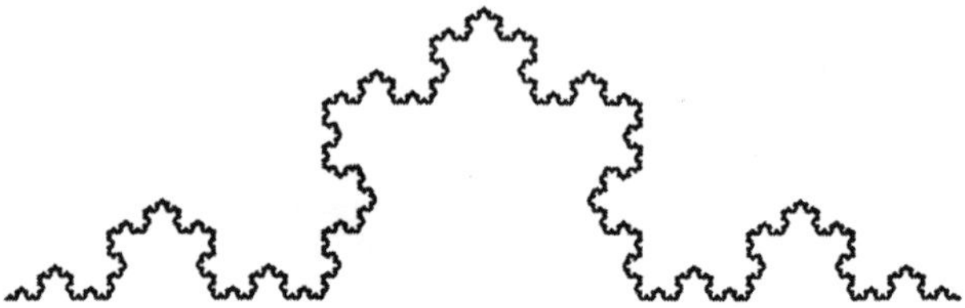

Figure 1.2

their own meaning. John Briggs and F. David Peat (1989) asserted that in the future fractals will undoubtedly reveal more about how chaos hides within regularity and how stability and order can arise out of turbulence and chance. New ways of doing and being may be contained within the old. Unusual and surprising patterns may emerge when least expected. If teachers were to look deeply within themselves for answers, hidden patterns, and universal themes, perhaps they could generate novel purpose and vitality to science education.

IMPLICATIONS OF FRACTALS FOR BRAIN-COMPATIBLE SCIENCE

Three implications of fractals for brain-compatible science are (1) wait for simple truths to reveal greater complexities, (2) construct new meaning from the old, and (3) search for repeating patterns and different perspectives. Parallels exist linking fractal theory to brain-compatible science. Teachers need only to look at the many natural patterns surrounding them to understand the innate ability of the human brain to make connections by constructing new meaning from the old.

Wait for Simple Truths to Reveal Greater Complexities

Wheatley and Kellner-Rogers (1996) raised significant questions about the role of structure. They wondered what people could accomplish if they stopped trying to impose structure on the world and instead found a simpler way of doing things by working with life's natural tendency to organize. Educators might ask this question of themselves as they begin a lesson with their students. Life's events are patterned similarly yet differently each day. Their beautiful, fractal patterns occasionally reveal themselves, often times taking people by surprise. Will people be receptive to the simple truths of life's events when patterns emerge? Perhaps fractals can teach educators something about simplifying the educational process.

Teachers tell students to line up, get it straight, sit up straight, don't get out of line, toe the line, stay on the mark. But where is the line? Where are the mark and the straight? Perhaps they are still back in the age of machines and clockwork precision. Teachers' zest for lesson planning, structuring, and assessing often overshadows the sparks of creative insight that they forget to look for. In a frenzy to get things done and to prepare for tomorrow or next week, teachers rush from one thing to the next, missing out on beautiful moments of fractal simplicity. Perhaps teachers need to slow down, allowing their brains to reveal the simple truths hidden in the complex schedules and endless lists of things to do. Freed from the complexities that get in the way of life's natural tendency to organize, teachers may find a much more creative and energetic form of complexity, one that leads to new discoveries and new understandings about the educational process.

Construct New Meaning From the Old

Geoffrey and Renate Caine, current leaders in brain and learning theory, believe in the brain's constructivist capacity to make patterned connections among the learning task, current experiences, past knowledge, and future behavior. Learning occurs when new information is added to the existing information within the brain and linkages develop between the old and new elements. Students construct their own meaning by reflecting on and integrating new science knowledge with the old. As concepts "construct," broader and more inclusive concepts develop. In one of their 12 mind/brain principles (see Introduction), the Caines (2006) stated that learning involves both conscious and unconscious processes as understanding continues to construct in the brain long after the original learning experience. Teachers need to present material in different ways, using real-life examples to make learning meaningful.

Stephanie Pace Marshall (1999) compared the old educational paradigm with the new in her 13 "principles for the new story of learning," which closely connect to recent theories about learning and the human brain. She explained how the purpose of education is a lifelong acquisition of wisdom, and that prior learning is essential to future learning. Learning is a dynamic process of constructing meaning through personal inquiry and pattern formulation. Students must be fully engaged through the reflective exploration of essential and deeply human questions.

In his constructivist dimensions of learning model, Robert Marzano (1992) described how acquiring and integrating knowledge occur when information already known and understood is used to make sense out of newly acquired knowledge. Then knowledge is extended and refined as students develop new insights, ideas, and discoveries about things they already know through questioning, comparing, classifying, inducing, deducing, and analyzing errors. Finally, students learn to use new knowledge meaningfully as they reflect on the knowledge and apply it to their everyday lives. Using knowledge meaningfully involves the use of higher-level thinking skills, decision making, investigation, experimental inquiry, problem solving, and invention.

For example, in a third- or fourth-grade lab about static electricity, begin with a short discussion about personal experiences the students have had with this form of electrical energy. Many students have at some time rubbed balloons against their hair and experienced it standing on end. Students usually mention being shocked while walking across a rug, touching a light switch, or when combing their hair on a dry day. Groups of four students can go on to experiment with a variety of materials to investigate static electricity as an energy source. They can try various methods to get balloons to stick to the wall. They can rub two balloons with pieces of wool

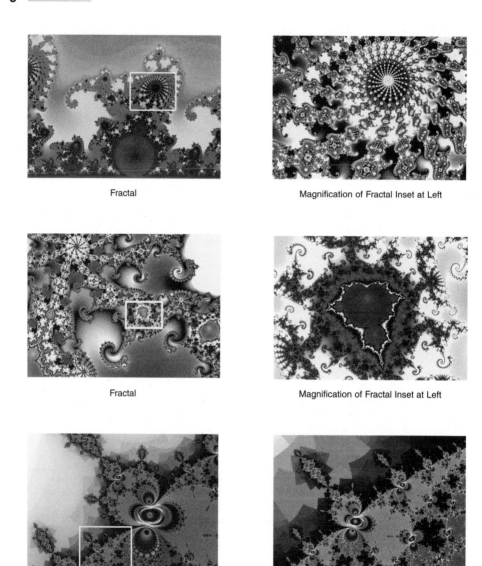

Fractal

Magnification of Fractal Inset at Left

Fractal

Magnification of Fractal Inset at Left

Fractal

Magnification of Fractal Inset at Left

Figure 1.3

Fractal images by Jock Cooper. © 2006. Used by permission.

Fractal

Magnification of Fractal Inset at Left

Fractal

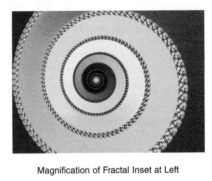

Magnification of Fractal Inset at Left

Fractal

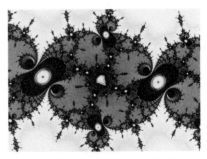

Magnification of Fractal Inset at Left

Figure 1.3

(Continued)

Fractal images by Jock Cooper. © 2006. Used by permission.

or fur and watch the balloons push away from each other. Show the students how to charge a comb with static electricity by rubbing it with wool or fur. Then bring the comb close to little bits of tissue paper. Invite students to create a static electricity experiment of their own using confetti, puffed rice, salt, pepper, dried parsley flakes, saran wrap, tinsel, and the like. Throughout the lesson encourage communication and positive interaction.

After cleaning up the materials, ask the students to explain their exciting discoveries, sharing what they have learned about static electricity. Reflect upon their experiences by writing and/or drawing pictures of their new understandings. What additional activities would the students like to try? Perhaps give them ideas to do and share with family at home.

Continue the lesson the next day with a discussion about lightning. What is lightning? What causes it to occur? What are some lightning safety rules? How do the students feel during a bad thunderstorm? Darken the room and rub two balloons against some fur. Then hold the balloons, almost touching, and observe a spark jump between them. When clouds and objects on the ground become charged with static electricity, electrons jump from an area with a negative charge to a positively charged area, producing a lightning bolt!

Howard Gardner (1991) concluded that children often grow into adults harboring deeply entrenched concepts about the world. For example, they might believe that lightning and thunder occur when two clouds bump into each other or that the Sun travels across the sky each day and disappears at night. Gardner contended that education for understanding occurs only when students integrate prescholastic with scholastic and disciplinary ways of knowing.

> All understandings are partial and subject to change; far more important than arrival at a "correct view" is an understanding of the processes whereby misconceptions are reformulated or stereotypes dissolved. (Gardner, 1991, p. 152)

Even with advanced training, students too often regress back to their view of the world from the perspective of a 5-year-old child (Gardner, 1991).

When students leave school at the end of a school day, teachers should not assume that students make the connection between the taught lessons and their lives outside of school. Cynthia Crockett (2004) discussed how educators must lead students to deeper scientific understanding by helping them first to identify their ideas and then to reflect on evidence to support their ideas.

> Understanding science requires students to learn a vast array of facts, processes, and skills. To ensure that this understanding is accurate, we need to know what the students think and why they think it. . . . As educators, we can expose students' misconceptions and help them unravel their false ideas. We must then provide students with the opportunity and support to develop a more accurate set of beliefs on which to build true scientific understandings. (Crockett, 2004, p. 37)

Student understanding is constructed through thoughtful discussion and careful assessment.

Many misconceptions appear when students are asked to explain how the Earth, Moon, Sun, and stars relate to each other. To raise their level of understanding, students begin by comparing four ancient models of the Earth, explaining how the Earth, Moon, Sun, and stars relate and interact. They invent their own ancient models of the world to describe the motion of the Sun in the sky, how it rises in the East, goes overhead, and then sets in the West. Next, they present their ideas and, after each presentation, encourage their classmates to ask questions and to engage in further dialogue. Students see that many different models can be used to explain the same set of observations. Later, students work in cooperative groups to discuss the implications of the ball-shaped Earth model to help them develop insights about Earth's shape and gravity. They support their ideas with arguments or demonstrate using globes (Sneider, 1989). Finally, students can participate in kinesthetic activities to physically act out the relationships of the Earth, Moon, Sun, and stars. Through the process of reflection, and by confronting their misconceptions, students reconstruct their understanding of Earth and beyond, encompassing a more sophisticated and scientific view.

Many perspectives and dimensions of learning exist. Science educators must encourage students to look at the world from differing points of view, nudging them toward complex, real-life experiences and creative problem solving. Learning takes on a fractal scaling dimension as newly constructed meanings intertwine, web, and build—the old contained within the new like nesting boxes.

> One has to look for different ways. One has to look for scaling structures—how do big details relate to little details. . . . Somehow the wondrous promise of the Earth is that there are things beautiful in it, things wondrous and alluring, and by virtue of your trade you want to understand them. (Feigenbaum in Gleick, 1987, pp. 186–187)

Getting the "right answer" is not as important as the critical-thinking skills that students develop while struggling to apply their mental models to real and imaginary situations.

Search for Repeating Patterns and Different Perspectives

The world is filled with many natural patterns, the result of nature's efficiency. Nature uses the same pattern over and over again, if the pattern is suitable for the purpose that nature has in mind. The spiral is one of the many basic designs that seems to repeat itself in many natural systems. Spiral patterns on hurricane maps, spiral-shaped galaxies, spirals on pinecones, and spiral-shaped seashells and snails are a few examples. Additional natural patterns include branching, ripples and waves, hexagons in beehives, bubbles, and radial symmetry.

Several of Caine and Caine's (2006) brain-based learning principles deal with the human brain's strong need to make sense of the world through patterning (see Introduction). The Caines believe that through patterning the search for meaning happens naturally. Making sense of life experiences is innate as the brain works to understand patterns and express them in uniquely creative ways. Patterning and interconnecting are central to learning and understanding. Human brains want learning to occur, making connections and seeking out patterns from the constant information flow of life experiences. A combination of novelty and familiarity are needed in a learning environment to ensure that true understanding takes place. Embedded activities linked to students' prior experiences lead to meaningful and genuine learning situations.

In their work to initiate a paradigm shift in education, Caine and Caine (1997a) identified three perceptual orientations, each reflecting a different perspective for teaching and learning. Perceptual Orientation 1 is the traditional approach, with the teacher in control and a fragmented curriculum. Perceptual Orientation 2, a more complex perspective, uses complex materials and engaging experiences to create meaning. With this approach, teachers may see links between some subjects while maintaining strong conceptual boundaries between others. According to the Caines, the ideal perspective is Perceptual Orientation 3, which they envisioned as brain based, learner centered, and more dynamic, "with educational experiences that approach the complexity of real life" (p. 25).

> Teachers at this orientation are open to the multiple possibilities of inter-connectedness. They know or sense that every subject in the curriculum is a way of organizing human experience and is therefore interconnected at a deep level. Thus, they do not see the ideas in the curriculum as standing alone—they relate them to life experience. . . . (Caine & Caine, 1997b, pp. 128–129)

Caine and Caine averred that the key to transforming education lies in the ability of teachers to transform themselves as they search for and evaluate the many options open to them. The Caines (1997a) identified five indicators of the instructional approaches that seem significant to differentiate among the three orientations; instructional objectives, use of time, sources for curriculum and instruction, dealing with discipline, and approaches to assessment. No one of the five indicators in isolation, however, can determine a teacher's educational approach. As teachers grow into Perceptual Orientation 3, instructional objectives become more connected to life experiences; assessment, more authentic; and use of time, more flexible and student centered. These teachers use multiple sources for curriculum and instruction and replace traditional discipline procedures with the creation of collaborative communities focused on order, trust, and respect.

Each day teachers unravel their way through endless lists, schedules, meetings, lesson plans, and science curricula, which can easily lock them into a structure that is too confining for the nonlinear, constantly evolving world. Teachers must see what is going on at every level for the clarity of vision to make change possible. They need to step back from their science curricula and instructional strategies to gain a new and perhaps enlightening perspective and to look for themes and patterns instead of isolated causes and facts.

APPLICATION FOR BRAIN-COMPATIBLE SCIENCE

The following lesson plan, *Changing Perspectives*, introduces the chaos theory principle of fractals into a science/geometry lesson involving a simple snowflake shape viewed from several different perspectives. Teachers discover that changing the scale redefines the snowflake's outer edge much in the same way that the human brain is shaped by life experiences. Following the lesson plan is a web to incite more creative ideas (Figure 1.10) and a chart to navigate the road to change in the brain-compatible, science classroom (Figure 1.11).

Lesson: Changing Perspectives

Chaos Theory Principle: Fractals
Grade Level: K–8, Gifted and Talented

Chaos Connection

- The Koch snowflake is a fractal pattern that repeats itself on increasingly smaller scales.
- The perimeter of the snowflake is infinite even though the snowflake always fits within a finite area.
- When viewed from a variety of perspectives, coastlines become increasingly longer as more detail is included in the measure.

Curriculum Connection

- Geology
- Weather
- Measurement
- Maps
- Geometry

National Science Education Standards

- Content Standard A; 1–9
- Content Standard D; 1, 2

Objectives (Students will ...)

- Investigate the Koch snowflake as having an infinitely long perimeter and compare it to a lake or coastal shoreline viewed from a tiny insect's perspective.
- Use critical thinking skills to analyze the potential complexity of a simple fractal shape.

Materials

- ❑ Koch snowflake transparency (use Figure 1.4)
- ❑ Koch snowflake handouts (Figures 1.5, 1.6, 1.7, 1.8, and 1.9)
- ❑ Thin string or yarn
- ❑ Compasses
- ❑ Transparency circles and/or laminated construction paper circles
- ❑ Crayons or markers
- ❑ Scissors

Preactivity Discussion

1. Introduce the Koch snowflake with the transparency, triangle, and six-pointed star, followed with the more complex snowflake figures (see Figure 1.4). Ask the students to look closely at the outside edges of the snowflakes and to explain how they are drawn. What repeating pattern do they notice? (Students will see triangles and will comment on their size and the number).

Koch Snowflake Views

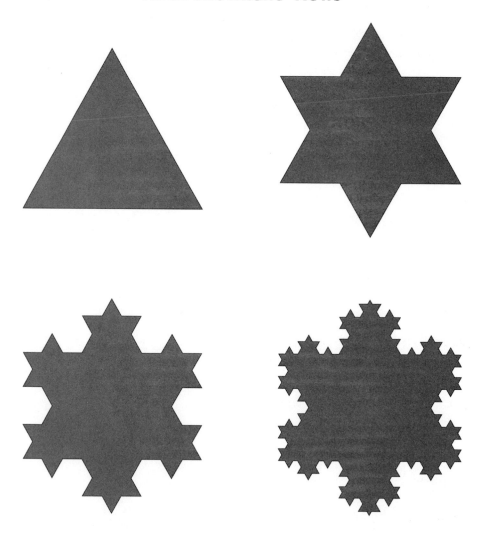

Figure 1.4

2. Discuss the following questions with the students: If we lay a string around the large triangle and then around the six-pointed star, which string will be longer? Why? How will the length of the string change if we lay it around the other two snowflake figures? Predict what will happen when we draw circles around the triangle, star, and snowflake figures. How will the size of the circles change?

Procedure

Organize the students into cooperative groups of two to four. Pass out handouts of the circle, the triangle, the star, and the two snowflake shapes (use Figures 1.5, 1.6, 1.7, 1.8, and 1.9). Invite the students to experiment freely with the patterns. Give them the following ideas to get started:

1. Color and cut out the snowflake patterns.

2. Experiment with positioning the patterns in different ways.

3. Hold the patterns up to the light to discover how they fit together.

4. Construct more triangles within triangles.

5. Use string to measure around the edges of the figures to discover which shape is the longest.

6. Use a compass to draw circles around the triangle and snowflake shapes.

7. Use transparency circles or laminated construction paper circles to discover that the figures all fit inside a finite area.

Closure

1. Circulate among the groups and discuss the students' observations. Ask students why the patterns always remain within a finite area of congruent circles.

2. Use the transparencies on an overhead projector to illustrate the relationships among the circle, triangle, six-pointed star, and the two Koch snowflake views.

3. Encourage students to share their pattern experiments.

Questions and Extensions

1. Ask students to think about how many self-similar snowflake figures they could make. How small will the sides eventually get? Can we keep on going to the molecular level? To the level of atoms? To infinity? Just how long could the outside of the Koch snowflake get? (Infinitely long!) What special tools might we eventually need for measuring?

2. Continue with a discussion of a trip to the beach. How long is the beach shoreline? How would the shoreline look when viewed from the air? From up on a bluff looking down? From a student's point of view? From a snail's point-of-view? Which view is the longest? What if a small sand insect travels around each tiny pebble and grain of sand? If we could follow the shoreline journey of a microscopic organism, how long would that take? Will the edge of the snowflake ever be a perfectly straight line? Why not?

3. Discuss why various encyclopedias, atlases, and other reference books may give different mileage for the same shoreline or boundary. How many fine details do maps tend to smooth out? What kinds of maps give the least detail? The greatest detail?

4. Have students choose one of the Koch snowflake patterns (Figures 1.8 or 1.9) and complete the following activity. Cut carefully around the outside edge. Fold first in half and then in sixths, matching the pattern on the edge. Cut lacy patterns from the folds. Open and compare with classmates to see that no two snowflakes are ever the same.

5. Repeat the triangle exercise with a square. Have students draw a large square first and two more complex views. All three must fit within congruent circles.

6. For a bodily/kinesthetic, experience or for younger students, enlarge the patterns so that they are big enough for the students to walk around. Time how long it takes to walk once around each. Provide rhythm by playing music in the background to keep the students' steps consistent.

7. Have students compare a map of the same area drawn on three different scales. Which map shows the greatest detail?

Technology Connection

Browse the following Web sites to find exciting new ideas for teaching science. Remember to use links and keywords to search even more science-related sites.

A Fractals Lesson
http://math.rice.edu/~lanius/frac/

The Spanky Fractal Database
http://spanky.triumf.ca/

Fractals (many images)
http://astronomy.swin.edu.au/~pbourke/fractals/

Exploring Fractals
http://www.math.umass.edu/~mconnors/fractal/fractal.html

These Web site addresses were accurate at the time of printing; however, as these sites are updated, some of the addresses may change.

Circle

Figure 1.5

Triangle

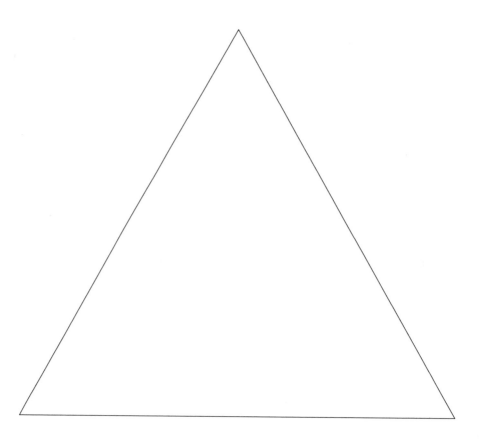

Figure 1.6

6-Pointed Star

Figure 1.7

Koch Snowflake 1

Figure 1.8

Koch Snowflake 2

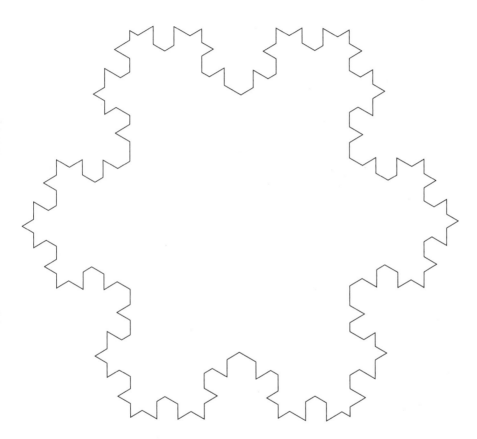

Figure 1.9

Web for Applying Fractals

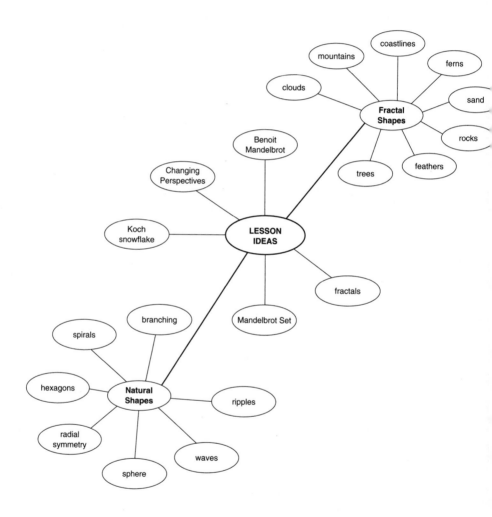

Figure 1.10

NAVIGATING THE ROAD TO CHANGE IN SCIENCE EDUCATION

Fractals

Too Much Order	On the Edge	Too Much Chaos
• Overplan, structure, and assess.	• Simplify by working with life's natural tendency to organize.	• Do not bother to structure, organize, or plan.
• Focus on isolated causes and facts.	• Look for meaning in patterns and themes.	• Overemphasize the importance of patterns and themes.
• Overemphasize previous learning with tedious review.	• Construct new meaning from old with higher-level thinking skills.	• Ignore previous learning.
• Disregard student misconceptions.	• Confront student misconceptions to raise level of understanding.	• Allow discussion of student misconceptions to shift away from the focus of the lesson.
• Dwell too long on connections.	• Connect instructional objectives to life experiences.	• Forget to make connections.
• View science education with tunnel vision.	• View science education from a variety of perspectives for a balanced outlook.	• View science education from an idealistic view by going with every new trend.

Figure 1.11

2

Iteration

A Metaphor for Change in Science Curriculum and Information Management

Scientific knowledge is constantly changing. As more research is conducted and advanced technology enhances our ability to make observations, our knowledge of the world changes. Knowing that science is a continuous process of inquiry helps students understand its dynamic nature and recognize that in science change is the rule rather than the exception.

Lawrence Lowery (1997, p. 35)

BACKGROUND: WHAT IS ITERATION?

Iteration appears all around in the world: in relationships, in replacement of human body cells, in changing weather systems, in constant encoding of DNA, and in bending and folding of the Earth's crust. Iteration, commonly known as *feedback*, is a simple process in which a complicated behavior as the output of one equation becomes the input for the next. Children understand it as the telephone game when they eagerly wait to find out how information changes as it iterates through a system of giggling children at a birthday party. Benoit Mandelbrot (1983) produced his set of highly complex and hauntingly beautiful shapes (see Chapter 1) by using the mathematical process of iteration.

John Briggs and E. David Peat (1989) described one way to visualize iteration. They suggested picturing a baker kneading bread dough. The baker stretches out the dough, folding and refolding it in on itself. The stretching process causes the individual molecules of dough to move about on the bread dough plane in a seemingly random manner. Molecules starting out close together may eventually end up far away from each other. Although no one can ever say just where a given molecule of dough might be in the continually changing system or if it will ever return to precisely the same position again, one can say that the dough molecules will remain contained within the finite shape of the bread dough. Mathematicians call this type of iteration the *baker transformation.*

> When a geometer iterates an equation instead of solving it, the equation becomes a process instead of a description, dynamic instead of static. When a number goes into an equation, a new number comes out; the new number goes in, and so on, points hopping from place to place. A point is plotted not when it satisfies the equation but when it produces a certain kind of behavior. (Gleick, 1987, p. 227)

If Mandelbrot had simply solved his first equation, he never would have discovered the magnificence of his famous fractal set (see Chapter 1). Through the continual feedback process of iteration, the Mandelbrot Set was unveiled for the world to ponder.

In the 1960s, at the same time that Mandelbrot was busy contemplating geometrical shapes and coastlines, a young physicist, Mitchell Feigenbaum, was studying self-similarity in systems. Interested in the onset of turbulence when orderly systems become chaotic, Feigenbaum observed that at precisely the point when an ordered system begins to break down into chaos, a consistent sequence of period-doubling transitions occurs (Gleick, 1987). Later in the 1970s, while looking to uncover mathematical principles to explain how the human mind sorts through the chaos of perception, Feigenbaum discovered universal theory.

James Gleick (1987) explained how Feigenbaum began with a simple population biology equation, which he repeated endlessly as a feedback loop. With a hand calculator, he began calculating, concentrating his efforts on the boundary region between order and chaos. As the numbers converged geometrically at a constant rate, Feigenbaum found an unexpected regularity hidden within system after system (Gleick, 1987). Every period-doubling equation he studied scaled with a certain order of self-similarity preserved from calculation to calculation. Feigenbaum's numerical constant, known to mathematicians as the *Feigenbaum number,* controls the doubling process, showing that the results may apply to many chaotic systems, including the boiling of water and the magnetizing of metals (Gleick, 1987).

IMPLICATIONS OF ITERATION FOR BRAIN-COMPATIBLE SCIENCE

Three implications of iteration for science education are (1) emphasize dynamic process and flexibility, (2) look for similarities in systems, and (3) feed new information into the system. These elements are closely related to brain-compatible science education. Students learn science effectively when they actively participate in relevant activities embedded in their lives both in and out of school. The learning process, as well as the processes of science, continually feed back on themselves creating a depth of understanding that fosters energy and revitalization.

Emphasize Dynamic Process and Flexibility

Iteration suggests a chaos theory paradox that stability and change are not opposites. Dynamical systems exhibit both in their iterating cycles through time. To remain healthy and renewed, systems must evolve and change.

Chaos also seems to be responsible for maintaining order in the natural world. Feedback mechanisms not only introduce flexibility into living systems, sustaining delicate dynamical balances, but also promote nature's propensity for self-organization. Even the beating heart relies on feedback for regularity. (Hall, 1991, p. 10)

To foster brain-compatible science teaching and learning, teachers need to search for new activities, stay receptive to new information, welcome new ideas and questions from students, search out new strategies, and be adaptable and flexible rather than inflexible. As Geoffrey and Renate Caine (2006) suggested, teachers must seek out the windows of opportunity for learning. The classroom dynamics, like a living system, are always changing and so must teachers.

Each day, life iterates anew in thousands of classrooms. The equation of teaching becomes an ongoing, dynamic process, not a solution. The constants in the classroom are the teacher and the students, and the cycling iteration is the science curriculum. The output of one day's lesson becomes the input for the next. Unlike in the days of Sir Isaac Newton, who assumed that inputs and outputs were measurable (Caine & Caine, 1997b), the interplay among the teacher, students, and curriculum slowly reveals a hidden pattern, a moving design of connections and growth contained within the constantly evolving classroom dynamics. Teachers can expect surprises and trust in universality. Hidden within class after class, an unexpected regularity appears as long as teachers feed in the right information. Teachers need to be watchful as the order emerges.

Howard Gardner (1991) reminded people that young children naturally ask questions. He further suggested that teachers must strive to cultivate a reflective attitude in children.

The scientifically oriented teacher not only encourages questioning but also reinforces the inclination to observe, to try out small-scale experiments, to note the results of those experiments, and to relate them back to the question that motivated them initially. (Gardner, 1991, p. 213)

Scientists participate in the process of science. Students must do the same. Students learn science by doing and participating in hands-on, minds-on activities rather than by simply reading and discussing science textbooks, writing reports, and viewing science videos. Because the science knowledge base is constantly growing and changing, content in a science curriculum should be derived from the science process, the inquiry skills that enable students to construct their own knowledge.

For example, fourth graders can brainstorm a list of devices using electrical energy and then discuss where inventors' ideas come from (See Invention Bifurcations lesson in Chapter 5). They can go on to use science process skills as they experiment with electricity, using balance and vibration to invent methods of putting together small DC motors, and assembling wires and batteries to create electric pencils, fans, and other small inventions. Students can continue experimenting with strategies to improve, further develop, and evaluate the effectiveness of their inventions. They can then reflect on what worked and what did not work as they repeatedly cycle through the steps of the scientific method in a nonlinear, webbed fashion.

In another example, fifth graders can use science process skills to build a home-made space capsule containing an egg to represent an astronaut (Figure 2.1). In the

A Unique "Eggsperiment"

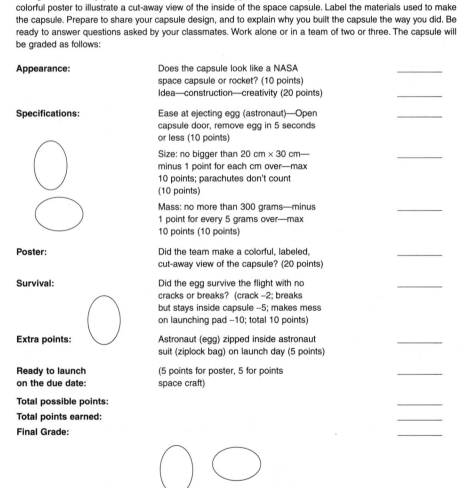

Assignment/Problem:

Build a rocket or space capsule containing an egg to represent an astronaut. You will drop the capsule from a height selected by your teacher to observe if the egg survives the flight. Name your capsule and make a colorful poster to illustrate a cut-away view of the inside of the space capsule. Label the materials used to make the capsule. Prepare to share your capsule design, and to explain why you built the capsule the way you did. Be ready to answer questions asked by your classmates. Work alone or in a team of two or three. The capsule will be graded as follows:

Appearance:
Does the capsule look like a NASA space capsule or rocket? (10 points) _____
Idea—construction—creativity (20 points) _____

Specifications:
Ease at ejecting egg (astronaut)—Open capsule door, remove egg in 5 seconds or less (10 points) _____

Size: no bigger than 20 cm × 30 cm—minus 1 point for each cm over—max 10 points; parachutes don't count (10 points) _____

Mass: no more than 300 grams—minus 1 point for every 5 grams over—max 10 points (10 points) _____

Poster:
Did the team make a colorful, labeled, cut-away view of the capsule? (20 points) _____

Survival:
Did the egg survive the flight with no cracks or breaks? (crack –2; breaks but stays inside capsule –5; makes mess on launching pad –10; total 10 points) _____

Extra points:
Astronaut (egg) zipped inside astronaut suit (ziplock bag) on launch day (5 points) _____

Ready to launch on the due date:
(5 points for poster, 5 for points space craft) _____

Total possible points: _____
Total points earned: _____
Final Grade: _____

Figure 2.1

experiment, students drop the capsule from a ladder to observe if the egg can survive the flight. Beforehand, students bond with their eggs by drawing faces on their eggs and designing all sorts of imaginative contraptions to provide for their "astronaut's" safety. Materials for the contraptions can include rubber-band suspension systems, Velcro® seat belts, parachutes, and even gelatin. Students *love* this activity!

According to the *NSTA Pathways to the Science Standards* (Lowery, 1997, p. 35), students should be able to do the following science processes by the time they finish eighth grade:

- Ask questions that can be answered by scientific investigations.
- Design and conduct a scientific investigation.
- Use appropriate tools and techniques to gather, analyze, and interpret data.
- Develop descriptions, explanations, predictions, and models based on evidence.
- Think critically and logically to discover the relationship between evidence and explanations.

The methods that scientists use to actually do science are as important as the actual science content.

Holloway (2000) described the research of Sprenger (1999), who recommended science lab experiences where students would participate regularly in science processes such as observing, communicating, comparing, measuring, organizing, relating, inferring, and applying. Sprenger reasoned that frequent repetition of the science processes enables the brain to store information in easier to retrieve, procedural memory. The output of one experience with science inquiry becomes the input for the next experience. Science teachers feed in the right information and marvel as students grow in their understanding of how scientists go about their work (for a "colorful" example, see Figure 2.2).

Look for Similarities in Systems

Another of the Caines' (2006) principles (see Introduction) is that learning engages the entire physiology with the body and mind totally interconnected and involved. The brain is a complex, adaptive system as well as a parallel processor, functioning simultaneously on many different levels. Teachers can engage both body and brain by looking for similarities in systems. For example, in a first-grade rock lab, students used their senses to examine a collection of rocks to investigate their characteristics and explain how the rocks were alike and how they were different. When asked to describe what the rocks reminded them of, the students found many similarities in systems. Like Feigenbaum and his universal theory, the students' ideas were never ending (Figure 2.3).

These first-grade students easily made connections between rocks and minerals and their life experiences as they discovered their own version of universal theory where seemingly unrelated ideas follow the same rules. Performing many functions at once, the first graders' parallel-processing brains explored and gradually wove information about the rocks into a coherent whole. Sorting, ordering, and finding similarities in systems, the students' brains naturally did what they were designed to do (Caine & Caine, 2006). Through the process of generating a list of things the rocks reminded them of, the students' analytical thinking processes raised their existing knowledge to a higher level.

Color Lab

Objectives: Students will . . .

1. develop the abilities necessary to do scientific inquiry including using appropriate tools and techniques to gather, analyze, and interpret data.
2. develop skills in measuring with a graduated cylinder to record liquid volume.

Materials:

- three small beakers
- red, yellow, and blue water (teacher-prepared ahead with food coloring)
- test tube rack
- six test tubes
- 50 mL graduated cylinder

Procedure: (Check off each one as you do it)

_____ 1. Label the test tubes A, B, C, D, E, F.

_____ 2. Pour 30 mL of each color (red, blue, yellow) into separate beakers.

_____ 3. Into test tube **A** measure 19 mL of **red** water.

_____ 4. Into test tube **C** measure 18 mL of **yellow** water.

_____ 5. Into test tube **E** measure 18 mL of **blue** water.

_____ 6. From test tube **C** measure 4 mL and pour it into test tube **D**.

_____ 7. From test tube **E** measure 7 mL and add it to test tube **D**. Mix.

_____ 8. From the beaker of **blue water** measure 4 mL and pour it into test tube **F**.

_____ 9. From the beaker of **red water** measure 7 mL and add it to test tube **F**. Mix.

_____10. From test tube **A** measure 8 mL of water and pour it into test tube **B**.

_____11. From test tube **C** measure 3 mL and add it to test tube **B**. Mix.

Observations:

Complete the data table below by recording the final colors in each test tube. Then measure and record the final volume of colored water in each test tube. (Remember to label with mL). Use the third column to mathematically check your answers.

Test Tube	Color of Water	Total Volume of Water	Mathematical Check
A			
B			
C			
D			
E			
F			

Figure 2.2   *(Continued)*

Conclusions: Answer in complete sentences.

1. Why is it important to follow directions exactly?

_____

_____

_____

_____

_____

_____

2. What would have happened (or did happen) if your measurements were inaccurate?

_____

_____

_____

_____

_____

_____

3. How many mL of liquid did you have at the end of the lab? _____ How many should you have? _____ What are some reasons why you may have more or less than when you started?

_____

_____

_____

_____

_____

_____

Figure 2.2 (Continued)

Answers

Test Tube	Color of Water	Total Volume of Water	Mathematical check
A	Red	11 mL	$19 - 8 = 11$
B	Orange	11 mL	$8 + 3 = 11$
C	Yellow	11 mL	$18 - 4 - 3 = 11$
D	Green	11 mL	$4 + 7 = 11$
E	Blue	11 mL	$18 - 7 = 11$
F	Purple	11 mL	$4 + 7 = 11$

1. Why is it important to follow directions exactly?

If you do not follow directions exactly, the measurements will not be accurate.

2. What would have happened (or did happen) if your measurements were inaccurate?

If measurements were inaccurate, the amounts in the test tubes would not all be the same and the colors would not be a perfect rainbow.

3. How many millimeters of liquid did you have at the end of the lab?

Answers will vary

How many should you have?

Students should have 11 mL in each test tube or a total of 66 mL.

What are some reasons why you may have more or less than when you started?

Reasons for having more or less liquid in a test tube may be that:

Students did not measure accurately.

Students spilled some of the liquid.

Students did not read the graduated cylinder correctly.

Figure 2.2

(Continued)

Student Responses for Rock Comparisons

This rock looks like a water rock.

This rock looks like mountains.

This rock looks like honeycomb.

This rock looks like a wave.

This rock looks like the ocean. (It was Cochina, a rock made of shells.)

This rock looks like people.

This rock looks like a rainbow.

This rock looks like tiger skin.

This rock looks like outer space.

This rock looks like the night stars.

This rock looks like a fancy floor.

This rock looks like a chocolate chip cookie.

This rock looks like the fossil of a ladybug.

There's a heart in the middle of this one.

This one reminds me of hot tar.

I think this came out of a volcano.

I like this rock because it looks glittery.

I like this one because it's really sparkly.

I like this one because there are crystals inside.

This rock reminds me of a mammoth brain.

I think I'm going to be a scientist when I grow up!

(First graders at Cumberland School, Whitefish Bay, WI, 1997)

Figure 2.3

One of the nine instructional strategies (see Introduction) identified by researchers at Mid-continent Research for Education and Learning (McREL), as a strategy to improve student achievement across all content areas and grade levels, is identifying similarities and differences in a concept (Marzano, Pickering, & Pollock, 2001). Students should be engaged in activities that allow them to compare, classify, and create analogies. Thus, teachers can lead students to an understanding of complex problems by analyzing them in a simpler way.

A strategy often used by teachers to enable students to look for similarities, as well as differences, in systems is graphic organizers, which help students to organize information in a way that actually allows them to visualize their thinking. Explaining the power of graphic organizers, Gayle Gregory and Carolyn Chapman wrote, "Graphic organizers give visual representations of facts/concepts and . . . show the relationship between and among new facts and previous information. They also are used to plot process and procedures" (Gregory & Chapman, 2002, p. 87). Teachers who engage students in learning experiences to determine how topics are alike and how they are different can empower students to construct new

Name _____

Complete a Venn diagram to compare and contrast science, technology, and exploration. How are they alike, and how are they different? Include at least two points in each of the seven sections.

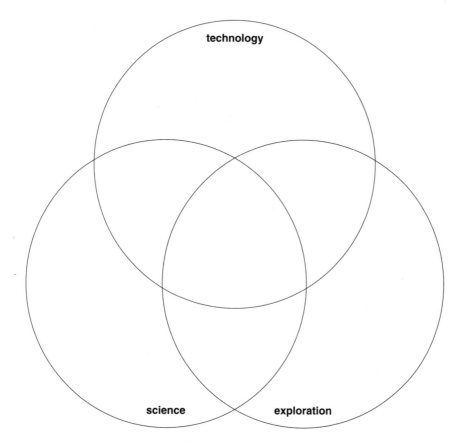

Figure 2.4

knowledge by intensifying their understandings and expanding their ability to use the new knowledge meaningfully.

Concept or mind maps, webs, sequence charts or flowcharts, and Venn diagrams are the organizers most commonly used as tools to organize student thinking. The Venn diagram enables students to compare and contrast two or three topics (See Sand Patterns, Chapter 7). In a unit on the nature of science, students use a three-circle Venn diagram to compare and contrast science, technology, and exploration (Figure 2.4). Teachers can incorporate graphic organizers into cooperative learning activities, asking students to create graphics on a large piece of paper that can be shared with the entire class. Students are encouraged to participate and empowered to think.

Feed New Information Into the System

Rapidly changing computer technology has profound implications for science education of the future with its windows of information existing inside of windows, all containing fractal layers of information. People work back and forth between the windows on a computer screen in a nonlinear fashion. They click on a Web site, which leads to more icons to click. Computer windows have a mesmerizing, fractal quality. People easily lose their way when searching among windows upon more windows of ideas.

> To fully understand technology, one has to participate in it. . . . No culture in history has been asked to move this fast. For millions of years, we were hunters and gatherers; for thousands of years, we were agricultural workers; for a few hundred years, we were urban industrial workers. Now brain technology is an instant reality and we already are moving on to a service and information-based economy. (James, 1995, p. 23)

In this age of information overload, students need more than ever to find methods to manage information. According to Eric Jensen (1998), the quality of the information is more important than the quantity. Meaning making occurs when the topic is personally relevant, emotions are engaged, and context and pattern making are considered.

Margaret Wheatley (1994) viewed information as the underlying structure and dynamic aspect of evolution, defining growth and life itself. The source of all change, information provides for new growth, power, and renewal. The information age surrounds people with more scientific information than they can ever possibly assimilate, compelling them to make sense of it all. And information need not obey the laws of matter and energy. Science educators must find ways to manage these vast quantities of information as they go about making curriculum decisions. Information is not a thing, although many teachers view it as such when they try to control it and expect to manage it in their plan books. Like a life force, information has an energy all its own—moving, flowing, and transforming through the educational process.

Wheatley (1994) believed that information must be continually generated for a system to remain alive. To expect a single textbook to have all the curriculum answers is no longer viable and far too limiting. When designing science curricula, teachers need to look at great quantities of information from many different sources, listen to different interpretations, process the interpretations together in committed teams, and thoughtfully infuse technology into the curriculum. The information amplifies as it is iterated, building in significance with each new interpretation and eventually disclosing its hidden complexity. Wheatley (1994) wrote, "The fuel of life is new information—novelty—ordered into new structure" (p. 105). When teachers develop their own curriculum by engaging in the curriculum writing process, the process and product become one, revealing clarity and simplicity.

The science reform initiatives, stressing that more is not better, recommend that educators teach fewer topics but teach them in greater depth; whereas the old way was to give a broad overview of many topics. Jensen (1998) agreed that fewer but more complex projects provide students with more challenging opportunities to foster pattern making in the brain. A science program with many iterations, starting and stopping in a disjointed fashion, does not reveal the same depth of understanding that a continuously iterating, more connected, and concentrated curriculum provides. The constant feeding of current but relevant information into educational programs is essential to energize schools with new direction and purpose and to cultivate brain-compatible science.

APPLICATION FOR BRAIN-COMPATIBLE SCIENCE

The following lesson plan, *Magma Mix*, introduces the chaos theory principle of iteration into a science lesson with a geology focus. By hypothesizing about the inside of the Earth through a simulation with a magma-like substance, students learn how molecules continuously feed back in on themselves in a constantly cycling motion. Science understandings must continuously feed back in on themselves, as well, in the developing minds of students. Following the lesson plan is a web to incite more creative ideas (Figure 2.6) and a chart to navigate the road to change in the brain-compatible, science classroom (Figure 2.7).

Lesson: Magma Mix

Chaos Theory Principle: Iteration

Grade Level: 3–8

Chaos Connection

- Iteration, better known as feedback, involves the continual reabsorption or enfolding of what has come before.
- Iteration appears in relationships, in the replacement of body cells, in changing weather systems, and in the bending and folding of the Earth's crust.
- One way to visualize iteration is to picture a baker kneading bread dough. (Mathematicians call this type of iteration the *baker transformation*.)
- Another way to visualize this same mathematical idea is to imagine repeatedly stretching and folding taffy back on itself.

Curriculum Connection

- Plate tectonics
- Volcanoes
- Oceanography

- Astronomy
- Chemical change
- Properties of matter
- Polymer chemistry

National Science Education Standards

- Content Standard A; 1–9
- Content Standard B; 1
- Content Standard D; 1, 2, 3

Objectives (Students will ...)

- Investigate how scientists, using indirect evidence, hypothesize about the inside of the Earth, without seeing it directly.
- Design experiments to observe the unique, magma-like properties of slime.
- Model the movement of magma to explain how the Earth keeps iterating.

Materials

- ❑ Borax
- ❑ White glue (Elmer's® glue recommended)
- ❑ Water
- ❑ Water-based markers
- ❑ Small plastic or paper cups (two for each student pair)
- ❑ Plastic spoons or wooden craft sticks
- ❑ Teaspoon and measuring cup
- ❑ Plastic gallon containers
- ❑ Magma Mix Activity Log (Figure 2.5)

    Optional

- Beads
- Plastic resealable bags

Preactivity Discussion

Prior to the lesson, discuss these questions with the students:

1. Using indirect evidence, how can scientists hypothesize about the inside of the Earth without actually seeing it?

2. Where must scientists use indirect evidence to find out about the Earth or the universe? (In fields such as astronomy, volcanology, and oceanography, the scientists may not actually go to these places to study them directly.)

3. What if scientists discovered a slimelike substance inside the mantle of the Earth? How would they go about studying it? What kinds of experiments could they set up?

Procedure

Make the Slime . . .

1. Before the students arrive, prepare a half water and half glue mixture, depending on how much slime you want each student to make ($1/2$ cup of each makes approximately 1 cup of slime). Prepare a concentrated borax solution by mixing approximately 4 teaspoons of borax for each cup of water. Shake well to mix thoroughly. (Empty plastic milk containers work nicely for the glue and borax mixtures and also provide for easy storage of leftovers.)

2. Organize the students into cooperative groups of two within each group, number them ones and twos. Ask ones to come get $1/2$ cup of the glue-water mixture and the craft stick; they are the stirrers and drainers. Ask twos to come get $1/2$ cup of borax solution; they are the pourers and splitters. The ones (stirrers) begin by stirring the glue-water mixture. The twos (pourers) pour the borax solution into the glue mixture, while the ones continue to stir. The ones (drainers) drain the extra liquid into a tub or down the sink. (Tell students to be careful not to lose the slime.) The ones hand the slime over to the twos (splitters), who knead the slime until it firms up like modeling clay and then split it to share with their partner.

3. If students express an interest in making their own slime at home, and many will, provide them with this recipe for a single batch (approximately $1/2$ cup) of slime. Dissolve 1 teaspoon of borax in $1/4$ cup of water in one small cup. In a second small cup mix $1/8$ cup of white glue with $1/8$ cup of water. Stir well with the craft stick. Pour the borax solution into the glue mixture and stir. Pour off the excess liquid, and knead the remainder into a uniform mixture.

Experiment With the Slime

Have the students do the following experiments with the slime. You might also ask them to record their observations in a science journal (see Figure 2.5).

1. Roll the slime into a ball and set it in the palm of your hand. Does the ball keep its shape?

2. Put the slime between your hands, and try to make a thin film. Hold the film at one end and observe. Can you see through it?

3. Drop a ball of slime on your desk. What happens?

4. Make imprints in the slime. How long do they last?

5. Roll the slime into a long cylinder shape, and slowly pull it apart while holding it at both ends.

6. Make another cylinder shape, and pull it apart quickly. Note how, like the Earth, the slime is able to both stretch and break.

7. Make a snail, a bracelet, a braid, and a figure eight. Try other shapes.

8. Shape the slime into a flat pancake. Place on top of your closed fist and observe what happens.

Experiment Further With Chaos Theory

Students can continue with these additional experiments that directly relate to the chaos theory principle of iteration and the baker transformation.

1. Shape the slime into a sausage-like cylinder.

2. Using water-based markers, draw circles approximately 1 centimeter each at the ends of the slime cylinder, one color at one end, a second color at the other end.

3. Discuss how the marker molecules are presently as far away from each other as they can be. What would be the easiest way to bring them close together? (Fold the cylinder into a U-shape). How close are the colors to each other now? Try other colors, designs, and shapes. Try beads.

Closure

1. Discuss with the students how the slime mixture is similar to magma in the Earth's mantle. (The slime has properties of both solids and liquids. It can flow like a liquid and break like a solid). Ask the students what previous experiences they may have had with slime or slimelike products such as Gak® or Silly Putty®. (Tip: To keep the slime from drying out, place inside a resealable plastic bag, and store it in the refrigerator.)

2. Explain to the students that iteration, better known as feedback, involves the continual reabsorption or enfolding of what has come before. Iteration appears all around in the world: in relationships, in the replacement of cells, in changing weather systems, and in the bending and folding of the Earth's crust.

3. Explain to students that one way to visualize iteration is to picture a baker kneading bread dough. The baker stretches out the dough, folds it in on itself, stretches and folds, stretches and folds over and over again. The process of stretching causes the points to move about on the plane in a seemingly random and independent manner. Individual molecules of dough, which may have started out close together, could eventually end up far away from each other. Mathematicians call this type of iteration the baker transformation.

4. Explain to students that another way to visualize this same mathematical idea is to imagine repeatedly stretching and folding taffy back on itself. Individual points in the taffy system are stretched around the taffy's finite shape over and over again. One can never say just where a given molecule of taffy might be in the continually changing system; however, one can say that the taffy molecules are all contained within the finite shape of the taffy itself as it is folded and stretched. The Earth behaves similarly as new crust is created while the old is destroyed. The stuff of the Earth is continually recycled, iterated, and enfolded. "No sooner is a continental mountain thrust up than all the forces of nature conspire to level it" (Carson, 1961, p. 73).

Questions and Extensions

At the close of the activity, pose these questions to students to elicit a discussion, or have students reflect on these questions in journals.

1. How is it possible for the colors to be far away from each other one minute and right next to each other the next?

2. How did the colors mix?

3. What colors, designs, and shapes were you able to create?

4. What will happen if you place two beads in the slime while you continue to fold and stretch it? Can you somehow figure out a method to graph where the beads will appear after each phase of folding? Can you predict where the beads will show up next? How are the beads like the marker colors? (If beads are placed in the center of the slime as you fold and stretch

it, the beads are unlikely to appear in exactly the same place more than once; however, the beads remain contained within the slime itself as it is folded and stretched. If we could graph this changing system, ultimately the complex order of the whole would reveal itself.)

Technology Connection

Browse the following Web sites to find exciting new ideas for teaching science. Remember to use links and keywords to search even more science-related sites.

United States Geologic Survey
http://www.usgs.gov/

The National Earthquake Information Center
http://neic.usgs.gov/

Global Volcanism Program
http://www.volcano.si.edu/

Volcanic Activity Reports
http://www.volcano.si.edu/reports/usgs/

This Dynamic Earth
http://pubs.usgs.gov/publications/text/dynamic.html

Plate Tectonics
http://www.cotf.edu/ete/modules/msese/earthsysflr/plates1.html

These Web site addresses were accurate at the time of printing; however, as these sites are updated, some of the addresses may change.

Magma Mix Activity Log

1. Roll the slime into a ball, and set it in the palm of your hand. Does the ball keep its shape?

2. Put the slime between your hands, and try to make a thin film. Hold the film at one end and observe. Record your observations.

3. Drop a ball of slime on your desk. What happens?

4. Make imprints in the slime. How long do they last?

5. Roll the slime into a long cylinder shape, and slowly pull it apart while holding it at both ends. Explain what happens.

6. Make another cylinder shape, and pull it apart quickly. How is pulling the slime apart quickly different from pulling it apart slowly?

7. Make a snail, a bracelet, a braid, and a figure eight. What other shapes might you try?

8. Which shapes work the best?

9. Shape the slime into a flat pancake, and place it on top of your closed fist. What happens?

10. Describe the properties of the slime. How is the slime different from the glue-water mixture and the borax-water mixture at the beginning of the activity?

Figure 2.5

Web for Applying Iteration

Figure 2.6

NAVIGATING THE ROAD TO CHANGE IN SCIENCE EDUCATION

Iteration

Too Much Order	On the Edge	Too Much Chaos
• Implement single-text, knowledge-based curriculum.	• Derive curriculum content from science process and knowledge base.	• Stress process only, with little connection to the knowledge base.
• Overuse graphic organizers.	• Use graphic organizers to show relationships.	• Never use graphic organizers.
• Focus on differences and classification of things.	• Focus both on how things are alike and how they are different.	• Focus on how things are alike with no attempt to classify.
• Move quickly and efficiently from subject to subject with no time for reflection.	• Cultivate a reflective attitude in students.	• Wander off on useless tangents, with pointless exploration.
• Ignore technology.	• Thoughtfully infuse technology into the curriculum.	• Emphasize technology with no regulation.
• View information as a thing that must be managed and perfectly organized.	• View information as energy flowing through educational process.	• Show indifference to sources of information and how information is handled.
• Offer a disjointed overview of too many, teacher-selected topics.	• Teach fewer topics but in greater depth (more is not better).	• Allow students total control over learning choices.

Figure 2.7

Sensitive Dependence on Initial Conditions

A Metaphor for Change in Gender Equity and Diversity

In my
science class
the teacher never calls
on me, and I feel like
I don't exist.
The other night I had
a dream that I
vanished!

Sadker, Sadker,
Fox, & Salata (1993–1994, p. 14)

BACKGROUND: WHAT IS SENSITIVE DEPENDENCE ON INITIAL CONDITIONS?

In 1961, Edward Lorenz, a meteorologist at the Massachusetts Institute of Technology, discovered how iteration leads to chaos. Examining weather sequences with a computer weather-forecasting model, Lorenz rounded off a number in an equation to three decimal places instead of six. Assuming that the small difference would prove inconsequential, he took a coffee break. When he returned, Lorenz discovered that his rounded-off number had greatly grown out of proportion as it iterated through the weather system. Tiny changes in the data eventually resulted in big changes in the output. Lorenz's discovery led him to conclude that long-term weather forecasting is impossible, laying the foundation for the new science called *chaos theory* (Gleick, 1987).

In the classical Newtonian world, large causes resulted in large effects; and small causes, in small effects. Weather systems are nonlinear with unpredictable outcomes. Known as the *butterfly effect* in chaos theory, small, seemingly unrelated events may have a great impact on patterns elsewhere in the universe. For example, the beating of a butterfly's wings in Beijing could lead to a major storm in New York.

> Lorenz had discovered the fact that very simple differential equations could possess sensitive dependence on initial conditions. Moreover, the Lorenz model has been shown to be a strange attractor, an extremely complicated geometric object on which the study of solutions of the differential equations reduces to the study of the chaotic behavior of an iterated function. (Devaney, 1992, p. 118)

Long-range forecasts in virtually every field are unreliable as small scales intertwine with large (Gleick, 1987). The world is a sensitive paradox.

Lorenz was the first to see a strange attractor (see Chapter 4, Figure 4.1). Resembling an owl's mask or a butterfly's wings, the Lorenz attractor became an emblem for the early explorers of chaos theory. The attractor revealed the fine structure hidden within a disorderly stream of weather data, a figure-eight shape looping around forever, never repeating itself or intersecting (Gleick, 1987).

> Sensitive dependence on initial conditions serves not to destroy but to create. A growing snowflake falls to earth, typically floating in the wind for an hour or more, the choices made by the branching tips at any instant depend sensitively on such things as the temperature, the humidity, and the presence of impurities in the atmosphere. The six tips of a single snowflake, spreading within a millimeter space, feel the same temperatures, and because the laws of growth are purely deterministic, they maintain a nearly perfect symmetry.
>
> But the nature of turbulent air is such that any pair of snowflakes will experience very different paths. The final flake records the history of all the changing weather conditions it has experienced, and the combinations may as well be infinite. (Gleick, 1987, p. 311)

A single snowflake is a delicate crystal; however, many snowflake crystals acting together can shut down an entire city.

IMPLICATIONS OF SENSITIVE DEPENDENCE ON INITIAL CONDITIONS FOR BRAIN-COMPATIBLE SCIENCE

Three implications of sensitive dependence on initial conditions for science education are (1) pay attention to details, (2) show sensitivity to unique dynamics, and (3) accept the impact of changing demographics. These elements, promoting brain-compatible science education, illustrate how things that seem inconsequential may magnify in significance as they iterate through science curricula and classrooms. Replace the snowflake and weather words in Gleick's quote with words associated with education such as child, classroom, teacher, curricula, assessment, teaching strategies, learning strategies, and so on, for a whole new perspective. The dynamics of each class are different. Teachers must approach all students and situations with sensitivity and understanding for science education to be truly brain compatible.

Pay Attention to Details

Another of Geoffrey and Renate Caine's (2006) mind/brain principles (see Introduction) states that learning involves both focused attention and peripheral perception. The human brain absorbs information of which it is directly aware, as well as information beyond the nearby focus of attention. To enable students to tap into the information beyond immediate recall, teachers need to involve students in learning experiences involving higher-level thinking skills. Teachers must nudge their students away from the simple recall of information to connect meanings that are known with those that the students are on the brink of discovering. Learning is constructed from contexts that students hardly ever consciously attend to.

Critical-thinking skills will not develop spontaneously. Teachers must pay attention to details, guiding and modeling critical thinking as students ask questions, draw inferences, make observations, note contradictions, propose alternatives, and validate claims ("Thinking and Learning," 1993). Research indicates that because critical-thinking skills are most effectively taught within the context of a subject area, critical thinking is dependent on a sufficient knowledge base. To think critically about something of which one knows nothing is impossible. Critical-thinking skills are brain compatible, attending to the details necessary for students to create meaningful learning. For a lesson encouraging the use of higher-level and critical-thinking skills, see *Nature Patterns*, Figure 3.1.

Another brain-compatible, critical-thinking strategy, one of the nine instructional strategies (see Introduction) identified by researchers at Mid-continent Research for Education and Learning (McREL), as a strategy to improve student achievement across all content areas and grade levels, consists of cues, questions, and advance organizers (Marzano, Pickering, et al., 2001). Teachers must pay careful attention to details as they vary the way they start a lesson. Should they tell a story, show a video clip, do a mind-grabbing science demonstration, observe an experiment already in progress, turn to a partner and share ideas, skim the text, or discuss an interesting newspaper article? Teachers can expose students to information before the students learn it in many ways that will enable them to use what they already know about a concept to construct additional learning.

Teachers may consider the bare walls and cluttered counters on the peripheries of their classrooms to be of minor relevance or importance. Brain-based learning

Nature Patterns

Earth's Eye

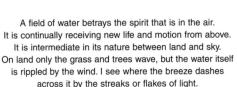

A field of water betrays the spirit that is in the air.
It is continually receiving new life and motion from above.
It is intermediate in its nature between land and sky.
On land only the grass and trees wave, but the water itself
is rippled by the wind. I see where the breeze dashes
across it by the streaks or flakes of light.

—HENRY DAVID THOREAU, *Walden*

OBJECTIVES (Students will . . .)

Study nature pattern pictures and a variety of natural objects to discover patterns, connections, and holistic meaning in our world.

MATERIALS

- Nature pattern pictures from old calendars and nature magazines
- Natural objects such as rocks, minerals, fossils, snake skin, feathers, shells, coral, starfish, tree rings, bark, flowers, leaves, pine cones, bubbles, fur, ferns, branches, etc.
- Microscopes and/or magnifying lenses

PROCEDURE

1. Hold up some natural objects. Ask, *How are these natural objects connected?* Briefly discuss several of the students' ideas.

2. Organize the students into cooperative groups of four. Give each group a set of nature pattern pictures, and a variety of natural objects. Explain that they will look at the pictures and natural objects to find patterns and connections between them. Complete the "Patterns in Nature" lab sheet.

3. Proceed with the activity. Circulate from group to group, offering assistance when needed and encouraging connections!

4. If microscopes are available, suggest that the students have an up-close look at small pieces of the natural materials.

5. When the students have completed the activity, ask them to share their groups' findings. Discuss the following questions:

   - What patterns did you find? What patterns seem to repeat themselves?
   - How were the patterns formed by forces of nature?
   - How can the forces of nature, which are frequently so chaotic, produce such perfectly organized, repetitive patterns? What forces cause rapid change? Slow change?

Figure 3.1

- Where else do we see patterns such as these?
- The photographer captured one moment in time in a picture. How might the image be different if taken the next day? During a different season? In a year? In a million years?
- What changes in these natural patterns will continue to occur over time?
- How many grains of sand are needed to form a pattern? What pattern does just a single grain make? Two grains? Four? Eight? Millions? Discuss how sand is a system composed of millions of tiny individual parts working holistically to create patterns.
- Are we able to predict where individual grains of sand will move in a sand system?
- Can we predict sand pattern shapes forming over time? Give examples.
- What might we learn about ourselves and the human race as a whole by studying patterns in nature?

6. Have the students use their notes and the nature pattern images to complete one of the following:

- Write a one page composition entitled, "Nature Patterns."
- Write a poem, story, or myth to go with one or more of the pictures. Here are some title suggestions to get you started. Choose one, or think of your own.

Wave Patterns	Ladybug Patterns
Butterfly Designs	Rainbow Connections
Universal Connections	Earth Patterns
Planet Earth Connections	Tomorrow and Beyond
A Portrait in Time	Time Continuums

- Look at the pictures and make up a game dealing with how the pictures connect to each other. Pay attention to colors, patterns, shapes, textures, uses, food chains, ecosystems, stories, and songs the pictures remind you of. Perhaps call your game "1 - 2 - 3 - Connect" or "Earth Circles."
- Lay the pictures out to form a pattern, for example, square, circle, triangle, rectangle; or arrange the pictures to tell a story. Join up with two more students. Explain your connection idea to them, and they will explain their idea to you. Join up with at least one more group of two and do the same.
- Compose a pattern song or chant.
- Make a "Nature Patterns" mobile.
- Make a series of nature sketches including microscopic views.

7. Younger children might work in groups of four with their desks clustered closely together to prepare a "museum display" with the nature pictures and natural objects. Provide 5x8 cards folded in half for labels and sketches.

8. Bring closure to the lesson by sharing projects.

LITERATURE CONNECTION

Pattern by Kim Taylor, John Wiley & Sons, 1992
Brother Eagle, Sister Sky by Susan Jeffers, Scholastic, 1992
The Butterfly Book by Donald and Lillian Stokes & Ernest Williams, Little, Brown, 1991
Bees by Gallimard Jeunesse, Ute Fuhr, & Raoul Sautai, Scholastic, 1997

Figure 3.1   *(Continued)*

Nature Patterns

1. What patterns can you find? What patterns seem to repeat themselves?

_____

_____

_____

2. How were the patterns formed by forces of nature? How can the forces of nature, which are frequently so chaotic, produce such perfectly organized, repetitive patterns?

_____

_____

_____

3. What forces cause rapid change? Slow change?

_____

_____

_____

4. Choose one picture to answer this question. The photographer captured one moment in time in a picture. How might the image be different if taken the next day? In a month? During a different season? In a year? In a million years?

_____

_____

_____

5. What might we learn about ourselves and the human race as a whole by studying patterns in nature?

_____

_____

_____

Figure 3.1 (Continued)

principles, as well as the chaos principle of sensitive dependence on initial conditions, teaches them otherwise. Even unconscious signals, revealing teachers' own value structure, impact students more than they realize. Discussing enriched environments, Eric Jensen (1998) states that classrooms filled with posters, maps, and mobiles will both inspire and feed the brain. Likewise, the Caines (2006) believe that teachers must pay considerable attention to all aspects of the educational environment.

The small things teachers do make a major difference: their words of encouragement, their smiles and hellos, their remembering to call students by name, and their waiting for a few extra moments for hesitant girls to raise their hands rather than always calling on eager boys first. Should teachers arrange the students in groups of two or four? How many microscopes? How many learning stations? What about the mirrors, flashlights, and balloons? These seemingly simple decisions can have more impact than teachers realize. Although life has numerous variables and is much too nonlinear for long-term predictions, teachers must understand that the choices they make each day in their classrooms are powerfully significant. Teachers' daily decisions lead to larger ramifications, quickly amplifying through their classrooms, their schools, and the lives of their students.

One simple adjustment in materials or grouping could change the whole complexity of the lesson, providing the magic iteration, leading to a bifurcation of insight into how to make the lesson work. Teachers can input more or different information into the classroom equation by trying another strategy. They can then rejoice as the lessons reorganize themselves, emerging as new entities specifically adapted to the system of the classroom. If teachers ignore the new input information by sticking to their original plans, following them sequentially, step by step with absolutely no flexibility, they will shut out the output, flow, and interchange of ideas from which true change and new visions are born. The true potential of the lessons may never be realized. Although some of the strategies may throw a class into chaos, too often teachers forget to wait for the order. In a brain-compatible science classroom, teachers remember to watch for the order to reemerge.

Show Sensitivity to Unique Dynamics

As cultural diversity in the United States continues to increase, and as science teachers prepare to work effectively in classrooms of transition, change, and diversity, sensitive dependence on initial conditions takes on new significance. Teachers need appropriate knowledge, attitudes, and skills to work effectively with increasingly diverse groups of students. Teachers must be adaptable, thriving on the possibility of change, and sensitive to the unique dynamics of each classroom and the individual personalities within.

One obvious and relevant example in today's science classrooms is the issue of multiculturalism. To ensure the future quality of the nation and the world, all Americans, regardless of gender or ethnic background, must be scientifically literate by the time they complete high school (Rutherford & Ahlgren, 1989). Similarly, the *National Science Education Standards* (National Research Council, 1996) were designed as a vision to enable the nation to meet the goal that all students should achieve scientific literacy.

Elaine Hampton and Charles Gallegos (1994) described several teaching strategies to make science accessible to all. Teachers must have high expectations and carefully communicate those expectations to girls and minority students, as well as to boys. Teachers must vary the learning, focusing on relevant, hands-on, problem-solving activities, and allow students to work in groups. Teachers can develop a positive relationship with students through attention, appreciation, acceptance, affection, and assistance. They can overcome language barriers with process science and demonstrations that are the same in any language. Teachers can also respect different cultural mores and traditions by staying informed. They must confront gender and cultural inequities through discussion and examinations of equity in classroom management to avoid teaching only to high-profile students and white males. Teachers must provide strong female and minority role models and use the culture and home environment as a vehicle for making the learning relevant.

The National Council for the Social Studies (1992) recommended that teachers modify their instruction to facilitate the academic achievement of students from diverse racial, cultural, gender, and socioeconomic groups. The council also recommended using a variety of teaching styles consistent with the wide range of learning styles found in various cultural, ethnic, and gender groups. The curriculum and teaching strategies chosen by science educators profoundly affect future choices made by girls, boys, and minorities with respect to science education and science-related careers.

Science for All Cultures (Carey, 1993) is a collection of articles compiled from the National Science Teachers Association (NSTA) journals. The articles state repeatedly that science and technology in the United States does not originate solely from white, European roots but rather from many countries and cultures. A summary of some of the research findings includes the following:

- Educators should avoid curriculum containing gender or minority stereotypes (Atwater in Carey, 1993).
- Students with limited English proficiency should learn science by doing and participating in hands-on, minds-on activities (Mason & Barba in Carey, 1993).
- Both genders and many cultures have made significant contributions to the field of science (Barba, Ooga Pang, & Tran in Carey, 1993).
- Educators must nurture every child's potential to understand science, including girls and minorities, because the future world cannot afford to lose vital contributions and discoveries (Blake in Carey, 1993).
- African American and Hispanic American students must participate in relevant science experiences and must be exposed to strong science role models (Clark, Rakow, & Bermudez in Carey, 1993).

During the 1990s major studies exposing the inequities that occur daily in classrooms across the United States showed how this imbalance in attention results in lowering girls' achievement and self-esteem (The American Association of University Women, 1992; Sadker & Sadker, 1994; Sadker et al., 1993–1994). Despite the advances of feminism, sexism in the classroom causes girls to stifle their creative spirits and natural impulses and ultimately their sense of self. These reports conclude that much remains to be done to provide equal educational opportunities for female students. One of the ironies of gender bias in schools is that much of it goes unnoticed by educators. Although personally committed to fairness, many teachers are unable to see the inequities surrounding them (Sadker & Sadker, 1994).

The synthesized findings include:

- Teachers communicate more often with boys than with girls in the classroom.
- Teachers praise boys more often for the content and quality of their work, while praising girls more for neatness and form.
- Boys dominate, demanding more teacher time, attention, and energy than do girls.
- From grade school to graduate school, girls receive less teacher attention and less useful teacher feedback.
- Teachers encourage more assertive behavior in boys than they do in girls.
- Girls talk significantly less than boys do in class, and when they do speak in class, they often begin with remarks such as, "I'm not sure this is right."
- Female students become targets of unwanted sexual attention from male peers, teachers, and even administrators.
- Female voices are heard less often in science classes, and their names are less likely to be seen on lists of national merit finalists.
- Although girls are ahead of boys academically in the early elementary years, they achieve higher standardized test scores in every area but science.
- By middle school female test scores begin a downward spiral that continues through high school, college, and even graduate school. This drop in test scores begins around the same time that girls experience a loss of self-esteem.
- As a group, women are the only students who actually lose ground the longer they stay in school.

David Sadker (1999) reported that although much progress had been made with gender equity issues in schools, much still remained to be done. He explained the top 10 gender bias updates, including one heralding both good and bad news. The math and science gender gap is getting smaller, with more girls enrolling in science and math classes, including honors and advanced placement courses. Girls favor biology and chemistry, while physics is preferred by boys, who are also more likely to take all three core sciences. Although the gender gap has decreased in recent years, boys continue to outscore girls on high-stake tests such as the SAT (American Association of University Women, 1992; Sadker, 1999).

The fifth report from the U.S. Commission of Civil Rights on equal educational opportunity analyzed and evaluated the efforts of the U.S. Department of Education to enforce Title IX of the Education Amendments Act of 1972. The report agreed with David Sadker, in that while gender gaps in math and science have narrowed, there are still barriers to overcome. The report revealed that in math, science, and technology pursuits women do not have the same educational opportunities as men. Chapter 7 of the report reminds educators that "to be effective in meeting the educational needs of each student, educational programs must be structured in ways that address differences across age groups, ability levels, and interests; appropriate curriculum content; and differences in family and socioeconomic backgrounds" (U.S. Department of Education in "Gender Gaps Remain in Science Education," 2000/2001).

Accept the Impact of Changing Demographics

A metaphor for change, sensitive dependence on initial conditions reminds educators that equal science education experiences are for all students. Sensitivity to initial conditions must be considered with multicultural and gender issues and must also be provided for students with special needs and students at risk. If teachers are not already doing so, they will soon teach classes with multicultural student populations of diverse ethnic, racial, language, socioeconomic class, gender, and religious backgrounds. "Each year the nation's public school classrooms contain increasing numbers of at-risk students who are poor, non-English speaking, mainstream disabled, culturally different, or who come from dysfunctional and/or single parent families" (Barr & Parrett, 2003).

In their book *Saving Our Students, Saving Our Schools,* Barr and Parrett reminded educators of the disparities that exist between the well educated in our society and those who lack education. In addition, a greater number of children live in poverty, many are abused or neglected, and too many are in child care outside of the home. Educational research concludes that all children can learn, schools and teachers make a difference, immediate gains are possible, low-performing schools can become high-performing schools, and best practices work for low-performing and other at-risk students (Barr & Parrett, 2003, p. 14).

Examining classroom strategies, researchers discovered that effective classroom teachers and managers interacted with specific types of students. A cross section of students in a typical classroom might include passive students who fear relationships or failure; aggressive students who are either hostile, oppositional, or covert; students with attention problems; students who are perfectionists; and students who are socially inept. Rather than treating all students the same, effective teachers used different strategies with different types of students. Ineffective classroom managers did not appear sensitive to the diverse needs of students (Marzano & Marzano, 2003). Quite obviously, educators must be sensitive to the unique dynamics of a diverse student population to promise a brain-compatible atmosphere for students to learn and grow.

Change begins by acknowledging that there is a problem. As teachers confront cultural biases and prejudices and work collaboratively with both genders, different minorities, and special needs and at-risk students, they may begin to develop effective curriculum for all students, whatever their culture, gender, or special need. Students and teachers learn and grow together in awareness of their similarities and their differences as they continue to change and evolve. Students are empowered or disabled, depending on how they interact with their teachers.

Because they interact daily with children, teachers' seemingly insignificant actions carry more weight than they realize. To provide equal opportunities for all students in a rapidly changing and multicultural world, educators must transform their educational institutions, empowering all students to fully participate in classroom activities and in society.

> The problem is that when systems are moving toward "the edge of chaos," they can change radically; but the change cannot be controlled. The practical implication is that traditional procedures for solving problems do not work. One reason is that small actions can have large and unintended consequences, while large actions and interventions may have no impact whatsoever. In effect we need to internalize a fundamentally new way of conceiving of and responding to the situation in which we find ourselves. (Caine & Caine, 1997a, p. 13)

True empowerment comes from within as students are challenged out of their silence to pose and to seek solutions to those problems. Teachers' sensitivity or lack of sensitivity may make all the difference.

APPLICATION FOR BRAIN-COMPATIBLE SCIENCE

The following lesson plan, *A Closer Look at Crystals,* introduces the chaos theory principle of sensitive dependence on initial conditions into a science lesson, explaining how sensitive dependence on conditions of temperature, pressure, and humidity lead to an endless variety of intricately beautiful crystal patterns. No two students are alike; no two brains are alike. Each thought process, as unique as a crystal snowflake, depends sensitively on the melding of past and present thought processes as new understandings crystallize in a brain-compatible classroom.

Following the lesson plan is a web to incite more creative ideas (Figure 3.3) and a chart to navigate the road to change in the brain-compatible, science classroom (Figure 3.4).

Lesson: A Closer Look at Crystals

Chaos Theory Principle: Sensitive Dependence on Initial Conditions
Grade Level: 3–8

Chaos Connection

- Known in chaos theory as the butterfly effect, sensitive dependence on initial conditions implies that small, seemingly unrelated events may have great implications on patterns elsewhere in the universe.
- Nonliving matter grows into crystals with tiny changes in temperature and pressure or during the process of evaporation.
- Crystals form when atoms collect on a nucleus or tiny piece of crystal consisting of a cluster of atoms.
- No two snowflake crystals are ever exactly alike; each depends sensitively on the initial conditions of temperature and humidity as its dendritic branches grow and change with additional deposits of frozen water.

Curriculum Connection

- Weather—precipitation
- Rocks and minerals
- States of matter
- Physical change
- Microscopy
- Space shuttles

National Science Education Standards

- Content Standard A; 1–9
- Content Standard B; 1
- Content Standard D; 1

Objectives (Students will . . .)

- Create crystal straw blowings with a concentrated solution of Epsom salt.
- Observe the growth of Epsom salt crystals.
- Use a microscope to view developing Epsom salt crystals and discover their delicate beauty and sensitivity to surrounding conditions.
- Use a microscope to view a snowflake.

Materials

- ❏ Epsom salt
- ❏ Water
- ❏ Large cup
- ❏ Spoons or eyedroppers
- ❏ Glass jar
- ❏ Black construction paper
- ❏ Straws
- ❏ Magnifying lenses
- ❏ Glass microscope slides (clear yogurt lids or petri dishes may be substituted)
- ❏ Microscopes or microscope viewers

Optional

- Sugar, salt, alum, and copper sulfate
- Flat tray
- Clear lacquer spray
- Cotton and glitter
- Paint and brushes

Preactivity Discussion

Prior to the activity, discuss the following questions with students:

1. What is a crystal? (Crystals are solids composed of atoms arranged in orderly patterns under certain conditions. Well-developed crystals have a distinctly regular shape as a result of their geometrically ordered arrangement of atoms.)

2. How do crystals form? (Resulting from tiny changes in temperature and pressure or during the process of evaporation, various substances grow into crystals. Crystals form when atoms collect on a nucleus or tiny pieces of crystal consisting of a cluster of atoms. Atoms continue collecting on the nucleus as the crystal increases in size in an expanding network of structural units.)

Procedure

1. Before the students arrive, prepare a saturated Epsom salt solution. Pour a large cup of very hot, but not boiling, water into a glass jar. Add a tablespoon of Epsom salt to the water and stir until the crystals dissolve. Continue adding Epsom salt, one spoonful at a time, until the crystals no longer dissolve in the water. Allow the solution to cool slightly.

2. Have students use a spoon or an eyedropper to place a dime-size drop of Epsom salt solution at the bottom center of a piece of black construction paper.

3. Show the students how to blow slowly through a straw to spread the Epsom salt drop out into a feather tree design.

4. Move the straw around the paper directing the stream of air in different directions until the treelike design resembles a Japanese watercolor painting.

5. As the water evaporates, have students observe the Epsom salt crystals left behind in frosty patterns on the black paper. Let them use a magnifying lens for an up-close view of the feathery crystal shapes. For an artistic touch, add bits of cotton, sprinkles of glitter, or dabs of paint.

6. Have students make crystal slides with small drops of Epsom salt solution placed in the middle of a clean glass microscope slide, a clear plastic yogurt lid, or a petri dish.

7. Tell students to wait for some of the water to evaporate (about 5 or 10 minutes).

8. Have students carefully place the slide or plastic lid under the low power of a microscope and observe the crystals growing right before their eyes as the water continues to evaporate, leaving Epsom salt crystals behind on the slide. Tiny changes in one part of the crystal solution lead to bigger changes as more and more atoms cluster together. In time, a feathery crystalline structure appears.

9. Let students view the Epsom salt crystals first under the low power. Then have them change to the medium power for a closer view. Finally, tell them to use the high power for still a closer perspective. Epsom salt crystals have a fractal pattern as they repeat on smaller and smaller, self-similar scales (see Chapter 1).

10. Invite students to make drawings of the crystal microscope views.

Closure

At the close of the activity, pose these questions to the students to elicit a discussion, or have students reflect on these questions in journals.

- Crystal growth experiments are conducted regularly aboard space shuttle flights. How would crystals grow differently if they were grown in outer space? (Space crystals are larger and more symmetrical with fewer imperfections due to the absence of gravity in outer space. There are fewer initial conditions for the crystals to be sensitive to.)
- Explain this statement: A single snowflake is a delicate crystal. Many snowflake crystals acting together can shut down an entire city.

Questions and Extensions

- Have students write Japanese haiku poetry to accompany their beautiful crystal straw blowings.
- Grow additional crystals with sugar, salt, alum, or copper sulfate. Discuss how they are alike and how they are different from Epsom salt crystals.
- If you live in an area with snowy winters, make snowflake slides to view under a microscope. Either you or your students can place several glass slides on a flat tray. Chill the slides and a can of clear lacquer spray in the freezer. Wait for a snowy day and quickly carry the slides and the lacquer outside. Spray a thick layer of lacquer evenly over the slides, and allow a few snowflakes to fall on the slides. Leave the slides outside for 24 hours in a sheltered area. Bring the completed slides inside and view them under a microscope. Discuss how snowflakes are all different because of their sensitive dependence on initial conditions.

- Enjoy the extraordinary snowflake photographs in the book *The Snowflake Winter's Secret Beauty*, text by Kenneth Libbrecht (2003) and photography by Patricia Rasmussen.
- Pose the following questions to students:

  What is snow, and where does snow come from? (Composed of small crystals of frozen water, snow crystals form as atmospheric water vapor condenses around solid nuclei at temperatures below zero degrees centigrade. When snow crystals fall through the atmosphere, they cluster together as snowflakes.) What causes the infinite variety in snowflakes? (The shapes of snow crystals depend on air temperature and on atmospheric humidity. Crystal size depends mainly on the moisture content of the air. Snow crystals formed at higher temperatures tend to grow larger than those at lower temperatures because the moisture content of the atmosphere increases with increasing temperatures; see Figure 3.2.)

Technology Connection

Browse the following Web sites to find exciting new ideas for teaching science. Remember to use links and keywords to search even more science-related sites.

Exploratorium
http://www.exploratorium.edu

Snow Crystals.Com
http://www.its.caltech.edu/~atomic/snowcrystals/

Snowflake Images
http://www.its.caltech.edu/~atomic/snowcrystals/photos/photos.htm

Paper Snowflakes
http://www.papersnowflakes.com/

Weather Underground
http://www.wunderground.com/

These Web site addresses were accurate at the time of printing; however, as these sites are updated, some of the addresses may change.

Seven Types of Snowflakes

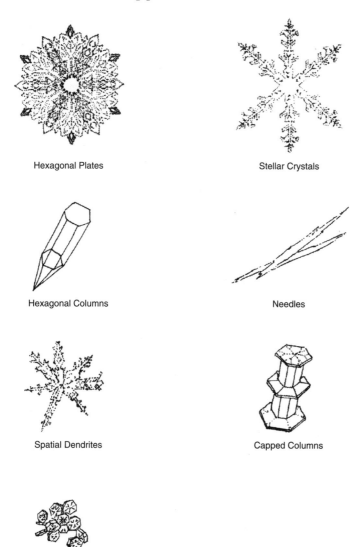

Hexagonal Plates

Stellar Crystals

Hexagonal Columns

Needles

Spatial Dendrites

Capped Columns

Irregular Crystals and Particles

Figure 3.2

Web for Applying Sensitive Dependence on Initial Conditions

Figure 3.3

NAVIGATING THE ROAD TO CHANGE IN SCIENCE EDUCATION

Sensitive Dependence on Initial Conditions

Too Much Order	On the Edge	Too Much Chaos
• Pay attention to every detail, demanding absolute perfection.	• Pay attention to details, believing that small things have large consequences.	• Ignore small things, believing that they are inconsequential.
• Ignore peripheral perception with too little stimulation.	• Tune into peripheral perceptions with well-balanced stimulation.	• Overemphasize peripheral perception with too much stimulation.
• Maintain high expectations from only high-level students and those who will seek out science careers.	• Maintain high expectations from all students, regardless of gender, ethnicity, or special needs.	• Have indifferent and mediocre expectations from all students.
• Underplay gender and minority bias.	• Encourage participation by all to enhance learning and self-esteem.	• Encourage haphazard participation of students.
• Emphasize a male-dominated curriculum and classroom.	• Balance female, male, and minority roles.	• Overemphasize contributions to science by women and minorities, underrepresenting the contributions by men.
	• Note contributions to science by men, women, and minorities.	

Figure 3.4

4

Strange Attractors, Phase Space, and Phase Portraits

A Metaphor for Change in Learning Environments and Habits of Mind

A chaotic system wanders wildly, never repeating itself. Each behavior is new and unpredictable. Moment to moment the system is free to experiment. And yet there is a hidden geography to its experimentation. Something unknown calls to its wanderings and the system answers by keeping its explorations within bounds. The attractor calls the system to a certain terrain, to a certain shape.

—Margaret Wheatley and Myron Kellner-Rogers (1996, p. 61)

BACKGROUND: WHAT ARE STRANGE ATTRACTORS, PHASE SPACE, AND PHASE PORTRAITS?

In chaos theory, a *strange attractor* is randomness with an underlying order, the shape that indecision traces (Briggs & Peat, 1989). Strange attractors exist everywhere in the universe, appearing in all chaotic systems including weather systems. The circulating heated and cooled air in convection currents moves randomly, exploring infinite possibilities. Displaying chaotic randomness with an underlying order, the air molecules stay within the defined phase space of their convection attractor. The air molecules circulate in the convection system, drawing out a phase portrait of two circles looping around forever, never revisiting the exact space in time twice.

In chaos theory this shape is known as the Lorenz attractor (see Chapter 3). Although the hot and cold molecules of air never end up in the same place twice, they still always remain within the convection system boundary of moving air. The molecules wander unpredictably at the same time that they trace out a phase portrait within the phase space of their strange attractor. As energy transforms molecules of air into self-similar patterns, a convection system that looks chaotic reveals a deeper order within.

> The strange attractor lives in phase space, one of the most powerful inventions of modern science. Phase space gives a way of turning numbers into pictures, abstracting every bit of essential information from a system of moving parts, mechanical or fluid, and making a flexible road map to all its possibilities. In phase space the complete state of knowledge about a dynamical system at a single instant in time collapses to a point. That point is the dynamical system— at that instant. At the next instant, though, the system will have changed, ever so slightly, and so the point moves. (Gleick, 1987, p. 134)

The butterfly-shaped Lorenz attractor (Figure 4.1) stays within the defined space of its strange attractor.

Beginning in phase space, with a point representing the complexity of a changing system, the initial equation begins to iterate, and the system's complexity is gradually revealed (Briggs & Peat, 1989). As the iterations continue, points move about chaotically, never returning to the same place twice. Gradually the points fill in, and a shape defining the system emerges. More intricate details appear the longer the equation runs.

While the equation iterates in three-dimensional phase space, the strange attractor traces out a phase portrait or picture that stays within the boundaries of its phase space, the place in space where a system changes over time. The phase space sets the parameters for the system, as well as determining a range of variations. The equation numbers trace out a design depicting the system's long-term behavior. David Ruelle described the aesthetic appeal of strange attractors:

Lorenz Attractor

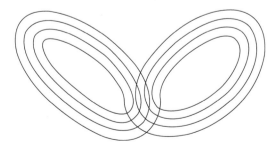

Figure 4.1

These systems of curves, these clouds of points suggest sometimes fireworks or galaxies, sometimes strange and disquieting vegetal proliferations. A realm lies there of forms to explore, and harmonies to discover. (Ruelle in Gleick, 1987, p. 153)

Like the weather, which is globally stable but locally unpredictable, the iterated points trace shapes that are predictable in form but not in the placement of specific dots. Gradually the dots reveal their secret pictures.

IMPLICATIONS OF STRANGE ATTRACTORS, PHASE SPACE, AND PHASE PORTRAITS FOR BRAIN-COMPATIBLE SCIENCE

Implications of strange attractors for science education are (1) trust in the inherent order, (2) set invisible boundaries with freedom to expand, (3) offer greater freedom and flexibility, and (4) believe in the power of guiding principles and values. These implications stress the importance of providing a learning environment and productive habits of mind that are conducive to brain-compatible science teaching and learning. Human brains innately search for meaning (Caine & Caine, 2006). Teachers must ensure that the search is brain compatible.

Trust in the Inherent Order

Unpredictable events follow a pattern known as the strange attractor. Teachers might miss the pattern because they are trapped in linear, two-dimensional thinking, but the pattern is there. Teachers need to trust that it will reveal itself. Wheatley (1994, p. 8) posed questions that may have parallels to science curriculum and teaching strategies: What are the sources of order? How do we create organization coherence where activities correspond to purpose? How do we create structures that move with change, that are flexible and adaptive, that enable rather than constrain? How do we simplify things without losing control?

Strange attractors in the classroom can take the shape of a dynamic environmental curriculum, a solar system unit, or a student's question sparking a thematic study of toys and energy. A day of launching student-made rockets, a Cartesian diver learning center, and a bubble-blowing activity also provide focus and act as strange attractors, as can a teacher's calming voice or an enthusiastic colleague, a science fair or school open house, the strong purpose and guiding values and principles provided by a school staff as a whole—the list could go on forever. Figure 4.2 show an example of an activity that can act as a strange attractor.

In her book *Brain Compatible Classrooms,* Robin Fogarty (1997a) describes the relationship between learning and the brain and how learning depends on memory. She suggests that the use of big ideas and curricular themes, by providing an overall pattern for the brain to perceive, assist in the learning process. "The brain is always seeking the big picture—the pattern of thought that is created by repeated use of familiar neural pathways"(p. 39). Perhaps the pattern of thought is a strange attractor, creating an inherent order through patterning, which enhances memory, which in turn enhances learning.

Toying With Toys

Grade Level: 2–4

OBJECTIVE

Students will use their knowledge of scientific principles to analyze favorite toys and household utensils.

PRELAB

Students should find a toy or a household utensil that illustrates a scientific principle. Some scientific principles include:

- Gravity and balance
- Newton's Laws (inertia; speed, motion, force; action-reaction)
- Friction
- Pushes and pulls
- Pulleys
- Levers
- Wheels
- Wheel and axle
- Inclined planes
- Wedges
- Screws
- Gears
- Energy—potential, kinetic, sound, heat, light, mechanical, electrical

Bring the toy to science class to analyze and share. Be prepared to explain how it works and what scientific principles it illustrates.

POSTLAB

Complete sharing and analyzing the toys and utensils; then make diagrams or write explanations explaining how the toys work. Students may wish to design, invent, or create their own toys.

Figure 4.2   *(Continued)*

Toying With Toys
Activity Log

1. What toy or utensil did you bring with you to share today? (If you forgot to bring one, which was your favorite?)

_____

_____

_____

_____

_____

2. What scientific principles does the toy/utensil illustrate?

_____

_____

_____

_____

_____

3. How does the toy/utensil work? You may draw a diagram to help you with your explanation.

_____

_____

_____

_____

_____

Figure 4.2 (Continued)

Dear Students,

On _____ you will participate in a fun science activity called "Toying With Toys." To prepare for the activity, please bring a toy or a small household utensil that illustrates several of the following scientific principles:

- Gravity

- Balance

- Speed, motion, force

- Inertia

- Action-reaction

- Friction

- Pushes and pulls

- Pulleys

- Levers

- Wheels and axles

- Gears

- Energy (light, heat, sound, electrical, magnetic, mechanical, potential, kinetic)

Bring the toy or utensil on _____ to analyze and share with your class. Be prepared to explain what scientific principles the toy/utensil illustrates and how it works. Make sure to choose something safe and something that fits in with the main ideas listed above. (No sharp edges, points, weapons, dolls, or stuffed animals, please.) If you wish, you may design and create your own toy.

Sincerely,

Figure 4.2   *(Continued)*

Strange attractors may be tangible or intangible, energy or things, people or values, anything that provides meaning, pulling teachers together in their educational quest, calling them to the shapes that they help define. During Geoffrey and Renate Caines' work with schools to implement brain-based teaching and learning, when teachers began questioning their deepest beliefs about teaching and learning, a new sense of order emerged. As the schools experienced an improvement in atmosphere and personal relationships, the Caines wondered if perhaps their theory about the process of educational change was somehow acting as a strange attractor (1997a, p. 199). The Caines (2006) believe that learning takes place when the brain self-organizes the tangled flow of information shaping meaning from thoughts, feelings, and past experiences. Information flows around the strange attractor in peoples' values and beliefs that they hold most central to their existence.

Set Invisible Boundaries With Freedom to Expand

In his dimensions of learning model, Robert Marzano (1992) discussed how positive attitudes and perceptions affect learning. In a positive learning environment, teachers accept their students, and students accept each other. Students sense comfort and perceive order in the classroom, and they believe that the tasks that they are required to do have relevance and value. Students understand what is expected of them. Serving as a strange attractor for students, teachers provide invisible boundaries by being aware of their students' needs; their physical, mental, and emotional health; and the importance of meeting those needs to ensure optimum learning. Only then may teachers effectively present new material to help students acquire knowledge and integrate that knowledge into previous concepts learned.

One of Caine and Caine's (2006) principles for brain-based learning (see Introduction) states that emotions are critical to patterning. Emotions and mind-sets influence learning. Webbing and shaping each other, emotions and thoughts cannot be separated. A lesson or life experience may trigger emotions that linger long after the specific event, again reminding educators of the importance of the chaos principle of sensitive dependence on initial conditions (see Chapter 3). Students' expectations, personal biases and prejudices, self-esteem, and the need for social interaction require a healthy emotional boundary surrounding learning situations.

Eric Jensen (1998) reviewed the research on how emotions are central to the thinking and learning process. Emotions drive students' attention, health, learning, meaning, memory, and survival. Because emotions, thinking, and learning are all linked, an engaging environment is a vital prerequisite to learning. According to Jensen, long-term memory encoding in the brain is enhanced by the presence of strong emotions during or after a learning experience.

Marzano (1992) believed that people's mental habits influence everything they do and that poor habits of mind usually lead to poor learning, regardless of the level of skill or ability. Teachers must plan to develop productive habits of mind in their students before effective learning may take place. By encouraging students to seek accuracy and clarity, be open-minded, resist impulsive answers, and show sensitivity to the feelings and ideas of others, teachers effectively train students to think critically. Teachers can encourage creative thinking by helping students pursue answers to problems, even when no easy solutions appear. Productive habits of mind provide invisible boundaries surrounding students with direction and purpose.

Teachers set the stage for brain-compatible science learning by making the phase space within their classrooms and schools as appealing as possible. Some teachers are lucky to have well-equipped science labs with running water and abundant supplies; others are not so fortunate. Wherever teachers teach, they face the challenge of providing an engaging learning environment for their students, brimming with bright science posters and inviting learning centers. A science news bulletin board, experiments in progress, aquariums and terrariums, and an invention center with parts from broken appliances can draw students into the learning experience. Lesson plans need to be carefully thought out with the freedom to expand beyond the invisible boundaries and with the assurance that the emotional needs of students will be met.

Offer Greater Freedom and Flexibility

Recent developments in the learning process reinforce that the search for meaning and understanding is basic to the human brain (Caine & Caine, 2006). The brains of learners search for patterns and connections, resisting meaningless and isolated bits of information that have no relevance. Learning will increase when new patterns of knowledge are linked with previous knowledge. Students must be given the opportunity to design their own patterns of understanding and to put ideas and skills together in their own way. Teachers can imagine what beautiful phase portraits could be drawn if students were given the freedom to learn within a much larger realm beyond the four walls of their classroom.

Most present-day schools were designed for a factory paradigm in Newton's linear age. School buildings can be so confining, with students sitting in desks in little rooms that are arranged up and down long hallways. Schools need not be static cubby holes with rigid boundaries, where students are constantly told to sit still, stop talking, raise their hands, and go back to their seats. How narrow are educators to expect children to learn and grow in such a limited and confining space? Schools need to be dynamic places of movement and activity where teachers guide their students to look at things in unique ways; welcome diverse ideas, understandings, and opinions; and enable students to trace out their own uniquely creative phase portraits.

Definitely the adoption of a single textbook series as the science curriculum for a school district can seriously limit learning. Science represents so much more than words, pictures, and diagrams in a series of books! Because of the rapid pace of modern scientific discoveries, science texts are outdated before they go to press. Educators must stop confining students to view science from the single perspective of the authors of a text. Instead they must view science from many perspectives, including scientists in the field who conduct experiments on the cutting edge. Although a good text may provide a strong science knowledge base, educators must consider widening the phase space to allow the strange attractor greater freedom to design increasingly more intricate patterns of understanding.

In their book *Windows on the Future: Education in the Age of Technology*, Ian Jukes and Ted McCain (2000) forecasted a shifting paradigm for education in the future. They envisioned 10 changes and explain the role of technology in these changes:

1. Education will not be confined to a single place.

2. Education will not be confined to a specific time.

3. Education will not be confined to a single person.

4. Education will not be confined to human teachers.

5. Education will not be confined to memorization.

6. Education will not be confined to paper-based information.

7. Education will not be confined to linear learning.

8. Education will not be confined to the intellectual elite.

9. Education will not be confined to childhood.

10. Education will not be confined to controlling learners.

Clearly Jukes and McCain understood the importance of widening the educational phase space to include more strange attractors, creating phase portraits of purposeful meaning.

Should teachers throw out all the traditional methods? Absolutely not! However, some activities, particularly in science, may require a new way of looking at the noise level and freedom of movement in the classroom. What if teachers could plot an idea and trace out a phase portrait as the idea iterated in a child's mind, building on previous knowledge and coming forth as newly constructed meaning? What if teachers expanded the phase space out into the community for science students to go to the woods, the pond, the prairie—out into the real world to run and explore, to see and gather? What if teachers allowed greater freedom and flexibility to tinker and wander, to muse and ponder?

Teachers encourage brain-compatible science and provide for greater freedom and flexibility by using computer technology to let their students visit Mars and Jupiter and volcanic vents on the ocean floor. Teachers can make the beach their classroom, where students will discover the interacting systems and diversity of life in a beach ecosystem. Students can participate in a beach scavenger hunt, create beach drawings and sketches, and look for signs of weathering, erosion, deposition, and patterns in the sand and water (see Sand Patterns lesson plan in Chapter 7).

Students can also grow a garden of prairie flowers and watch the monarch butterflies interact with the marsh milkweed. Anyone who has ever seen the splendor of purple prairie coneflowers in full bloom understands the impression that something beautiful and real has on a child's developing imagination. Observing beauty in the surrounding world may help students discover what is real and of value to them in their everyday lives.

Believe in the Power of Guiding Principles and Values

Research conducted by Robert Marzano (2003) concluded that classroom management decisions made by teachers impact student achievement more than decisions regarding curriculum and assessment. A poorly managed classroom is not conducive to learning. Teachers need to find a balance between the setting of clear consequences for unacceptable student behavior and the recognition of and reward for acceptable behavior. In his book *Classroom Management That Works*, Marzano introduced nine key "variables" essential to effective classroom management:

1. Establish clear expectations and consequences.

2. Establish clear learning goals.

3. Exhibit assertive behavior.

4. Use appropriate levels of cooperation with students.

5. Provide flexible learning goals.

6. Take a personal interest in students.

7. Use equitable and positive classroom behaviors.

8. Be aware of and understand high-needs students.

9. Don't leave relationships with students to chance.

Behaving as a strange attractor, the nine variables go to work in the phase space of the classroom, drawing out a phase portrait of improved relationships, student achievement, and classroom behavior.

In a later work on classroom management, Robert and Jana Marzano (2003) interpreted research findings and concluded that of all the variables essential to effective classroom management, the quality of student-teacher relationships is the most important. They found that teachers who had high-quality relationships with their students had fewer discipline problems than did teachers who did not.

Why are certain topics central to teachers' ideas about what children should know? Why do teachers choose certain classroom management strategies? Teachers' values determine the decisions they make as educators. Margaret Wheatley stressed the power of guiding principles and values:

> The structure is capable of maintaining its overall shape and a large degree of independence from the environment because each part of the system is free to express itself within the context of that system. Fluctuations, randomness, and unpredictability at the local level, in the presence of guiding or self-referential principles, cohere over time into definite and predictable form. (Wheatley, 1994, pp. 132–133)

Teachers must determine what principles and values guide them to teach the way they do.

Wheatley (1994) believed that when teachers begin to examine the meaning behind their beliefs, they may begin to understand reasons for change. As the Caines discovered (1997a; 1997b), teachers must face their new understandings, using them as strange attractors to help them discover new meaning in their teaching. These new understandings guide teachers as they forge ahead by generating new order for their science curricula, providing meaningful purpose to their teaching, and assuring that their science classrooms are truly brain compatible.

APPLICATION FOR BRAIN-COMPATIBLE SCIENCE

The following brain-compatible lesson plan, *Dancing Raisins*, introduces the chaos theory principle of strange attractors into a science lesson featuring the interaction of solids, liquids, and gases. Through an exploration of changes in density, when bubbles of carbon dioxide cling to small objects in carbonated water, students observe a dynamical system in action while their brain neurons trace out phase portraits of newly constructed meanings. Following the lesson plan is a web to incite more creative ideas (Figure 4.4) and a chart to navigate the road to change in the brain-compatible classroom (Figure 4.5).

Lesson: Dancing Raisins

Chaos Theory Principle: Strange Attractors, Phase Space, and Phase Portraits

Grade Level: 2–8

Chaos Connection

- Strange attractors exist everywhere in the universe, appearing wherever systems behave randomly, including the chaotic movements in a bubbly jar of dancing raisins and popcorn kernels.
- A single tiny bubble, with its sensitive dependence on initial conditions, may determine whether a raisin or popcorn kernel sinks or floats in the fizzy water.
- Displaying chaotic randomness with an underlying order, the dynamical dancing raisin system stays within the defined space of its strange attractor. Although the bubbles and dancing objects never exactly follow the same path twice, they always remain within their watery, liquid boundary.
- The bubbles, raisins, and popcorn kernels wander unpredictably at the same time that they trace out a phase portrait within the phase space of their strange attractor.

Curriculum Connection

- Physical and chemical change
- Properties of matter
- Density
- Solids, liquids, gases
- Convection

National Science Education Standards

- Content Standard A; 1–9
- Content Standard B; 1
- Content Standard D; 1

Objectives (Students will . . .)

- Observe changes in density when bubbles of carbon dioxide cling to small objects in carbonated water.
- Observe raisins, popcorn kernels, and other small objects interacting in a bubble system.

Materials

- ❏ Large jar
- ❏ Baking soda
- ❏ Vinegar
- ❏ Water

❑ Raisins
❑ Popcorn kernels
❑ Dancing Raisins Activity Log (see Figure 4.3)

Optional

- Spaghetti (cut in 1-inch sections)
- Rice
- Bean seeds
- Black-eyed peas
- Other small objects
- Clear soda instead of baking soda and vinegar

Preactivity Discussion

1. Discuss the meaning of density. Why do some things sink while others float?

2. How can you get something that sinks to float?

3. How can you get something that floats to sink?

Procedure

1. Organize the students into cooperative groups of four.

2. Give each group the following materials:
   - Large jar filled three-fourths with water
   - Approximately two tablespoons of baking soda
   - Approximately one-eighth cup of vinegar
   - Raisins, popcorn kernels, and the like

3. Have the students pour the baking soda into the jar.

4. Gradually add the vinegar, and observe what happens.

5. Add the raisins, popcorn, rice, spaghetti, and so forth.

6. Continue to observe.

7. Complete the Dancing Raisins Activity Log.

Closure

1. Circulate among the groups, and discuss the students' observations.

2. Discuss the Dancing Raisins Activity Log.

Questions

At the close of the activity, pose these additional questions to students to elicit a discussion, or have students reflect on these questions in journals.

1. What happens when baking soda is added to the jar of water? (The baking soda will sink to the bottom of the jar.)

2. What happens when the vinegar is poured into the jar? (The baking soda and vinegar will fizz.)

Dancing Raisins Activity Log

1. What happened when baking soda and vinegar were poured into the jar of water?

2. What gas was produced?

3. Explain what happened to the small bits of matter that were dropped into the jar.

4. Why did some sink?

5. Why did some float?

6. Why did some dance up and down?

7. Make a drawing of the jar, including the raisins, noodles, rice, popcorn, etc.

Figure 4.3

3. What kind of a reaction is this? (A chemical reaction)

4. What gas is produced? (Carbon dioxide)

5. Why do the raisins and other add-ins dance up and down? (Raisins and popcorn kernels have a low density, very close to 1, which is the density of water. For this reason they just barely sink in the water. When bubbles of carbon dioxide collect on the raisins' surface, the raisins become more buoyant and rise to the top. When the raisins reach the surface, the bubbles burst, and the raisins lose their buoyancy, thus sinking back to the bottom. Popcorn, rice, and other small objects behave in a similar manner, although some may require more or fewer bubbles to rise and sink again.)

6. Why do some of the small bits of matter stay floating on the top? (If the raisins, etc., are less dense than water, they will float.)

7. Why do some of the small bits of matter sink to the bottom? (If the raisins, etc., are denser than water, they will sink.)

8. Imagine a single raisin or popcorn kernel tracing out a little line of red ink as it travels up and down in its watery world. What kind of strange shape would eventually emerge?

9. How could the raisins escape their strange attractor? (The jar could break or spill.)

Extensions

1. Demonstrate a convection current by heating a beaker of water over a hot plate or alcohol lamp. Add some confetti or paper dots, which will at first sink to the bottom. Bring the water to a boil and observe what happens to the dots. (As the water warms, the dots will begin jumping around at the bottom of the beaker. Then, as the water gets hotter, they will rise to the top, along with the heated, less dense water. At the top, the water cools, becomes denser, and drops back down to the bottom, carrying the dots along.) Add a drop of food coloring, and observe its motion. (The food coloring will move downward and then upward in a quick, circular motion.) Shine a flashlight through the beaker to highlight the action. Have students watch a single piece of confetti and draw a diagram to show how it moves. What shape does the piece of confetti trace out? (It traces out a circular shape, half of the butterfly shape of the Lorenz attractor). Explain that the shape is the strange attractor for this chaotic system of water currents. Behaving like air in massive weather systems, the circulating molecules of water never go beyond their strange attractor. Molecules move within the defined phase space of the beaker. Convection systems such as this occur in the atmosphere and oceans of the Earth. Convection currents also exist deep within the mantle of the Earth as rock layers are continually folded, faulted, and recycled.

2. Fill a 5-gallon or other large-sized clear container three-fourths full with room-temperature water. Pour hot water with red food coloring into a small baby food jar. Pour icy cold water with blue food coloring into a second baby food jar. Place lead weights in the jars to keep them from floating. Cover both jars with aluminum foil, and secure with rubber bands. Place both jars on the bottom of the container, one on each end. Use a pencil to carefully poke holes in the foil. Observe how the less dense, hot water rises while the denser, cold water sinks, creating still another convection current.

3. Other activities to illustrate the principle of strange attractors, phase space, and phase portraits include activities with pendulums, stream tables, ripple tanks, evaporating water, and tornado tube bottles. All of these are dynamical systems changing in time.

Technology Connection

Browse the following Web sites to find exciting new ideas for teaching science. Remember to use links and keywords to search even more science-related sites.

Hurricane Storm Science
http://www.miamisci.org/hurricane

Lesson Plan Central
http://lessonplancentral.com/lessons/Science/

Lorenz Butterfly
http://www.exploratorium.edu/complexity/java/lorenz.html

Chaos Theory and Strange Attractors
http://www.alunw.freeuk.com/chaos.html

These Web site addresses were accurate at the time of printing; however, as these sites are updated, some of the addresses may change.

Web for Applying Strange Attractors, Phase Space, and Phase Portraits

Figure 4.4

NAVIGATING THE ROAD TO
CHANGE IN SCIENCE EDUCATION

Strange Attractors, Phase Space, and Phase Portraits

Too Much Order	On the Edge	Too Much Chaos
• Continue to offer a linear and two-dimensional curricula. • Concentrate on fact retention. • Initiate a box paradigm with rigid boundaries. • Train students to think alike. • Disregard the impact of emotions on learning. • Base science curriculum on a single text. • Insist on quiet and perfect adherence to the rules at all times. • Rules are made and enforced by the teacher. • Leave relationships with students to chance. • Dictate principles and values with zero flexibility.	• Trust in the inherent order of nonlinear, multidimensional curricula. • Use big ideas and curricular themes to generate thought patterns. • Provide a positive learning environment. • Develop productive habits of mind. • Consider the impact of emotions on learning. • Provide the freedom to learn within a much larger realm both in and beyond the classroom. • Generate science curricula from multiple sources. • Take a new look at noise level and freedom of movement in the classroom. • Establish a contract of rules between students and teachers. • Develop positive relationships with students. • Feature guiding principles and values.	• Offer neither pattern nor linearity in the curriculum. • Overdo the holistic approach. • Feature a totally free learning environment. • Ignore habits of mind. • Exaggerate the impact of emotions on learning. • Implement science curricula containing any and all perspectives. • Totally ignore noise; give students free reign. • Throw out the rules. • Indulge students with too much attention and praise. • Hide from simple truths.

Figure 4.5

5

Bifurcations and Period Doubling

A Metaphor Featuring Choices, Joy, and Surprise

The concepts that run in tandem with the idea of bifurcation points are emergence and self organization. Although a great deal of effort was spent on "inducing" the change, there was something about such change that was not "managed. . . ." Rather, the critical factor was the jelling of the individual groups. This process was an emotional/intellectual process that just happened, then was translated into the school as a whole.

Geoffrey and Renate Nummela Caine (1997a, p. 199)

BACKGROUND: WHAT ARE BIFURCATIONS AND PERIOD DOUBLING?

In her exceptional picture book *One Grain of Rice,* Demi (1997) told the tale of Rani, a clever village girl who does a good deed for the raja. When the raja offers her a reward, Rani asks for just one grain of rice to be doubled every day for 30 days. Through the surprising power of bifurcation and period doubling, one grain of rice grows into more than one billion grains of rice. In the process, Rani teaches the raja a lesson about the true meaning of wisdom and fairness.

A bifurcation, or forking, occurs in a dynamical system when a single happening, perhaps as small as a photon, a butterfly's wings, or a smile, amplifies so greatly by iteration that the system takes off in a whole new direction. A continual branching process is set into motion as large swirls break into smaller swirls and into still smaller swirls. The whole process from order to turbulence and unpredictability involves endless bifurcations at smaller and smaller scales, as with Benoit Mandelbrot's famous fractal set or sand at the beach (see Chapters 1 and 7). Perhaps the boundary between smooth and turbulent actually exists at the molecular level.

77

Life is filled with endless bifurcations, or phases of transition, as people face choices and challenges on a daily basis. Sometimes the seemingly insignificant choices, the small things representing the daily process of living, profoundly affect people's futures. What college? What job? What city? Which turn in the road? People can only guess where the decision will lead. Nonequilibrium thermodynamics chemist Ilya Prigogine explained that in the evolution of living systems, when bifurcation points are reached, new choices and freedoms lead to still more bifurcations and a complexity of iterations that keeps recycling the past history of the system (Prigogine & Stengers, 1984). Encoded genetic information iterates from generation to generation, and systems stabilize through their connectedness in time.

As the state of the system changes, the bifurcations begin with period doublings, which are a common factor in the way order breaks down into chaos. First the system splits into 2, 4, 8, 16, and then after a huge number of bifurcations and infinite number of choices, the onset to turbulence ensues. The chaos continues until the system is driven further by still more iterations. In time, a new structure appears. Then the period doublings begin again with a 6, 12, 24, and so on. Mitchell Feigenbaum saw period doubling as he performed his breakthrough mathematical calculations in the early 1960s (Gleick, 1987). Feigenbaum knew that the boundary between order and chaos was like the mysterious boundary between smooth flow and turbulence in a fluid. The windows of order emerge inside of chaos at the boundary between the two.

In the 1970s biologist Robert May (1976) helped to develop the explanation of the "period-doubling route to chaos," a period being defined as the amount of time it takes for a system to return to its original state. May's work studying biological systems, in particular, the growth rate of fish populations, led him to understand that biological systems behave both erratically and nonlinearly. Before May's breakthrough studies, population biologists had believed that changing animal populations followed orderly cycles, more in keeping with the Newtonian paradigm. May believed that chaos theory should be taught to better prepare future scientists to deal with the nonlinear nature of the world.

The Caines described three possible outcomes for schools that undergo a process of change. Each of these outcomes occur at bifurcation points. "The process might die out, and the school revert to former practices," resulting in resistance to change and burnout. "The school might evolve" with a dramatically changed belief system into a more complex means of working and learning together, and "The school might disintegrate" as a result of deeply entrenched values and beliefs. "Capitalizing on and managing these bifurcation points are the real mastery of transformation" (Caine & Caine, 1997a, pp. 244–245).

IMPLICATIONS OF BIFURCATION AND PERIOD DOUBLING FOR BRAIN-COMPATIBLE SCIENCE

Three implications of bifurcation and period doubling for science education are (1) recognize more than one right way by providing choices, (2) seek out turmoil and surprise, and (3) provide a joyful classroom atmosphere. These implications directly coincide with four of Geoffrey and Renate Caine's (2006) mind/brain principles (see Introduction): The mind/brain organizes memory in at least two different ways, learning is developmental, learning is enhanced by challenge and inhibited by threat, and every mind/brain is unique. Today's students need preparation for the modern world awaiting them. Real-life problems are not easily solved. The nonlinear world is amazingly complicated, and yet, hidden within life's complexities, lie bifurcations of knowledge and the potential for unimaginable understandings.

Recognize More Than One Right Way by Providing Choices

Brain-compatible science education requires that teachers offer choices in teaching, learning, assessing, and designing curriculum to provide for divergence and bifurcations of new knowledge for all students. Rather than focusing their efforts on teaching science, teachers in brain-compatible classrooms concentrate on teaching children.

Choices in Teaching

Teachers need to teach in different ways by using a combination of strategies to reach diverse learning styles. Teachers must resist their inclination to exclusively use only teaching strategies that are comfortable for them. Instead, teachers should take risks by trying out new methods and approaches. Believing that all students can learn and that science is for all, teachers must respect student differences and modify instruction to meet diverse needs. Students need variety for creativity and imagination to flourish. Educators need to teach the children they have, not the children they used to have or wish they had. Teachers need to provide fewer convergent and more divergent activities for students to enable greater bifurcation and period doubling of knowledge to occur. Many right ways and many different perspectives exist.

Integrate visual, auditory, and kinesthetic experiences into science lessons in hopes of addressing multiple intelligences, as well as reaching out to girls and minorities. Working in cooperative learning groups, students share materials, ideas, and enthusiasm for learning. When designing lessons, look closely at developmental levels of students, matching activities with what students are ready to learn. Consider how to organize materials and meaningful activities most effectively to help students develop a love for science. Embed activity-based experiences with an emphasis on creative and critical thinking skills (e.g., questioning, collecting data, analyzing data, and explaining), designed to generate excitement and curiosity.

Caine and Caine (2006) stated that learning is developmental. Windows of opportunity for learning occur in developmental stages. The brain is composed of billions of neurons, which when used connect to other neurons and when not used may die. Heredity and environment determine the ability of the brain to wire itself within certain critical periods or windows of opportunity that open and then slam shut, generally early in the development of a child. There is no limit to the human capacity for growth and learning. All learning builds on previous learning accompanied by physiological changes in the brain. Differences in the maturation and development of students need to be taken into account.

Teachers need to find a balance between what they teach and how they teach, using teaching strategies and models to draw out the very best in students, while at the same time having a deep and committed knowledge of science. Good technique is a must for subject matter to be transferred from the brain of the teacher to the brain of the learner.

Knowing what you are trying to teach is essential to good teaching, but knowing how to teach it is what distinguishes good teachers from mere content experts. (Gunter, Estes, & Schwab, 1995, p. 349)

Science teachers need a combined knowledge of science content, effective techniques, and an extensive understanding of children and how they learn before they can design meaningful instruction. Brain-compatible science teachers create meaningful instruction to ensure bifurcations of meaningful learning in their science classrooms (Figure 5.1).

Choices in Learning

Because of the uniqueness of individuals, bifurcations of knowledge occur at different times and at different rates. Some students work well in groups. Others prefer to learn alone. Some thrive on excitement and change. Others like quiet and dim lights. Some students are self-starters with an amazing sense of purpose and motivation. Others need constant nudging from their teachers. All learners display differing learning styles, talents, and intelligences. The Caines (2006) put forth the notion that every brain is uniquely organized yet paradoxically similar. Students need many choices and a wide variety of multisensory experiences to learn effectively.

Stating that an individual's intelligence offers a pluralistic view of the mind, Howard Gardner's (1983) theory of multiple intelligences presents an in-depth understanding of children and how they learn. An intelligence involves solving problems or fashioning products that have cultural significance. Gardner originally theorized the existence of seven or more intelligences: verbal/linguistic, logical/mathematical, visual/spatial, bodily/kinesthetic, musical/rhythmic, intrapersonal, and interpersonal (Gardner, 1983; 1995). In a later work (1999), reporting on how his theory of multiple intelligences is radically changing our understandings of education and human development, Gardner introduced three additional intelligences: naturalist, spiritual, and existential. Undoubtedly more intelligences will surface over time.

Gardner's multiple intelligences theory embraces all cultures, encouraging teachers to teach children based on their strengths and interests. Understanding that children learn best when they are joyfully engaged in challenging activities that are consistent with individual learning styles, Gardner's works (1983; 1991; 1999) suggest a shift in education from how teachers teach to how students learn. Gardner averred that instructional strategies must invite rather than alienate students. When designing learning, teachers need to look for ways to incorporate all of the multiple intelligences and to address a wide range of learning styles (Gardner, 1999).

The three-story intellect with multiple intelligences is a model featuring the three stories of intellect using Gardner's multiple intelligences (Fogarty, 1997b) (Figure 5.2). First, students gather knowledge through research. Next, they process knowledge where ideas begin to crystallize. Finally, students apply their new understandings as they test their knowledge. Promoting higher-level thinking strategies, this model fosters brain-compatible science within a brain-compatible classroom. *With a Cluck Cluck Here* is an engaging science lesson incorporating all of the multiple intelligences (Figure 5.3).

(Text continues on page 87)

Science Lesson Plan Guide

Title of Lesson _____

Grade Level _____

1. What are the district learning standards/benchmarks for this science lesson?

2. What understandings will the students gain as a result of this science lesson?

3. Where does this science lesson fit in the unit of study?

4. What instructional strategies and activities will occur in this science lesson?

5. What special conditions (materials, student needs, other) may be present during this science lesson?

6. How will you accommodate for students with diverse learning needs in the context of this science lesson?

7. How will you provide students with feedback during this science lesson?

8. How will you evaluate this science lesson?

Figure 5.1

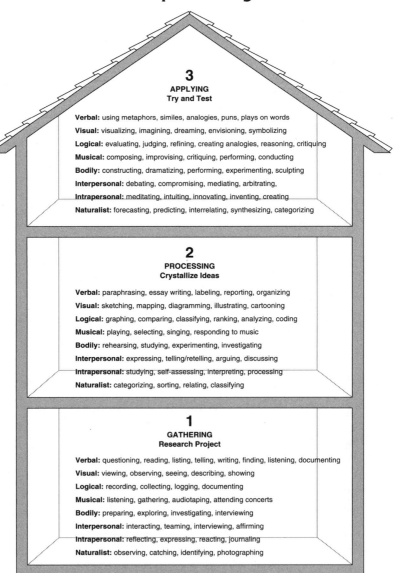

The Three-Story Intellect
With Multiple Intelligences

3
APPLYING
Try and Test

Verbal: using metaphors, similes, analogies, puns, plays on words
Visual: visualizing, imagining, dreaming, envisioning, symbolizing
Logical: evaluating, judging, refining, creating analogies, reasoning, critiquing
Musical: composing, improvising, critiquing, performing, conducting
Bodily: constructing, dramatizing, performing, experimenting, sculpting
Interpersonal: debating, compromising, mediating, arbitrating,
Intrapersonal: meditating, intuiting, innovating, inventing, creating
Naturalist: forecasting, predicting, interrelating, synthesizing, categorizing

2
PROCESSING
Crystallize Ideas

Verbal: paraphrasing, essay writing, labeling, reporting, organizing
Visual: sketching, mapping, diagramming, illustrating, cartooning
Logical: graphing, comparing, classifying, ranking, analyzing, coding
Musical: playing, selecting, singing, responding to music
Bodily: rehearsing, studying, experimenting, investigating
Interpersonal: expressing, telling/retelling, arguing, discussing
Intrapersonal: studying, self-assessing, interpreting, processing
Naturalist: categorizing, sorting, relating, classifying

1
GATHERING
Research Project

Verbal: questioning, reading, listing, telling, writing, finding, listening, documenting
Visual: viewing, observing, seeing, describing, showing
Logical: recording, collecting, logging, documenting
Musical: listening, gathering, audiotaping, attending concerts
Bodily: preparing, exploring, investigating, interviewing
Interpersonal: interacting, teaming, interviewing, affirming
Intrapersonal: reflecting, expressing, reacting, journaling
Naturalist: observing, catching, identifying, photographing

Figure 5.2

SOURCE: From *Problem-Based Learning & Other Curriculum Models for the Multiple Intelligences Classroom,* Robin Fogarty, 1997, Corwin Press.

With a Cluck Cluck Here!

Key Concept

Sounds differ in their frequency, pitch, intensity, loudness, and quality.

Objectives: Students will . . .

1. Discover how sounds differ in pitch, intensity, loudness, and quality.

2. Analyze what effect the size of the cup has on sound.

3. Experiment with other variables such as string length and width, and size of cup.

Content Focus

Sounds have three characteristics: pitch, loudness, and tone or quality. The pitch of a sound refers to how low or how high the sound is. Pitch depends on frequency, which is how fast or how slow an object is vibrating. The faster an object vibrates, the greater is its frequency and the higher its pitch. A shorter string on a stringed instrument vibrates more rapidly, producing a higher frequency, which results in a higher pitch. A longer string produces a lower pitch.

Loudness refers to the energy of the sound wave, or how strong a sound seems when it reaches our ears. The greater the intensity, the louder the sound. Frequency also affects a sound's loudness, with frequencies in the upper and lower limits of our hearing range sounding less loud than sounds of equal intensity in the middle frequencies. If you pluck a guitar or violin string very hard, it will make a loud sound. If you pluck the same string gently, it will make a soft sound.

Advance Preparation

Cut the sponges and strings, and poke holes in the tops of the cups. Cut small scraps of paper for the beaks and eyes. Organize all of the materials for easy distribution.

Tips

You may use commercial googly eyes if you wish, as well as construction paper feathers instead of real feathers. Feather dusters provide an inexpensive feather source. If all students are constructing a chicken, it may be helpful to pass out materials in the following order: cups with holes pre-poked, string, toothpicks, sponges. Students younger than third grade will need help tying their strings to the toothpicks and sponges. Put the orange and black construction paper and feathers on a table where children may help themselves when they are ready. Limit the feathers to two each, one sticking out on each side of the chicken. Make sure that you are prepared mentally for a noisier than usual activity!!

Figure 5.3   *(Continued)*

Materials

plastic cups, large, small, and medium

variety of other containers both large and small

string of various widths

small pieces of sponge

toothpicks

awl or compass for poking holes

orange and black construction paper

feathers

glue

scissors

Procedure

1. Use an awl to poke a small hole in the center of the cup base (do ahead).

2. Insert a string that will hang 30 or more cm below the inverted cup.

3. Tie a toothpick to the string at the top to prevent the string from pulling through the cup.

4. Wet a small piece of sponge and tie it to the other end of the string.

5. Decorate the cup to look like a chicken. Add eyes, beak, and feathers on the sides. (You may poke holes on the sides of the cup and insert a feather in each.)

6. Wet the sponge and dampen the string.

7. Pull the sponge quickly, and in a jerking motion, along the string to make the chicken cluck.

Extensions

1. Experiment with different sizes and kinds of cups, and lengths and thicknesses of string. How will changing these variables affect the pitch and volume of the sounds? How can you improve the quality of the cluck? A plastic ice-cream bucket makes a great-sounding dog! Try a bottle cap for a squeaky mouse. Make up an entire "Old McDonald's farm," including a dog, pig, duck, horse, and cat.

2. Read animal sound stories and sing animal sound songs (you will have your own chicken coop at Old McDonald's farm). Produce a chicken play complete with sound effects. Write animal onomatopoeia (sound) poetry. Invite other classes to share in the good "sound" fun!

Figure 5.3 (Continued)

Suggested Follow-up/Questions

1. What produces sound? (Vibrations of matter)

2. What is the purpose of the sponge? The string? (The sponge moving up and down causes the string to vibrate, and sound is produced.)

3. What is the purpose of the cup? (The cup serves as an amplifier to amplify the sound. The sound waves are prevented from spreading out in all directions.)

4. Try using just the string and sponge without the cup. What is the difference in the sound produced? (Without the cup the sound is reduced to a soft squeak because the sound waves are allowed to spread out in the surrounding air with no cup to provide amplification.)

5. What effect does the size of the cup have on the pitch of the sound? (The large cups produce the papa-sized, or low-pitched sounds. The medium cups produce the mama-sized sounds. The small cups produce the highest pitch, or baby-sized sounds.)

Unit/Curriculum Connections

Energy

Sound

Musical instruments

Animals

Onomatopoeia poetry

Literature Connections

Sounds My Feet Make by Arlene Blanchard

Through Grandpa's Eyes by Patricia MacLachlan

Ty's One-man Band by Mildred Pitts Walker

Figure 5.3   *(Continued)*

With a Cluck Cluck Here:
Using Eight Multiple Intelligences

Verbal/Linguistic:

Read stories and poems about chickens and animal sounds.
Write onomatopoeia (sound) poetry.
Read and discuss how sounds differ in pitch, intensity, loudness, and quality.

Logical/Mathematical:

Use the scientific method to predict which chicken will have the highest pitch.
Measure the string.

Visual/Spatial:

Make papa, mama, and baby chickens.
Create a face with eyes and beak and decorate with feathers.
Make additional "Old McDonald's farm" animals.

Body/Kinesthetic:

Participate in a hands-on learning activity.
Make up a play starring the chickens.
Using arm movement, act out the difference between high, medium, and low pitches.

Musical/Rhythmic:

Sing "Old McDonald Had a Farm."
Hum and dance the "Chicken Dance."
Experiment with pitch and volume.

Interpersonal:

Do the activity in cooperative groups or with partners.
Take turns listening to each other's chickens cluck.
Give the chickens names and introduce them to each other.

Intrapersonal:

Discuss how you felt while doing the activity, the humor in science and how much fun can be had.
Write a paragraph beginning, "Today in science we made clucking chickens."
How would the chickens cluck if they were happy? Sad? Angry? How would they say, "Thank you for the fun science activity?"

Naturalist:

Find out about chickens and their body structure.
Find out about how chickens are raised on chicken farms. What health issues
    sometimes make the headlines?
How must poultry be handled safely when prepared for cooking?

Figure 5.3 (Continued)

Choices in Assessing

Although science teaching strategies have developed and changed over the years, assessment methods have not always managed to keep up. Too often teachers rely on traditional forms of assessment, consisting of multiple-choice and fill-in-the-blank tests. State mandates and the national science education standards are forcing teachers to reexamine assessment methods and develop items that appropriately assess not only science content but also science processes. Assessment is no longer viewed as an end point to learning but rather an integral part of teaching. Once teaching strategies and assessment tools are in harmony, teachers will have a better measure of the outcomes their students have achieved. "Assessment should focus on students' use of knowledge and complex reasoning rather than on their recall of low-level information" (Marzano, 1992, p. x). Ultimately students must learn to evaluate themselves for continual lifetime growth.

Ken O'Connor (2002) described a grading for learning approach to the assessment process. His approach advocates connecting assessment to grading in a more meaningful way, involving students throughout the teaching and learning process, and relating grading procedures to the intended learning goals and standards. Assessment should be an ongoing process rather than an end-of-the unit measure of performance. The focus should be on what the student knows, not on how the student does. Feedback should be sought and given continuously with an emphasis on how to close the gap between the present performance and the desired goal. A grade should represent the achievement of a standard including measurable improvement. A grade should not measure student attitude, effort, or behavior.

One of the nine instructional strategies (see Introduction) identified by researchers at Mid-continent Research for Education and Learning (McREL), as a strategy to improve student achievement across all content areas and grade levels, is setting objectives and providing feedback (Marzano, Pickering, et al., 2001). Teachers must encourage students to personalize their goals by involving them in the goal-setting process. For example, to shift the focus to learning that occurred rather than a grade received, provide students with a goal sheet to set goals, and track their progress prior to each science unit. Before rather than after instruction, teachers must communicate their high expectations by presenting and discussing samples of high-quality student performance.

Performance assessment, frequently allowing for more than one correct answer, involves watching and noting how students go about solving problems and how they actually use the process of science inquiry. Used correctly, performance assessment more fully allows for special-needs students, cultural diversity, multiple intelligences, and differing learning styles. It enables all students to succeed in communicating their knowledge of both science content and process. Performance assessment more accurately models the kinds of activities that usually go on during science instruction. Portfolio assessment is a collection of student work containing examples of work completed over a specified time period. Portfolios of student work provide a holistic assessment of student understanding and progress (Figure 5.4).

Evaluation may also be accomplished through use of informal checklists, rubrics, activity logs or journals, and science lab reports. Informal checklists can be used to document a teacher's observation of assigned science tasks (Figure 5.5). Using a scale of points, rubrics usually feature an established set of guidelines for scoring or rating student work (Figures 5.6, 5.7, and 5.8). Science activity logs (see Figures 2.5, 4.2, and 4.3) or reflection pages (Figures 5.9, 5.10, and 5.11) provide opportunities to assess students' understandings and thinking, identify misconceptions, and provide a more in-depth view of students' scientific understandings (Dana, Lorsbach, Hook, & Briscoe in Shepardson & Britsch, 1997). Science lab reports provide a day-to-day assessment of how well students understand a particular science activity or experiment. Teachers can also ask students to assess themselves (Figure 5.12).

Benchmarks for Science Literacy (American Association for the Advancement of Science, 1993) states that children in third through fifth grade should be encouraged to observe more carefully, measure things with increasing accuracy, record data clearly in logs and journals, and communicate their results in charts and simple graphs, as well as in prose. To apply these recommendations, teachers need to develop specific descriptions of expectations. They must focus carefully on setting clear criteria and developing rubrics for scoring classroom performance to ensure that both students and their parents clearly understand the goals and objectives. Teachers are essentially clarifying the phase space within which bifurcations of student knowledge may period double to turbulence through the process of repeated iteration.

Science teachers must use a variety of assessment tools for evaluating students, including both traditional and performance assessment, which may easily be embedded within everyday science activities so that the assessment becomes an ongoing process rather than a culminating activity or test given at a specified time. Contained within the phase space of the science unit or lesson, the assessment is an integral part of the phase portrait, acting as a strange attractor to bring closure and order to a unit lesson. Embedded, ongoing assessment is much more consistent with modern learning theory (Gardner, 1991). Likewise, embedded, ongoing assessment is an essential component of a brain-compatible science classroom.

Choices in Curriculum

Bifurcations of knowledge occur faster than teachers can handle them as the new knowledge period doubles on route to chaos in a turbulent sea of ideas. To find their way through endless information and to design effective curriculum, teachers need to pause now and then, stepping back for a different perspective. Alternately, they can zoom in closer for a still greater understanding of the innovative patterns within classrooms and of the intricate dynamics of students as they learn and evolve.

Teachers should build on what they have already done, not in layers but by feeding their understandings back into the system. Curriculum should be a continuously evolving process, not a collection of never-read, spiral-bound documents lost in a file drawer. Curriculum is not a thing; it is not a single textbook adoption. Nor is it a document cranked out in a summer of frenzied writing. Curriculum is an ongoing process of creativity, a continued collection of successful ideas and strategies as teachers dialogue, collaborate, and share with their teams to initiate learning and growth in their students.

Seek Out Turmoil and Surprise

Caine and Caine (2006) explained, as another principle (see Introduction), how the mind/brain organizes memory in at least two different ways. The natural spatial memory allows people to instantly remember experiences. Always engaged and inexhaustible, the spatial system is motivated by novelty and surprise. The other system, motivated by reward and punishment, engages in the recall of unrelated information. The Caines concluded that students successfully learn facts, skills, and

(Text continues on page 98)

Science Portfolio Assessment

A science portfolio may contain the following:

❏ Laboratory investigations

❏ Field experiences (e.g., a trip to the beach, quarry, marsh, or desert)

❏ Research investigations

❏ Written accounts of current events in science (e.g., weather disasters, viruses and bacteria, earthquakes, volcanoes, space exploration, invasive species, endangered animals, etc.)

❏ Original stories and poems with a science theme

❏ Science sketches, drawings, and illustrations

❏ Lab reports and write-ups

❏ Ideas for experiments and science research

❏ Science journal entries

❏ Reflections on working in cooperative groups

❏ Science fair research and log book

❏ Science reports

❏ Long-term science assignments (e.g., logging results of environmental studies)

❏ Science lab reflections and activity logs (e.g., Bernoulli's principles, Newton's laws, physical and chemical change)

❏ Science assessments

❏ Technology projects

Figure 5.4

Science Experiment Checklist

Name of student _____   **Date** _____

Experiment _____

Behavior Observed   **Points Earned**

	1 Poor	2 Fair	3 Good	4 Excellent
States problem				
States hypothesis				
Sets up experiment				
Makes and records observations				
Draws a conclusion				
Explains what was learned with activity				
Comments				

Figure 5.5

Rubric for Endangered Species Box

Criteria / Performance	0 Poor	1 Fair	2 Good	3 Very good	4 Outstanding
Research the species, using a variety of reference books, Web sites, and additional materials.					
Decorate the sides and top of a small box with pictures, sentences, and short paragraphs to illustrate the endangered animal.					
Choose an object (or objects) to represent the animal, and place it inside the box.					
Complete the endangered species box on time.					
Present the endangered animal and box to the class.					

0—Poor: The student did not attempt or complete the endangered species box and showed little or no interest in or understanding of the activity.

1—Fair: The student attempted to complete the endangered species box, but showed very little understanding of the animal and its habits. The result was carelessly done, incomplete, not done on time, and/or did not follow directions.

2—Good: The student completed, or nearly completed, the endangered species box without errors or critical omissions, meeting most of the criteria. The result lacked creativity or originality. The box contained either drawings or written material, but not a sufficient amount of both.

3—Very Good: The student successfully created an endangered species box, followed all the directions, met all of the criteria, and prepared it on time. The cube contained a combination of drawings and writing, and it showed creativity or originality as well as evidence of careful preparation.

4—Outstanding: The student successfully completed an endangered species box on time, including all the requirements and containing a combination of drawings and writing. Over and beyond, expectations, the box exceeded the assigned task and contained additional, unexpected, or other outstanding features.

Figure 5.6

Open-Ended Rubric

Criteria　　　　Performance	0 Poor	1 Fair	2 Good	3 Very good	4 Outstanding

0—Poor: The student did not attempt or complete the task and showed little or no interest in or understanding of the activity.

1—Fair: The student attempted to complete the task, but showed very little understanding of the activity. The result was immature, carelessly done, not done on time, and/or did not follow directions.

2—Good: The student completed, or nearly completed, the activity without errors or critical omissions and met most of the criteria. The result lacked creativity or originality.

3—Very Good: The student successfully completed the activity, followed all the directions, completed the activity on time, and met all of the criteria.

4—Outstanding: The student successfully completed the activity, followed all directions, completed the activity on time, and met all of the criteria. Over and beyond, the student exceeded the assigned task with additional, unexpected, or other outstanding features.

Figure 5.7

Amusement Park Ride Rubric

Name(s) _____

Ride model demonstrates creativity and originality.	0 1 2 3 4
Ride drawing demonstrates creativity and originality.	0 1 2 3 4
Ride model demonstrates effort and hard work.	0 1 2 3 4
Ride drawing demonstrates neatness and precision.	0 1 2 3 4
Newton's 1st law of motion is explained in presentation.	0 1 2 3 4
Newton's 2nd law of motion is explained in presentation.	0 1 2 3 4
Newton's 3rd law of motion is explained in presentation.	0 1 2 3 4
Potential/kinetic energy transformations are explained in presentation.	0 1 2 3 4

Choose three or more additional laws of physics including speed, displacement, acceleration, velocity, momentum, balanced and unbalanced forces, friction, and so forth

_____ explained in presentation.	0 1 2 3 4
_____ explained in presentation.	0 1 2 3 4
_____ explained in presentation.	0 1 2 3 4
Safety features of ride are explained in presentation.	0 1 2 3 4
Student wisely used class time provided to work on project.	0 1 2 3 4

Total points _____

Scoring Key

4 points: correct, complete, detailed, over and beyond

3 points: partially correct, complete, detailed, nicely done

2 points: partially correct, partially complete, lacks some detail

1 point: incorrect or incomplete, needs assistance

0 points: no attempt

Figure 5.8

Science Activity Reflections

In science today the problem was _____

_____

First we _____

_____

Then we _____

_____

We also _____

_____

My hypothesis was _____

_____

I observed _____

_____

I think _____

and _____

I concluded that _____

_____

A question I have in science is _____

_____

Written by

_____

_____

Figure 5.9

Clouds of Science Reflections

Science is the most fun when . . .

One of my favorite experiments was . . .

I also liked when we . . .

I observed . . .

I think . . .

This year in science I hope . . .

I learned that . . .

I want to learn more about . . .

I will like science even more if . . .

Figure 5.10

???? Lab Write-Up Using the Scientific Method ????

Problem: What question are you trying to answer with this experiment?

Hypothesis: What do you think will happen?

Experiment: What steps will you follow, and what materials do you need to do the experiment?

Observations: What do you observe happening? (Discuss, draw, write)

Conclusion: What works? What doesn't work? Answer the question stated in the problem. What did you learn from the activity?

Figure 5.11

Self-Evaluation: Attitude and Effort in Science

Name: _____ Date: _____

Which answer BEST describes your attitude and effort in science class this past week?

_____ 1. **I participated in science class this week . . .**
4 = by volunteering often.
3 = by volunteering occasionally.
2 = only when I was called on.
1 = almost never or as little as possible.

_____ 2. **During group activities/labs, I . . .**
4 = stayed with my group and remained focused on the activity.
3 = occasionally wandered away from my group, but stayed focused most of the time.
2 = pretended to participate while looking for ways to interact with friends.
1 = wandered around room talking to friends and made little or no contributions to my group.

_____ 3. **My attitude in science class this week has been . . .**
4 = very positive.
3 = good—most of the time.
2 = okay, I guess.
1 = pretty negative.

_____ 4. **My behavior in science class this week has been . . .**
4 = excellent—I have been attentive and cooperative.
3 = good—occasionally I talked without permission or didn't pay attention.
2 = fair—talked to my peers instead of paying attention.
1 = poor—I disrupted the class repeatedly.

_____ 5. **I prepared for science class this week by . . .**
4 = bringing completed assignments and all needed books and supplies.
3 = bringing completed assignments but sometimes forgetting my books or supplies.
2 = not completing some assignments on time and forgetting my books and supplies.
1 = not completing most assignments or frequently forgetting my books or supplies.

_____ 6. **I worked to learn the science lessons at home and in class by . . .**
4 = reading and rereading the lessons, doing assignments very carefully, correcting my work in class, and seeking extra help when needed.
3 = doing assignments fairly carefully and seeking extra help when needed.
2 = doing assignments quickly but not correcting them carefully and not seeking extra help when needed.
1 = doing assignments carelessly or not at all and thinking about the lesson only when called on in class.

_____ **TOTAL POINTS OUT OF 24 POSSIBLE POINTS**

I generally agree / disagree with this self-assessment: _____
(teacher signature or stamp)

Additional Comments:

Figure 5.12

procedures when teachers embed and link them to complex experiences. The Caines also concluded that dynamic maps form in the mind/brain as the systems interact, interpreting experience and organizing further learning. Educators must be experts at getting things out of long-term memory and into short-term memory.

Another instructional strategy (see Introduction) identified by researchers at McREL to improve student achievement is the use of nonlinguistic representations such as models, movement, icons, charts, story boards, and diagrams (Marzano, Pickering, et al., 2001). McREL research shows that the more students use both linguistic and visual forms of storing knowledge, the greater their achievement.

As teachers search for alternative strategies for teaching and assessing students, teachers must seek out turmoil and surprise. Leonard Shlain (1991) quoted Hans Selye: "The true scientist never loses the faculty of amazement. It is the essence of his being" (p. 142). Margaret Wheatley (1994) suggested that teachers may actually want to seek out the surprises and relish the unpredictable events when they finally decide to reveal themselves. Surprise helps teachers discover the important principles behind their work. Explaining how experimentation leads to further insights and possibilities, Wheatley and Myron Kellner-Rogers (1996) recommended that teachers continue searching for what makes life work to experience the joy that comes with surprise. Scientists do not waste their time with experiments that they already know the answers to, nor should teachers.

King-Friedrichs and Browne (2001) presented the essential factors of memory encoding that are aligned with how the human brain learns naturally. Criteria necessary for later memory retrieval depend on the importance of the knowledge to the student. Are students able to relate the new knowledge to previous learning, is the learning experience novel and engaging, and is the learning rehearsed to heighten retention? Teachers deepen scientific understandings in their students by immersing them in rich learning experiences. "Planning and executing more activity-oriented lessons that cement students' memories for later recall can help our classrooms become more efficient and effective" (King-Friedrichs & Browne, 2001, p. 46).

Activities featuring discrepant or conflicting scientific events offer novel learning experiences that can help students create meaning with an element of surprise to catch students off guard and draw them into the learning experience (see activities *The Paper Cup That Would Not Burn* and *The Burning Candle* in Chapter 8). Using the conceptual change model developed by Joseph Stepans (1996), students are brought face to face with their own preconceptions about burning and are encouraged to confront and share their beliefs and resolve conflicts as they arise. Student extend the concept of burning by making connections between the concept learned and their daily lives. Students are encouraged to go beyond the lesson, pursuing additional questions and problems related to the concept.

Wheatley wrote of the importance of teachers involving themselves in the process of discovery, of wanting to participate more in the lesson rather than simply planning the lesson. Too much planning and inflexibility may lead to a stifling of creative bifurcations and mind-expanding period doublings. Wheatley explained how teachers fear surprise and retreat to caution. "We would rather know what's in store than be caught off guard by new possibilities" (Wheatley & Kellner-Rogers, 1996, p. 74). Teachers need not be afraid of change, of student questions, of some turmoil in lessons and labs. New bifurcations and branching occurs as a lesson takes off in a whole new direction, period doubling to new choices and freedoms for teaching, learning, assessing, and designing curriculum. Like scientists, brain-compatible science teachers must welcome the unknown.

Provide a Joyful Classroom Atmosphere

Caine and Caine (2006) found, as another principle (see Introduction) that a threatening environment inhibits learning. Although some anxiety and stress are a necessary part of most learning situations, teachers must strive to keep their expectations high, providing an atmosphere filled with high challenge and low threat, holding their students in a state of relaxed alertness for maximum learning to occur. Agreeing with the Caines, Jensen (1998) described how threats and high stress have a negative effect on the chemistry of the brain and learning. Sensing threats subconsciously, even before the body is aware, the emotional brain downshifts to a state of conscious alert (LeDoux in Fogarty, 1997a).

> Emotions drive attention, and attention drives logic and reaction. When people are emotionally on alert, they are attentive; therefore, they are at a higher state of readiness for whatever follows. (Fogarty, 1997, p. 28)

The Caines stated that above all else, students must believe in their ability to grow and learn. They must be guided instead of threatened. Alfie Kohn (1996) implied that teachers should replace restrictions and threats with a caring, trusting classroom atmosphere, a learning community where students are respected and decisions are made together. Instead of things being done to students to control how they act, teachers need to work with students to create educational communities where everyone feels valued and connected.

Robert Sylwester (1994) posited a body/brain system integrated by emotion. Before meaningful bifurcations of learning can take place, teachers must engage students in positive activities such as role playing, storytelling, and games. "A joyful classroom atmosphere makes students more apt to learn how to successfully solve problems in potentially stressful situations" (p. 61). Sylwester recommended encouraging students to deal positively with their emotions and show sensitivity to the feelings of others. Provide safe outlets for students to vent negative emotions such as anger and contempt. Activities involving social interaction and body movement tend to provide the most emotional support. Engaging activities are almost therapeutic for students who frequently have problems in more traditional learning situations.

Students are not little robots whose emotions teachers can turn on and off at will when it's time to do a science lab or to take a test. Recognizing that their students come to them with a mixed bag of emotions—some positive, some negative on a given day—teachers need to allow for a wide range of emotional expression in their classrooms. Call students by name, greet them at the door with a smile and a handshake, and talk with them about their interests and lives outside of school. Involve students in awe-inspiring, hands-on science activities that they can look forward to with joy and anticipation. Learners prosper in a caring environment, learning by trial and error, inquiry, and risk taking. In brain-compatible science classrooms, teachers encourage these behaviors, ensuring that their students' brains operate at their highest cognitive level (Fogarty, 1997a).

Another necessary component of the emotional backdrop for successful learning is a classroom climate where students feel safe when motivated and involved. Before students can be receptive to learning, they must feel welcome, comfortable, and accepted by their teacher and peers. Teachers must treat their students with understanding and respect, encouraging them to trust in themselves, think for themselves, come to their own conclusions, and make their own discoveries. Encourage laughter. Smile frequently. Let the students know that they are loved, appreciated, and valued.

APPLICATION FOR BRAIN-COMPATIBLE SCIENCE

The following brain-compatible lesson plan, *Invention Bifurcations*, introduces the chaos theory principle of bifurcation and period doubling into a science lesson involving invention and discovery. As students wire their inventions with electricity, they are also rewiring their brains with meaningful connections of scientific understandings. By exploring freely with batteries, small hobby motors, and found objects, students can discover that many problems have more than one right answer. Following the lesson plan is a web to incite more creative ideas (Figure 5.15) and a chart to navigate the road to change in the brain-compatible classroom (Figure 5.16).

Lesson: Invention Bifurcations

Chaos Theory Principle: Bifurcation and Period Doubling

Grade Level: 3–8

Chaos Connection

- A bifurcation occurs in a dynamical system when a single happening amplifies so greatly by iteration that the system takes off in a whole new direction.
- The process from order to turbulence and unpredictability involves endless bifurcations at smaller and smaller scales, as with Mandelbrot's famous fractal set or sand at the beach.
- By providing choices, the invention process encourages bifurcations and period doubling of knowledge.

Curriculum Connection

- Electricity
- Machines
- Inventors and inventions
- Scientific method

National Science Education Standards

- Content Standard A; 1–9
- Content Standard B; 3
- Content Standard E; 1–6
- Content Standard G; 1, 2

Objectives (Students will . . .)

- Experiment with electricity, balance, and vibration as they invent methods of putting together small DC motors, wires, batteries, and found objects to create small inventions.
- Practice problem-solving skills following the steps of the scientific method as they continue experimenting with strategies to improve, further develop, and evaluate the effectiveness of their inventions.
- Improve their ability to communicate scientific findings both orally and in writing.
- Explore bifurcation and period doubling as they search for meaning and connections in a divergent learning experience.

Materials

- ❏ Small DC hobby motors
- ❏ Batteries (variety of types)
- ❏ Bell wire
- ❏ Masking tape
- ❏ Found objects and recyclables such as cans, meat trays, craft sticks, twist ties, pipe cleaners, plastic berry baskets, rubber bands, string, yarn, foil, paper plates, paper or plastic cups, markers, pencils, small erasers, plastic spoons, paper tubes, and so forth.
- ❏ Invention Bifurcations Activity Log (Figure 5.13)

Preactivity Discussion

Prior to the activity, discuss the following questions with the students:

1. Brainstorm ideas for devices that use electrical energy. Compile the ideas into a class list. Where did all these ideas come from?

2. What kind of person becomes an inventor? Where do inventors get their ideas?

3. Ask the students to discuss some of their ideas for inventions using a hobby motor. What could they invent to make their lives easier, more fun, or more interesting?

Procedure

Session One

1. To get the students started, ask them how they could power a small DC hobby motor with a battery. Initiate a discussion of how to connect a battery with the two hobby motor wires to complete the electrical circuit.

2. Make available batteries, small hobby motors, bell wire, masking tape, and a wide variety of found objects and recyclables. Give students the freedom to work in small groups or individually to design an invention. Most will begin with simple fan devices or objects hooked up to the motor, enabling the objects to spin. Encourage the students to go beyond their original idea and to use critical-thinking skills to perfect their idea as much as possible.

3. Before the second and third sessions, ask the students to think of and share additional ways to design inventions. How can they improve their original model? Have students begin taking notes in a science journal.

Sessions Two and Three

1. Provide a second and a third invention period for students to freely explore their invention ideas. Encourage sharing and collaboration so that bifurcations of new knowledge occur. Students and teachers learn together as they celebrate each new success.

2. After each session, provide a reflection time for students to record their evolving bifurcations of knowledge. Ask them to share their new knowledge about electricity and magnetism as they continuously cycle through the invention process.

Closure

1. Ask the students to prepare an Invention Bifurcations Activity Log (Figure 5.13) by using the ideas they have included in their notes.

2. Use a rubric (Figure 5.14), the students' write-ups, and their finished products to evaluate the project.

3. Share the inventions with the class and with other classes as well. Organize the event into a school-sponsored Invention Convention.

Questions and Extensions

At the close of the activity, pose these questions to the students to elicit a discussion, or have students reflect on these questions in journals.

1. What worked? What didn't work?

2. How was your completed invention different from your first invention attempts?

3. What did you think about while working on your invention?

4. What problems did you encounter? How did you solve them?

5. What else did you learn from this activity?

Technology Connection

Browse the following Web sites to find exciting new ideas for teaching science. Remember to use links and keywords to search even more science-related sites.

Museum of Science and Industry
http://www.museumscienceindustry.com/

How Stuff Works
http://www.howstuffworks.com/

The Science Spot: Invention Links
http://sciencespot.net/Pages/kdzinvent.html

Invention Convention
http://www.eduplace.com/science/invention/overview.html#learning

Smithsonian Education
http://www.smithsonianeducation.org/

How Things Work

http://HowThingsWork.virginia.edu/

These Web site addresses were accurate at the time of printing; however, as these sites are updated, some of the addresses may change.

Invention Bifurcations Activity Log

Problem: How can you invent a method to put together small DC motors, wires, batteries, and found objects to create small inventions?

Hypothesis: What do you think will work?

Experiment: What materials did you use to create your invention? What steps did you follow?

Observations: Draw or write what happens.

Conclusion: What worked? What didn't work? Think of a way to improve your design, or try a completely different design. Be ready to cycle through the steps of the scientific method again. You may bring additional materials from home.

What did you learn from this activity?

Figure 5.13

Invention Bifurcations Rubric

0 (Poor)—The student did not attempt or complete the hobby motor invention and write-up and showed little or no interest in or understanding of the activity.

1 (Fair)—Although the student attempted to complete the hobby motor invention and write up, he/she showed very little understanding of the invention and its use. The result was carelessly done, incomplete, and not done on time, and the student did not follow directions.

2 (Good)—The student completed, or nearly completed, the hobby motor invention and write-up without errors or critical omissions, meeting most of the criteria. The invention lacked creativity and/or originality. The student partially explained how the invention works.

3 (Very Good)—The student successfully completed the hobby motor invention and write-up, followed all the directions, and was prepared on time. The invention and write-up showed creativity and originality as well as evidence of careful preparation. The student successfully explained how the invention works.

4 (Outstanding)—The student successfully completed the hobby motor invention and write-up on time, included all the requirements, and demonstrated both creativity and originality. Over and beyond, the invention and explanation, containing additional, unexpected, or other outstanding features, exceeded the assigned task.

Figure 5.14

Web for Applying Bifurcations and Period Doubling

igure 5.15

NAVIGATING THE ROAD TO CHANGE IN SCIENCE EDUCATION

Bifurcations and Period Doubling

Too Much Order	On the Edge	Too Much Chaos
• Use teaching strategies matching only the teacher's learning and thinking styles.	• Modify instruction to meet diverse student needs.	• Take constant risks by trying out one new strategy after another.
• Feature only convergent activities.	• Maintain a balance between convergent and divergent activities.	• Feature all divergent activities.
• Emphasize teaching strategies with little understanding about the learning process.	• Shift emphasis from how teachers teach to how students learn.	• Offer little or no teacher guidance with students in total control over learning.
• Teach primarily from verbal-linguistic or logical-mathematical perspectives.	• Provide many choices and multisensory experiences from all of the multiple intelligences.	• Provide too many choices, resulting in confusion and lack of focus.
• Assess in a traditional sense for knowledge and fact retention.	• Assess in many ways including performance, rubric, and portfolio assessment.	• Assess very little or not at all.
• View curriculum as a thing to be managed.	• View curriculum as a continuously evolving process.	• View curriculum as a day-by-day decision.
• Remain inflexible to change and wary of surprise.	• Seek out surprises and discrepant events to find what makes life work.	• Change for the sake of change.
• Use reward and punishment as tools for motivation.	• Provide a joyful classroom atmosphere featuring low threat and high challenge.	• Eliminate all anxiety and stress from learning situations.
• Stifle emotions and creativity with threats and harsh punishments.	• Deal with emotions positively.	• Encourage totally free expression of emotion (students "let it all hang out").
• Don't smile until after Thanksgiving.	• Smile and laugh frequently.	• Smile, laugh, and joke around constantly.

Figure 5.16

6

Turbulence

A Changing Perspective of
Discipline and Classroom Management

Discipline writers may solemnly inform us that it is not enough to stop misbehavior in the classroom; rather we must take action beforehand to limit its occurrence. But the real quantum leap in thinking is not from after-the-fact to prevention, where problems are concerned. It involves getting to the point that we ask, "What exactly is construed as a problem here—and why?" It means shifting from eliciting conformity and ending conflict to helping students become active participants in their own social and ethical development.

Alfie Kohn (1996, p. 77)

BACKGROUND: WHAT IS TURBULENCE?

Turbulence, the breaking up of orderly systems, occurs in nature in air currents, fast-flowing streams, tornadoes, tidal waves, and hot lava flowing from volcanoes. Turbulence arises when all the pieces in a system are interconnected, with each piece sensitively depending on every other piece and the resulting feedback. Order becomes turbulent when each part is so deeply intertwined that one small ripple quickly reverberates throughout the entire system, remaining contained within the defined phase space of the strange attractor (see Chapter 4). The study of turbulence focuses on the flow of liquids and gases (Briggs & Peat, 1989).

> When flow is smooth or laminar, small disturbances die out. But past the onset of turbulence, disturbances grow catastrophically. This onset—this transition—[becomes] a critical mystery in science. (Gleick, 1987, p. 122)

Gleick continued with a discussion of whirling waters, plumes of cigarette smoke, and wind tunnels, still more examples of turbulent systems.

Turbulence also occurs in a captivating science lab activity called *Magical Milk Colors* (see the lesson at the end of this chapter). Students add drops of red, blue, yellow, and green food coloring to bowls of milk and observe as the colors create swirling patterns when a drop of liquid soap is added to the middle. The molecules at the surface of the milk form a filmy layer called surface tension. When the detergent weakens the forces attracting the surface milk molecules, the stronger molecules at the edges of the bowl pull these weaker molecules toward them. The food coloring moves with the molecules of milk in one quick motion.

Swirling movements of color appear, remaining separate temporarily because of the drops of fat in the milk. As the drops of fat are broken into smaller particles by the detergent, they spread out, allowing more of the food coloring and milk to mix. The initial chaotic and random motions of the food coloring molecules in the milk spontaneously give rise to fractal like structures and patterns as the flowing milk and food coloring go from smooth to turbulent. The slightest fluctuation in one part of the milk system quickly magnifies as molecules of food dye assist in the spread of continuously changing, agate marbles of eddying color throughout the bowl.

In a sense, order emerges out of chaos with energy continuously supplied by the soap and milk reaction. Turbulence is a mess of disorder, small fractal eddies within larger ones, as larger swirls of color break up into smaller swirls, and these again break up. Each area of swirling colors seems connected to all the other swirling colors in the bowl. Eventually, because turbulence is unstable and the system's energy dissipates, the second law of thermodynamics and entropy set in. The milk and food coloring period double their way to a uniform pea-green color, and the excitement is over.

IMPLICATIONS OF TURBULENCE FOR BRAIN-COMPATIBLE SCIENCE

Three implications of turbulence for science education are (1) expect the order to reemerge, (2) loosen up and have some fun, and (3) let go of the control to keep it. Geoffrey and Renate Caine (2006) stated that students learn science effectively when their brains and entire physiology are totally immersed in the learning activity (see Introduction). Turbulence in educational systems and processes engender creativity and revitalization as new understandings generate from the old.

Expect the Order to Reemerge

John Briggs and F. David Peat (1989) posed an interesting question, and a chaos theory paradox, when they asked, "Is the breakup of order into turbulence—that strange attractor—a sign of the system's infinitely deep interconnectedness? In fact, of its wholeness?" (p. 52). If, beneath the turbulence, a new order waits to be discovered, implications abound for science education. As with the Lorenz attractor (see Chapter 3), whirling eddies of turbulence may be a necessary part of curriculum and instructional processes.

In their work with teachers, Caine and Caine (1997a) explained how the new way of thinking necessary to implement a paradigm shift in education cannot be taught. They asserted that the system would not change until educators changed as a result of personal transformation. "The source of resistance of schools to change lies in a system that is itself maintained by a set of absolutely compelling deep beliefs about learning, teaching, and the nature of reality itself" (p. 26). Educators need to look for the order to reemerge out of the turbulence, along with a new set of convictions.

In an interview by Elizabeth Donohoe Steinberger (1995), Margaret Wheatley spoke of her belief that there are natural sources of order in schools where creative energy will actually create order in a classroom. Wheatley said,

> Where we believe that a teacher's fundamental strength is in keeping order and control, then we become afraid of the energies that would lead to spontaneity, excitement, outbursts, emotions—all the things that we try to keep a lid on but are really indications that the child is interested in his or her own growth. (Wheatley in Steinberger, 1995, p. 19)

Brain-compatible classrooms feature students who take charge of their own learning. Teachers who truly inspire their students are those who, daring to welcome spontaneity and energy, teach on the turbulent edge where order begins to break down into chaos. In the process of letting go, new connections are found.

Loosen Up and Have Some Fun

The National Science Education Standards (National Research Council, 1996) encompass a movement away from rigidly following curriculum to a greater emphasis on selecting and adapting curriculum. The standards suggest placing less emphasis on the direct presentation of scientific knowledge through lecture, demonstration, and reliance on a single text. Instead the standards envision classrooms where groups of students, guided in active and extended scientific inquiry, discuss and debate with both teachers and students sharing the responsibility for their learning. To cultivate brain-compatible science education, this vision may require a greater tolerance for movement and noise in classrooms as students engage in a number of activities simultaneously while teachers guide their learning from the sidelines.

Rather than taking themselves too seriously, teachers need to give themselves permission to seek out excitement, novelty, and the freedom to play and experiment. Why are teachers so afraid of messes and disorder? "Life doesn't seem to share our desires for efficiency or neatness. It uses redundancy, fuzziness, dense webs of relationships, and unending trials and errors to find what works" (Wheatley & Kellner-Rogers, 1996, p. 13). Must teachers insist on structuring and maintaining total control, stifling student creativity and potential for learning? Must teachers grumble when an experiment does not turn out the way the textbook says it will? Life is too short to resent the time spent buying science supplies or to complain about organizing materials for science experiments. Teachers need to loosen up, go with the flow, and have some fun. Better than the best toy, science is infinitely playful and full of surprises.

Children naturally seek out the kinds of experiences that adults avoid. Children are motivated and energized by disequilibrium and novelty, loss of control and surprise. When teachers provide the materials and invite students to design their own experiments and to take charge of their own learning, many more brain cells are put to work, doing what brains are designed to do, make connections (Figure 6.1). Although teachers fear disorder and disturbances, fluctuations and imbalances are a source of creativity. Perhaps teachers need to welcome turbulence as a spark signaling growth, revitalization, and renewal. Dan Freeman (1998) warned educators not to overdo the fun, however. Conducting gee-whiz experiments, without connection to science content, is going too far in the opposite direction. Finding the right balance between science content and science process is key.

Design Your Own Experiment

Identify the dependent variable, independent variables, control, and constants for each of the following experiments.

How does the surface of a material affect how high a ball bounces?
    Dependent variable _____
    Independent variable/s _____
    Control _____
    Constants _____

How does the design of a paper airplane affect its flight?
    Dependent variable _____
    Independent variable/s _____
    Control _____
    Constants _____

How does dropping a battery affect its energy use?
    Dependent variable _____
    Independent variable/s _____
    Control _____
    Constants _____

What brand of paper towel is the most absorbent?
    Dependent variable _____
    Independent variable/s _____
    Control _____
    Constants _____

What insulators best keep heat from escaping?
    Dependent variable _____
    Independent variable/s _____
    Control _____
    Constants _____

Figure 6.1

Choose one of the following (or an original idea with teacher approval) and design your own experiment. Use the steps of the scientific method to plan, conduct, and analyze the results of the experiment. Prepare a short (3–5 minute) presentation to share your experiment with the class. Follow the attached rubric to complete a lab report, which will be turned in and rubric-graded on the day of the presentation. You may work alone or in groups of two or three.

How does temperature affect the rate at which materials dissolve?

How does temperature affect the rate that food coloring mixes in water?

Which metal conducts heat best?

How does the color of a material affect its ability to absorb heat?

How do different light sources affect shadows?

Do all colors fade at the same rate?

How is the strength of a magnet affected by glass, plastic, paper, and cardboard?

How does the size of a lightbulb affect its energy use?

How fast does a ball or a toy car roll down an inclined plane set at different angles?

On what kind of surface will a ball roll the fastest?

How fast does a pendulum swing per minute when the length of the string is varied?

How can you measure the amount of potential energy in splatters of paint?

How does the amount of air inside a basketball affect the height of its bounce?

How does temperature affect how rapidly an Alka-Seltzer® tablet dissolves?

How does the size of the pieces affect how fast chalk dissolves in vinegar?

How does the pH of water change as vinegar is added?

How much mass does a grape lose in a week?

Does sugar prolong the life of cut flowers?

How does temperature affect the water uptake in celery plants?

Does heart rate increase with increasing sound volume?

Which brand of glue has the best sticking power?

Which laundry soap can best clean a grass stain? (juice, coffee, etc.)

How do three brands of toothpaste compare in their whitening ability?

Which brand of battery makes toys run longer?

What brand of dishwashing liquid makes the longest lasting suds?

Which brand of diaper holds more water?

How does the length of a vibrating body affect sound?

Figure 6.1   *(Continued)*

Design Your Own Experiment Rubric

Problem Question

    4 3 2 1 0   Proposed a problem question that could be tested

Hypothesis Formulated

    4 3 2 1 0   Formulated an educated guess or prediction that could be tested
    4 3 2 1 0   Explained how the hypothesis was developed

Experimental Procedure

    4 3 2 1 0   Provided an accurate list of materials
    4 3 2 1 0   Organized a clear and workable procedure in chronological, numbered steps
    4 3 2 1 0   Selected independent variables
    4 3 2 1 0   Chose dependent variable
    4 3 2 1 0   Set up control
    4 3 2 1 0   Explained constants
    4 3 2 1 0   Stated number of trials

Observations / Data

    4 3 2 1 0   Completed a data table to record observations
    4 3 2 1 0   Constructed a graph to compare results, or stated qualitative observations and included a visual display if experiment did not require graphing

Conclusion / Analysis

    4 3 2 1 0   Assessed or answered the problem question, based on observations
    4 3 2 1 0   Evaluated the hypothesis
    4 3 2 1 0   Recorded experimental errors (both real and possible)
    4 3 2 1 0   Stated possible application or importance of what was discovered

Writing / Speaking Skills

    4 3 2 1 0   Lab report and presentation organized according to rubric
    4 3 2 1 0   Demonstrated use of writing conventions (spelling, punctuation, capitalization, grammar, sentence construction)
    4 3 2 1 0   Demonstrated presentation skills (eye contact, posture, voice quality, etc.)
    4 3 2 1 0   Presentation 2–5 minutes long

Total Score _____ **points = Final grade** _____

<u>**Scoring Key**</u>

    4 points = correct, complete, detailed, over and beyond
    3 points = correct, complete, nicely done
    2 points = partially correct, partially complete, lacks some detail
    1 point = incorrect or incomplete, needs assistance
    0 points = no attempt

Figure 6.1 (Continued)

The Caines (2006) stated, as a mind/brain principle (see Introduction), that learning engages the entire physiology with the human brain functioning according to physiological rules. Rather than remaining separate, the body and brain are totally interconnected and involved in learning situations, freely interacting with the surrounding educational environment. Successful learning experiences are interactive and diverse. They are joyful, exciting, challenging, and stimulating, and they link prior knowledge to new knowledge. Students are immersed in high-interest, relevant activities in a positive, nonthreatening atmosphere.

The educational experiences teachers choose to provide for their students determine whether teachers inhibit or facilitate learning. The best science labs are open-ended and divergent, involving the use of many materials and encouraging students to use their senses. They allow students to experiment, invent, and construct, using their own ideas rather than following teacher directions to cookbook science. With a high tolerance for noise, mess, and laughter, teachers can allow students to experiment with water, safe chemicals, slime, food coloring, and paint. Other favorite materials include flashlights, mirrors, bubbles, rocks, minerals, and sea shells. Students love to take things home, often asking, "Do we get to keep this?" "Are we doing this again tomorrow?" Relevant and connected to the outside world, the science is brain compatible.

Let Go of the Control to Keep It

Discipline can be a challenge for science teachers because of the lively nature of their programs. All teachers have students who equate the less-structured lab environment as an invitation to inappropriate behavior. These students tread the line, knowing just how close they dare get but sometimes venturing over the line into turbulence to test the phase space of the teacher's limits. Constantly pushing beyond the teacher's strange attractor, these students shout out, incessantly wondering *why* and *what if*. A glint forever gleams in their eyes. However provoking these students may be, teachers need them in their classrooms to hold teachers at the edge, energize their teaching, and continuously focus them in new directions.

Student motivation, or lack of it, is a huge concern for teachers. Jonathan Erwin (2003) compared external motivation, which relies on rewards and punishments, with internal motivation, which inspires students from within. Erwin reviewed William Glasser's choice theory, which states that internal motivation is driven by the five basic needs of survival, love and belonging, power, freedom, and fun. Teachers who consider these needs can transform their classrooms into places where students are motivated to learn and behave respectfully and responsibly (Glasser in Erwin, 2003, pp. 19–23). One of Stephanie Pace Marshall's principles for the new story of learning states that "collaboration, interdependence, and internal rewards are more powerful motivators for learning" (Marshall, 1999, p. 2).

Research by Alfie Kohn (1996) shows that extrinsic motivation, with the teacher in control, handing out sticker rewards and threatening consequences for misbehavior, is not as effective as intrinsic motivation. Students with an intrinsic sense of motivation understand the classroom expectations and conduct themselves accordingly. Kohn challenged teachers to foster a sense of community by developing problem-solving abilities that will nourish their students' natural curiosity. "When enough meaning making is going on, and when the learning is tied to student purposes, then the problems of discipline tend to fall by the wayside. The learning is what leads to order. Hence, little control is needed to make the learning happen" (Caine & Caine, 1997b, p. 163). When teacher control is too visible, they lose it. To get it back, teachers must let go.

According to Jensen (2000c), physical activity and movement can enhance learning, whereas too much sitting can have negative mental and physical side effects. Jensen suggested that simple movements like stretching and walking increase circulation and the body's release of natural chemical motivators to improve student performance. Allowing the brain to take short movement breaks provides time for information processing and increased memory formation. Jensen recommended that teachers include movement in learning situations—energizers, learning stations where students move around from station to station, a walk and talk review, and hands-on experiments.

As an introduction to an energy unit, young students will eagerly act out the differences between lots of energy, some energy, and a little energy. To review the differences between high, low, and medium pitches of sound, students can stand and make arm movements to simulate the differences in vibration. For a novel review of science vocabulary, students can toss a ball around the room, with the student catching the ball defining one of the words on an eye-catching vocabulary transparency and using the word in a sentence (Figure 6.2).

Jensen cited research and concluded that enrichment through the arts, especially exposure to music, can build "creativity, concentration, problem solving, self-efficacy, coordination, values attention, and self-discipline" (p. 36). Teachers can use appropriate music to prime neural pathways in the brain. The melodies in music can be used as a vehicle to "carry" words or concepts that need remembering, for example, learning the alphabet by singing the alphabet song or chanting in rap style "kingdom, phylum, class, order, family, genus, species" over and over until the brain connects the words to the rhythm for memory retention.

Jensen (1998) also wrote of the need to satisfy basic body needs before effective learning can take place. Students need a good night's sleep, fresh air, healthy food, and plenty of water to feed their brains. Linked to poor learning, dehydration can increase stress, causing a drop in attention. Water is so obviously basic to human survival that teachers should encourage rather than limit student access to it throughout the day. Perhaps teachers need to rethink their classroom procedures regarding water, healthy snacks, fresh air breaks, and even trips to the bathroom!

At times, teachers may offer too much freedom and too many choices, thus throwing their class into a state of chaos. They may need to limit the choices to keep student energy channeled productively, while at the same time challenging their students to learn and grow and to become accountable for their own behavior. Classroom management procedures should be consistent and supportive, with an emphasis on mutual respect. Lessons should be stimulating but not so overwhelming that they overtax the brain's capacity to process content and make connections to real life. Although they will give up some control in doing so, teachers must find more brain-compatible ways to arouse interest, bring students closer to the edge where the positive energy is focused, and give students a gentle nudge toward turbulence without going overboard.

APPLICATION FOR BRAIN-COMPATIBLE SCIENCE

The following brain-compatible lesson plan, *Magical Milk Colors,* integrates the chaos theory principle of turbulence into a spectacular activity with swirling eddies of color. At precisely the point where order breaks down into chaos, eddying patterns

Brain-Based Word Review

constructivist

brain-based

intrinsic   *emotions*

scientific
method

diverse   rubric

learning

low

assessment

higher-level thinking skills

inquiry   *hands-on*   integrated

teaching

science curriculum

embedded   stimulating

novelty

multiple learning styles

science is
for all   **multiple**

joy!   **energy**

high challenge

effective questioning strategies

science supplies   relevant

Figure 6.2

of color emerge revealing a new kind of order. Similarly, many learning situations enter a turbulent period before the order appears and new knowledge constructs. Following the lesson plan is a web to incite more creative ideas (Figure 6.4) and a chart to navigate the road to change in the brain-compatible classroom (Figure 6.5).

Lesson: Magical Milk Colors

Chaos Theory Principle: Turbulence

Grade Level: 2–8

Chaos Connection

- When the liquid detergent is added to milk, chaotic and random motions of the food coloring molecules spontaneously give rise to structures and patterns.
- The red molecules assist in the spread of red throughout the bowl; the blue, in the spread of blue.
- Order emerges out of chaos as the soap and milk reaction continues to supply energy.
- Larger swirls of color break up into smaller ones, and these again break up, known as turbulence in chaos theory.
- Eventually, as the system's energy dissipates, the milk and food coloring turn a uniform pea-green color.

Curriculum Connection

- Matter and energy
- Solids, liquids, and gases
- Solutions
- Physical and chemical change

National Science Education Standards

- Content Standard A; 1–9
- Content Standard B; 1

Objectives (Students will . . .)

- Add drops of food coloring to containers of milk and watch as the colors create swirling patterns when liquid soap is added to the middle.
- Discover how order emerges out of chaos in a turbulent system.

Materials

- ❑ Milk (whole milk works best)
- ❑ Toothpicks
- ❑ Dishwashing liquid
- ❑ Food coloring: red, blue, green, yellow
- ❑ Plastic bowls (cereal bowl size)
- ❑ Medicine cups for dishwashing liquid

❏ Baby powder, flour, or fine pepper (optional)
❏ Magical Milk Colors Chart (Figure 6.3)

Preactivity Discussion

Prior to the activity, discuss the following questions with the students:

1. What happens when food coloring is added to water without stirring? Try it and see.

2. What do you predict will happen with food coloring in milk?

3. How will the mixture differ from when food coloring is added to water?

Procedure

For students in Grades 2–5, you may want to pour the milk and add the drops of food coloring; the students can do the rest on their own with guidance.

1. Have the students work with a partner. Give each pair of students a small bowl.

2. Fill the bowl halfway with milk.

3. Into the bowl of milk add drops of food coloring at positions 12:00, 3:00, 6:00, and 9:00. (e.g., red at 12:00, blue at 3:00, green at 6:00, and yellow at 9:00).

4. Provide each pair of students with a tablespoon of dishwashing liquid in a medicine cup and a toothpick for each of them. Tell them to dip one end of their toothpick into the dishwashing liquid.

5. Have students take turns touching the soapy toothpick to the center of the bowl of milk and observe closely what happens.

6. Students may continue dipping the toothpick into the dishwashing liquid and then into the milk. Tell them to use the toothpick to gently swirl the food coloring to create colorful designs. (If they work slowly, pausing between swirls to observe, they will get better results and the experiment will last longer.)

7. Slightly before the colors seem to have reached their peak, invite the students to take a quick tour around the classroom to view the other magical bowls of color.

Closure

1. Have students use Figure 6.3 to draw the milk before and after the soap was added, when the turbulent reaction was at its peak.

2. Discuss with the students the interesting designs made and why the swirling takes place. (The food coloring will not mix and swirl when it is first added to the milk. However, when the soap is added, the surface tension is broken in the middle of the bowl, and the food coloring will be swept to the sides where it will begin to swirl and mix.)

3. Explain how the molecules at the surface of the milk form a filmy layer called surface tension. When the forces attracting the surface milk molecules are weakened by the dishwashing liquid, the stronger molecules at the edges of the bowl pull these weaker molecules toward them. The food coloring moves with the molecules of milk. As the drops of

fat are broken into smaller particles by the dishwashing liquid, they spread out, allowing more of the food coloring and milk to mix.

Questions and Extensions

At the close of the activity, pose these questions to students to elicit a discussion, or have students reflect on these questions in journals.

1. What differences do you observe in how the red, blue, green, and yellow food coloring spreads throughout the milk?

2. What makes the food coloring move to the edge of the bowl?

3. What does the dishwashing liquid do to the surface tension of the milk?

4. What interesting designs do you observe? Notice the eddies within eddies that form.

5. Observe one area of swirling colors. How do they seem to connect to all the other swirling colors in the bowl? What do these swirling colors remind you of?

6. Imagine that you could have a set of dishes with magical milk color designs. What else could the patterns be used for (fabric, wallpaper, wrapping paper, etc.)?

7. Compare and contrast the magical milk color designs How are they alike, and how are they different?

8. What would it be like to be teeny tiny and riding on a raft through the swirling milk colors?

9. Use water instead of milk and sprinkle baby powder, flour, or fine pepper in the dish. Try different kinds of milk. Try cold milk and milk at room temperature. Is there a difference in the results?

Technology Connection

Browse the following Web sites to find exciting new ideas for teaching science. Remember to use links and keywords to search even more science-related sites.

What Are Materials Made Of?
http://www.schoolscience.co.uk/content/3/chemistry/materials/match1pg1.html

Bill Nye, the Science Guy
http://nyelabs.com/flash.html?flashtarget=flash.html&noflashtarget=noflash.html

Chem 4 Kids
http://www.chem4kids.com/

Solids, Liquids, and Gases
http://www.apqj64.dsl.pipex.com/sfa/slg.htm

These Web site addresses were accurate at the time of printing; however, as these sites are updated, some of the addresses may change.

Magical Milk Colors Chart

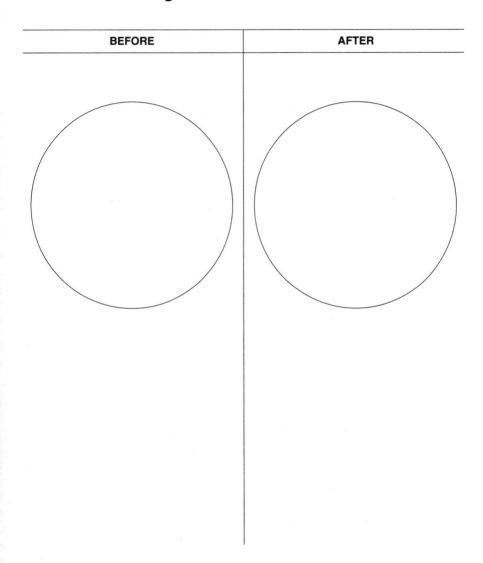

BEFORE	AFTER

Figure 6.3

Web for Applying Turbulence

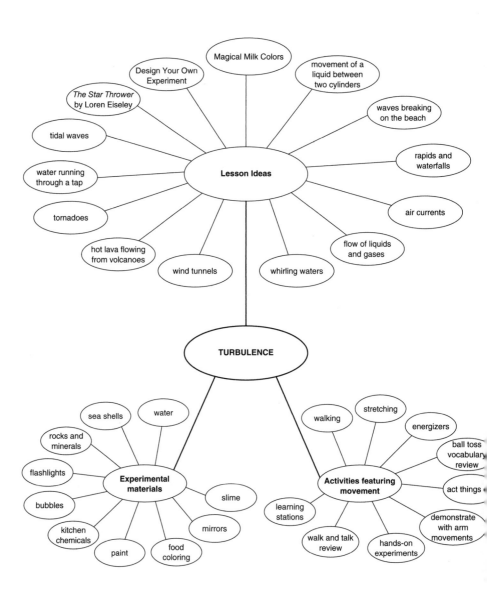

Figure 6.4

NAVIGATING THE ROAD TO CHANGE IN SCIENCE EDUCATION

Turbulence

Too Much Order	On the Edge	Too Much Chaos
• Rigidly follow curriculum.	• Select and adapt curriculum.	• Offer no curriculum guidelines.
• Present scientific knowledge through lecture, demonstration, and reliance on text.	• Expect turbulence as a necessary part of the curriculum and instructional process.	• Feature a number of activities simultaneously with little guidance.
• Remain overly serious and on task all the time.	• Guide groups of students in scientific inquiry and debate.	• Loosen up, go with the flow, school is a party.
• Structure lessons, maintaining total control.	• Teachers and students share responsibility for learning.	• Constant clutter, mess, confusion, and noise.
• Enforce quiet rule always, with students in perfect rows.	• Teachers guide learning from the sidelines with many activities happening simultaneously.	• Give students too much freedom.
• Avoid clutter, mess and noise.	• Look for excitement, novelty, and freedom to play and experiment.	• Over stimulate, agitate and unsettle.
• Teachers plan all activities.	• Include clutter, mess, and noise as part of the process.	• Provide little to no assistance.
• Direct, demand, and threaten.	• Guide, lead, rescue.	• Leave student motivation to chance.
• Provide too much assistance.	• Provide supportive assistance when needed.	• Give students total freedom to come and go as they please.
• External motivation provided by the teacher with discipline from the outside.	• Encourage internal, intrinsic motivation.	
• Regulate basic body needs to specific break times during school day.	• Satisfy basic body needs to ensure maximum learning.	

Figure 6.5

SECTION 2

New Science Principles

IMPLICATIONS OF NEW SCIENCE
PRINCIPLES FOR SCIENCE EDUCATION

Section 2 presents four new science principles and their implications for science education. The new science principles include evolutionary biology, self-organization, dissipative structures, and quantum mechanics. Used as metaphors for change in science education, the new science principles propose a much more connected and cooperative view of the universe. Constant interaction, nothing in isolation, exchange of matter and energy, and information recur throughout as major themes. The science-reform initiatives and the brain-based learning research, including the mind/brain principles proposed by Geoffrey and Renate Caine (2006), describe how teachers need to look at larger patterns, at the parts embedded in the whole, and the way that everything relates to everything else. When schools and society learn to understand this interconnectedness and recognize the potential of the human brain, science education will never be the same.

7

A New Look at Evolutionary Biology

A Metaphor for Change in Curriculum Integration and Localization

A good beach is a wide and generous place. . . . Were it small it would not work like a beach. It would not respond as expected to wind and water. . . . What we see at the beach would not be there in a tiny space; a pinch of sand is no beach.

Philip Morrison & Phylis Morrison (1987, p. 188)

BACKGROUND: WHAT IS EVOLUTIONARY BIOLOGY?

In the Galapagos Islands, 13 species of finches exist—the same finches that Charles Darwin (1895/1964) made famous more than one hundred years ago. Jonathan Weiner (1995) explained how some of the species look so much alike that during the mating season, the finches themselves have difficulty telling the difference. At the same time, the 13 finch species are stunningly diverse. Establishing invisible boundaries through their own behavior, the finches carve out unique niches by interacting with the whole environment and with each other. The borders between species are sensitive and adaptable as the finches become so interwoven with their surroundings that they regulate their own population numbers. The changes may occur within extremely short time periods.

Since 1973 Rosemary and Peter Grant have returned yearly to Daphne Major, a desert island in the Galapagos Islands, to study the finches. The Grants' (1989) findings show that evolution progresses constantly. After an excessively rainy season, when seeds are abundant, the range of finch beaks narrows. At the same time, the beaks display greater diversity, such as preferring certain seeds and each finch species settling into its own niche. When a drought occurs and much of the food source dries up, surviving finches find alternative food sources. Hard times force the evolution of finch beaks farther apart in one direction or the other, determined by which beak is best adapted to eat the available seeds. The difference in beak length of just one half a millimeter is significant enough to precipitate a bifurcation.

Sensitive dependence on initial conditions dwells everywhere in the world. Like the Galapagos finches, everything flows within living systems as the Grants, and other evolutionary biologists, watch changes occur through time. Shifting their efforts from the study of pattern and structure to the study of process and motion, they note what little stability exists in what appears to be the most fixed laws of life. A paradox exists because to have stability, people must have instability.

Weiner (1995) visualized living things oscillating back and forth within their lifetimes like waves upon a beach. As beach lovers walk along the shore, with the waves breaking constantly, they experience each undulating swell and pounding vibration. Both predictable and unpredictable simultaneously, the wave action stays within a fairly defined area and yet fluctuates greatly from moment to moment.

> People never know exactly when or where the next wave will break. Molecules of water may ride a current for miles in their tempestuous journey. When a wave trough approaches shore, eventually hitting the sandy lake bottom, the wave breaks and water molecules cascade into turbulence, agitating individual sand grains and tumbling rocks erratically. Side-by-side on a wave crest, individual molecules of water may end up in very distant places. Some form into bubble membranes, soon to disintegrate and evaporate into the sky. Other molecules flow back into the lake to join up with still another wave, while others linger behind in a cluster of lake-washed rocks. Every minute wave fluctuation depends sensitively upon every other fluctuation. (Mangan & Mangan, 1998)

The closer people look at life, the more rapid and intense is the rate of evolutionary change. And no two views will ever be exactly alike.

Like viewing a coastline or the Koch snowflake (see Chapter 1), the farther back in time people stand, the more fixed and stable the living world seems. In his *On the Origin of Species,* Darwin (1859/1964) described a steady, ongoing evolution spanning centuries, where living things evolve through the process of natural selection by competing intensely with each other for survival. With an updated view of Darwin, Weiner suggested that natural selection is only a mechanism that leads to evolution. "Natural selection takes place within a generation, but evolution takes place across generations" (Weiner, 1995, p. 79). The Grants witnessed natural selection working rapidly during both the drought and the heavy rains on the Galapagos Island of Daphne Major.

A growing number of modern-day theoretical biologists proposed a much more connected and cooperative view of evolution. Stuart Kauffman argued:

> Thirty years of research have convinced me that this dominant view of biology is incomplete. . . . [N]atural selection is important, but it has not labored

alone to craft the fine architectures of the biosphere, from cell to organism to ecosystem. Another source—self-organization—is the root source of order. The order of the biological world, I have come to believe, is not merely tinkered, but arises naturally and spontaneously because of these principles of self-organization—laws of complexity that we are just beginning to uncover and understand. (Kauffman, 1995, preface)

Kauffman asserted that classical Darwinism is not enough to explain the organization of the world. Kauffman explained how biological evolution is just one example of a self-organizing system balanced on the edge between steadiness and oscillation. Too much order precludes change. Too much chaos and continuity disintegrates.

Chaos theory suggests that mass extinctions may not require a catastrophic event to trigger them. Instead, they may arise naturally from the instability of the evolving system with a single small event bringing on the termination of an entire ecosystem. This natural biological order is alive and well today on the Galapagos Islands, as it was more than one hundred years ago when Darwin conducted his research. Darwin's vision of the tree of life was neater than Kauffman's tangled view, which intertwines with constant change and iteration. In Darwin's time, one species started where another stopped. In the modern view species flow into each other. Bifurcation points are messy and alive with constant teetering. This fuzzy region is where innovative adaptations and meaning create; where original entities, ingenious life-forms, and inventive new ways of being arise. Every tiny fluctuation depends sensitively on every other tiny fluctuation. One tiny detail may make all the difference!

Each of the Earth's ecosystems maintains a delicate balance. The various parts of all ecosystems interact and work together to achieve and maintain this balance. If people look at a system as a whole rather than as a sum of its parts, connectedness and relationships become more meaningful. Everything is related to everything else in a nonlinear manner. Every individual component in an ecosystem is totally connected and holistically interdependent. When one is removed or harmed, the rest of the system breaks down. No individual piece is more important than the next. All are equally a part of the whole.

Peter [Grant] suspects that the caltrop [a plant with a spiny fruit] is evolving in response to the finches. Where the struggle for existence is fierce, the caltrop that is likeliest to succeed is the plant that puts more energy into spines and less into seeds; but in the safe, more secluded spot, the fittest plants are the ones that put more energy into making seeds and less energy into protecting them. The finches may be driving the evolution of caltrop, while caltrop is driving the evolution of finches. (Weiner, 1995, p. 65)

People need to view the components of any ecosystem within the context of the whole system. Any individual component cannot and does not exist alone.

IMPLICATIONS OF EVOLUTIONARY BIOLOGY FOR BRAIN-COMPATIBLE SCIENCE

Four implications of evolutionary biology for science education are (1) be adaptable and expect to change, (2) teach in the boundary between steadiness and oscillation, (3) integrate curriculum for a holistic view, and (4) think globally, act locally.

Featuring integrated and holistic teaching and learning, the evolutionary biology implications pertain closely to brain-compatible science education. Brain-compatible science encourages young minds to discover new niches, adapt with change, learn creatively on the border between order and chaos, and develop naturally through everyday experiences.

Be Adaptable and Expect to Change

Loren Eiseley (1978) once observed a sunflower growing on a boxcar roof where a clump of soil had accumulated from the dust of the train's wanderings. Eiseley watched the flower grow throughout the summer. One day the train began to travel, taking the boxcar, with its swaying plant, on a journey. Eiseley knew that the sunflower would probably not survive for long, yet he wrote, "The flower seeds were autumn-brown. At every jolt for miles they would drop along the embankment. They were travelers" (pp. 200–201). Unknowingly, the sunflower had found a new niche and, in doing so, a new way to evolve and to spread its seeds.

Teachers need to find new niches as well, new ways of sowing their seeds to grow new gardens of understanding in their classrooms. Like Eiseley's sunflower, teachers must be adaptable as they face each new day, anticipating and expecting change. Teachers must be flexible and able to adjust constantly to the needs of their students, as well as to changing, evolving curricula. Highly adaptive species adjust successfully as conditions around them change. Species that are more sensitive to environmental change are able to adapt only by specializing to specific conditions within tightly defined boundaries (Garmston & Wellman, 1995).

In an ever-evolving, dynamic world, how can teachers possibly expect to stand still? Change is not necessarily slow and steady. Brain-compatible-science teachers understand that change may come in a torrent with one mind-expanding experience. Bifurcations of new knowledge bring new ways of looking at the constantly adapting world.

Human beings are not machines. Human beings are complex adaptive systems living on the edge of continuous ability to self actualize. We are creative, and in that creativity, we can reinvent our own lives by moving from the focus on problems to solutions. (Caine & Caine, 1997a, p. 86)

This is science—a creative, ongoing search for meaning in a world of constant flux.

Teach in the Boundary Between Steadiness and Oscillation

When Robert May focused on the boundary between steadiness and oscillation, he revealed another paradox (Gleick, 1987). Too much steadiness in May's fish populations resulted in extinction, whereas too much oscillation threw the whole system into chaos (see Chapter 5). The boundary between the two is where May saw the windows of order emerge inside of chaos. If the strange attractor were to stop iterating within its phase space, the system would die. If the strange attractor somehow broke out of its phase space, it would be lost, no longer a part of the beautiful, inner organization that comes from connecting. Equilibrium is not the desired state of an organization. Equilibrium eventually leads to death, boredom, and nothingness.

John Cleveland (1996) asserted that a preferred state exists when things are slightly off balance. Teachers dance on the edge of chaos, not into extreme turbulence but also not to the point of entropy. Cleveland explained that at the slightly off-balance edge, a mixture of structure and freedom resides where emergence, growth, evolution, and learning take place (Figure 7.1). If teachers lose their balance and fly into chaos, they disintegrate and fragment. If they file into order, they freeze to death with rigidity, repression, and perhaps even extinction. A paradox exists between the equilibrium and balance on one side of chaos and the disequilibrium and loss of balance on the other. The edge is where brain-compatible science teachers want to be with their science curricula and instructional strategies. The creativity and new life center at the edge where Darwin's finches fluctuate with constant transformation.

If teachers wish to learn, grow, and evolve, they must change their rules. Cleveland (1996) advocated less lecture and more active learning, greater variety in instructional media, ongoing student feedback, greater emphasis on the learning process as well as the content, different forms of assessment, more flexible learning environments, and learning outside of classrooms. He also promoted more student control and choice in the learning process, more interdisciplinary work, greater involvement of faculty in strategic planning, and more complex and rich interactions between educational institutions and the external environment. Cleveland believed that the world is changing far more rapidly than most educational institutions comprehend and that learning and knowledge creation are the key to the future health of institutions and social systems. Because what teachers know about learning has changed so dramatically in the last decade, improvement in learning must begin with a thorough understanding of the theories and practices of learning. Science teachers should thoughtfully consider Cleveland's recommendations when planning for brain-compatible science in their classrooms.

According to a study of what makes up high-quality science (and mathematics) instruction, U.S. schools fall short in providing exemplary instruction (Weiss & Pasley, 2004). In sync with Cleveland, researchers found that most science lessons include worthwhile science content, but agreed that significant content was not enough. Taking previous knowledge into account and building on it, students need to be positively engaged with the content as well. High-quality science classrooms are respectful and rigorous, with active participation by all students. Effective questioning strategies that encourage students to use higher-level thinking skills help students to make connections. Teachers must also be skillful in their ability to provide explanations for science content as the lesson unfolds to ensure that students are making sense of the concepts. There is no one-size-fits-all equation to this puzzle. All science teachers must choreograph their own dance, and the best venue is at the boundary between steadiness and oscillation.

Like the evolution of caltrop and finches, curriculum and instruction drive each other. Because they are so totally intertwined, teachers must look at the two holistically. What teachers do and how they do it are completely enmeshed, as is the intricate structure of a bifurcation diagram (see Chapter 5). Teachers cannot separate content and process into neat little charts or folders. The edges are fuzzy with shades of gray as they constantly overlap and work together. Knowledge is not layered. Rather, it is totally interconnected, with a nonlinear and infinitely deep structure.

Deck the School With Chaos Theory

To the tune of "Deck the Halls"

Deck the school with chaos theory
Fa la la la la, la la la la
Too much order is so dreary
Fa la la la la, la la la la
Too much chaos is so lurching
Fa la la, la la la, la la la
The edge is where we must be perching
Fa la la la la, la la la la.

A butterfly can cause bad weather
Fa la la la la, la la la la
Each grain of sand, each tiny feather
Fa la la la la, la la la la
Interacts in our great world
Fa la la, la la la, la la la
Each related and inter-swirled
Fa la la la la, la la la la.

Don't fall into either way
Fa la la la la, la la la la
Teach things differently each day
Fa la la la la, la la la la
Keep the lessons iterating
Fa la la, la la la, la la la
Strike a flowing balance swaying
Fa la la la la, la la la la.

Chaos thinking's so transcending
Fa la la la la, la la la la
On through time and never ending
Fa la la la la, la la la la
Fractals, patterns intertwining
Fa la la, la la la, la la la
Into schools for redesigning
Fa la la la la, la la la la.

by Peggy Mangan 11/27/96

Figure 7.1

Integrate Curriculum for a Holistic View

Research about the brain and learning shows that interdisciplinary, integrated, holistic, and embedded curricular themes help students make connections for meaningful knowledge acquisition (Caine & Caine, 2006; Fogarty, 1991; Fogarty & Stoehr, 1995; Marzano, 1992). One of Stephanie Pace Marshall's principles for the new story of learning, closely connected to recent theories about learning and the human brain, states that "concept integration is the most meaningful way to understand the unity of knowledge" (Marshall, 1999, p. 2). Marshall saw evidence that society is undergoing a transformation leading to a much more connected world where interdependence rather than independence is the rule (Marshall in Hesselbein, Goldsmith, & Beckhard, 1997).

In one of their 12 mind/brain principles (see Introduction), Caine and Caine (2006) stated that the brain and mind process parts and wholes simultaneously. When either is absent from the learning experience, students will have difficulty learning. The Caines implied that teaching with a big-picture experience at the beginning of the lesson will give students a sense of the whole on which they can link facts and details as the lesson unfolds. In a healthy individual both left and right sides of the brain are actively involved in the process of learning.

Caine and Caine (2006) assert that the brain is able to reduce into parts and to perceive things holistically at the same time. Accordingly, teachers must involve students in global ideas and curricula that make sense and connect to everyday life experiences. Too often teachers fragment content, reducing learning to the rote memorization of facts that have no personal meaning for the learner. Instead, teachers must provide complex, holistic learning experiences for their students. Teachers need to design activities that allow students' brains to make the meaningful connections that physiologically they want to make (see the *Sand Patterns* curriculum at the end of this chapter).

Resembling how people learn and work in the real world, an integrated curriculum is a renewed approach to teaching and learning that helps students to make powerful learning connections (Kotar, Guenter, Metzger, & Overholt, 1998). If teachers from many disciplines work together to provide integrated learning experiences, using a variety of models of integration, their students' learning will be more complete, enabling them to make valuable connections to their lives and world (Fogarty, 1991). Science educators need to integrate the various science disciplines, as well as integrate science with other subject areas.

An integrated curriculum makes lessons more meaningful and interesting to students and helps reach students with various learning styles. With an assumption that the whole is more than the sum of its parts, an integrated curriculum provides deeper understanding of science concepts, gives teachers the option for choice with students' subject preferences, allows students to apply science learning to other curricular areas, and offers opportunities for students to synthesize information from different sources (Atwater, 1995). Three of the most popular methods of integrating curriculum are literature-based units, theme-based units, and project-based units, although additional ways abound (Rakow & Vasquez, 1998).

Howard Gardner's (1983) multiple intelligence's theory (see Chapter 5) provides a more global way of integrating curricula (Fogarty & Stoehr, 1995). For example, in a dinosaur unit, students can measure and run off actual dinosaur lengths on the school playground to gain an appreciation for the size of dinosaurs (logical/mathematical and bodily/kinesthetic). Students can then construct a bar graph to compare dinosaur lengths (visual/spatial and logical/mathematical). They can draw their favorite dinosaurs on the playground or make clay dinosaurs and place them in a natural setting of grass consisting of radish and bean seedlings (bodily/kinesthetic and visual/spatial). Students can experience just how huge dinosaurs were by estimating and measuring how many of their own small feet fit into one apatosaurus footprint (logical/mathematical and bodily/kinesthetic). They can write dinosaur footprint stories, illustrate them with footprints and pictures, and display them with their large footprint cutouts (verbal/linguistic and visual/spatial). They can compose dinosaur raps to help them remember vocabulary (musical/rhythmic) and read dinosaur stories (verbal/linguistic). Students can observe footprints of other animals and compare them to the dinosaur footprint cutouts (naturalist). Students can do many of these activities in small groups (interpersonal), and they can make regular entries in science journals, where they reflect on their integrated learning experiences (intrapersonal).

In the chaos-theory-inspired *Sand Patterns* curriculum at the end of this chapter, students can write onomatopoeia (sound) poems about waves pounding the shore and create myths to explain how rocks turn to sand (verbal/linguistic). They can use a three-circled Venn diagram to compare and contrast the sand, water, and air of a beach ecosystem (logical/mathematical and naturalist), and make homemade musical instruments out of natural materials (musical/rhythmic). Students can collect water samples from various places along the beach shoreline and examine them under a microscope for signs of life (logical/mathematical and naturalist). They can create nature sketches of the beach (visual/spatial and naturalist) and play a food chain and energy pyramid game (bodily/kinesthetic). Using a cooperative-learning, jigsaw strategy (see Chapter 9), students can discuss why they need to protect beach ecosystems (interpersonal).

Students can lie down and look up at the sky, imagining how they would feel if they could soar above the lake like a gull or float across the sky with the clouds (intrapersonal). Along the shoreline of a beach, with the waves pounding continuously on the sand, students can create innovative adaptations and meaning in their minds. The rate of evolutionary change grows increasingly more intense with every closer view. An integrated curriculum allows learners to synthesize all the isolated parts of their learning into one.

Think Globally, Act Locally

Although chaos theory and the new science principles emphasize a global view, each student is an important entity in the same way that each of Darwin's finches, or each grain of sand at the beach, is a part of the whole. People who exist as individuals within a global setting are so totally connected that one little fluctuation in the system can make a difference. Teachers need to think globally while considering each child as an individual. If teachers look at a system holistically, connections and relationships become more meaningful. The whole is not more important than its parts because the whole system becomes one in its connectedness. Everything is related to everything else in a nonlinear manner. Individuals are not lost with a global view; they are found.

Margaret Wheatley (1994) maintained that to think globally and act locally is a quantum perception of reality and a sound strategy for changing large systems. Teachers should begin by working with the movement and flow of events within the small systems of their classrooms. Changes in small places precipitate large-system changes by sharing in the unbroken wholeness that has united them all along. Change in a system occurring through sensitive dependence on initial conditions works more effectively than linear change proceeding in a step-by-step sequence.

Thinking globally and acting locally has important implications for curriculum development. When teachers develop curriculum, the place to start is within their own communities. Teachers need to carve out curriculum niches in school gardens and local woods, ponds, lakes, and rivers to make the curriculum relevant to the lives of their students. Then, after providing students with prior understandings, they can branch out to study deserts, ocean communities, and other ecosystems of the world. A brain-compatible science curriculum will not look the same in any two communities as it is localized and as it continues to evolve.

APPLICATION FOR BRAIN-COMPATIBLE SCIENCE

The following brain-compatible curriculum, *Sand Patterns,* integrates the new science principle of evolutionary biology into a series of holistic lessons about the interacting systems of sand, water, air, and the diversity of life in a beach ecosystem. The curriculum begins with a big picture field trip to a beach ecosystem and then, in related lessons, proceeds to the individual parts of the system. Embedded with multiple intelligences theory, the lessons are integrated across curricular areas. The science disciplines of geology, weather, life science, and environmental science are integrated into the lessons for yet another layer of brain compatibility. Because more than one lesson is included in the *Sand Patterns* series, and also because of the nature of the lessons themselves, the lesson format is somewhat different from the lessons at the end of the other chapters in this book.

The field-trip experience outlined here could be adapted to other beaches and ecosystems. The idea is to localize the curriculum to provide students with opportunities to study a familiar area in depth. Following the lesson plan is a web to incite more creative ideas for teaching evolutionary biology (Figure 7.6) and a chart to navigate the road to change in the brain-compatible classroom (Figure 7.7).

LESSONS: SAND PATTERNS CURRICULUM

Lesson 1: A Sandy Beach

New Science Principle: Evolutionary Biology
Grade Level: 3–8

New Science Connection

- The beach as a whole—when viewed from a distance—seems static, constant, and never changing. Sand appears a drab tan from afar with little or no detail. Looking more closely, however, one can see more and more color, shape, and variety! Patterns exist within patterns, revealing miniature Grand Canyon designs. The sand, water, and air are interacting, inorganic systems forming the basis for life in the beach ecosystem.

- The constant wave action weathers the rocks, breaking them down into tiny grains. The waves and the wind work both to break rocks down into tiny sand particles and build the same sand back up into the sedimentary rocks of future eras. These forces, which seem to work against each other, are actually working together, harmoniously forming their own delicate balance. Each grain of sand represents a part of the whole, sculpting ripple designs and creating order out of chaos.
- The waves wash against the shore, stranding the heavy rocks while dragging the lighter rocks and sand back into the lake. The coarse bottom nearest the water's edge grades out into finer pebbles and sand as the water deepens.
- Geologists unravel the mysteries of eras past by looking at the size of sediment particles deposited in sedimentary rock layers. Larger particles were deposited at the edge of ancient shorelines. Smaller, finer particles settled offshore and under water. This action continues today as the rocks of the Earth constantly recycle.

Curriculum Connection

- Geology
- Weather
- Life science
- Environmental science
- Beach ecosystems
- Biomes
- Water

National Science Education Standards

- Content Standard A; 1–9
- Content Standard C; 1, 3, 4, 5
- Content Standard D; 1, 2
- Content Standard F; 2

Objectives (Students will . . .)

- Visit a lake or ocean beach to discover the interacting systems of sand, water, air, and the diversity of life in a beach ecosystem.
- View the beach holistically by participating in a beach scavenger hunt to locate a variety of natural objects.
- Create beach drawings and sketches.
- Write reflections of the beach trip.
- Discuss the geologic history and basic ecology of the beach.
- Record water, air, and sand temperature; pH; wind direction; and weather conditions.
- Look for signs of weathering, erosion, and deposition and patterns in the sand and water.
- View the shoreline from more than one perspective.
- Model a prey-predator relationship.

Materials

- ❏ Clipboards
- ❏ Pencils

❏ *Sandy Beach Reflections* sheet (Figure 7.2)
❏ Scavenger hunt list (adapt for local conditions)
❏ Ziplock bags
❏ Collecting bags or pails
❏ Jar with lid for water sample
❏ Thermometers
❏ pH paper
❏ Blindfolds
❏ Picnic lunches (optional)

Before the Trip

1. Assess student prior knowledge about the beach ecosystem by doing a simple concept webbing activity. Write the name of the beach in the center circle. Then ask the students to name some of the systems that they will see when visiting the beach. (Students may mention animals, plants, sand, water, clouds, fossils, and rocks.) Organize these around the center heading as topics and subtopics.

2. Cluster the students into cooperative groups of four. Number students 1–4 within each group. These numbers will enable you to group the students in a variety of ways throughout the field trip. Pass out clipboards with pencils attached and the *Sandy Beach Reflections* sheet. Explain all procedures thoroughly.

Procedure

1. On arriving at the beach, lead a focusing exercise with the students. Adapting for local conditions, say the following: Stand up straight. Take a deep breath. Breathe out slowly, and let yourself relax. Feel the cool breeze blow against your cheeks and the warmth of the sunshine on your face. Listen to the waves break against the shore. Watch the gulls circle above, waiting for a chance to dive for fish. Observe the clouds drift slowly overhead. Follow them down to the horizon where lake and sky meet. Look along the shore for as far as you can see. Focus on the sand. Continue to focus on the sand as you bring your eyes closer to where you are standing. Bend down and pick up a handful of dry sand. Observe it closely. How does it look? Feel its texture as you pour it from hand to hand and then let it slip between your fingers. How does it feel? How does the sand change as you view it up close?

2. Gather the students into their cooperative groups of four to participate in a beach scavenger hunt. Give each group a bag or ice-cream pail, a list of things to find, and a ziplock bag for sand. Assign group roles: Student #1: bag holder, Student #2: checker, Student #3: encourager, Student #4: reporter. Ask them to collect the following (adapt accordingly to local beaches): ziplock bag full of dry sand, shiny rock, pinkish-red rock, black rock, red speckled rock, black and white rock, gray rock, tan rock, one other special rock, five rocks containing fossils, small piece of driftwood, bird feather, shell, yellow leaf, brown leaf, and green leaf.

3. Rotate the students through any number or combination of the following activities. Invite parents to help with the leadership.

4. Find a quiet place to sit alone. On the *Sandy Beach Reflections* sheet, make a beach sketch, and write your thoughts or a poem about the beach. Record your feelings and perhaps reflect on the clouds.

5. Gather the students into their cooperative groups of four again, and assign group roles to complete the following: Student #1: Air temperature finder. Use a thermometer to find the air temperature. Student #2: Lake temperature finder. Use a thermometer to find the water temperature. Student #3: Sand temperature finder. Use a thermometer to find the sand temperature. Student #4: Lake pH finder. Use pH paper to determine how acidic or basic the water is. Then all report back to the group to share results.

6. Discuss the weather and wind conditions. What signs of pollution do you observe? Look for signs of living things, both plants and animals. What animals that you might not see may also be a part of this ecosystem? How do the plants and animals of the beach ecosystem live together in harmony? Record observations on the *Sandy Beach Reflections* sheet.

7. Look for signs of weathering, erosion, and deposition. Look also for patterns in the sand and lake. Discuss relevant portions of the background information contained in the "New Science Connection" section of this lesson.

8. On the *Sandy Beach Reflections* sheet, draw what you think the shoreline would look like when viewed from an airplane. Walk slowly along the beach. Draw your view of the shoreline. Draw the shoreline from the point of view of a tiny sand insect. Imagine laying a string down along the shore. Whose view would make the longest line if we could straighten out the string?

9. Before leaving the beach area, and in cooperative groups, go through the scavenger hunt bags. Prepare the following to take back to the classroom for further study: ziplock bag filled with dry sand, five rocks (all different), five fossil rocks, and other special finds.

10. Play Prey-Predator Hide-and-Seek. Find a thicket or woodsy area where students can safely hide. Blindfold one student who will pretend to be the "predator." The predator slowly counts to 20, while the others hide by blending into their natural surroundings. The students hiding must be able to see the predator at all times. After counting, the predator removes the blindfold and looks for "prey." The predator may turn around, squat, or stand on tiptoes, but not walk around or change location. The predator looks for hiding students, and when one is spotted, the predator calls the student's name out loud and describes where he or she is hiding (e.g., I see Alex standing behind that big oak tree). The identified student is then considered "eaten" and becomes a predator. When the original predator cannot see any more hidden students, all the predators put on blindfolds. After the original predator counts aloud to 20, all the remaining prey move in to a closer hiding place. The predators remove their blindfolds and take turns naming students they can see. Repeat the process if several students are still hidden. When only one or two students are left hidden, they are declared the winners, and a new predator is chosen.

11. After playing several rounds of the game, gather the students together for a brief discussion. What made a good hiding place? How were you able to use camouflage? How did it feel to be a predator? A prey? What predator-prey relationships exist naturally in this ecosystem?

Closure

1. Explain to the students that they will once again organize into their cooperative groups of four. Find a quiet place to sit and reflect upon the day's activities. Complete the *Sandy Beach Reflections* sheet. Discuss what you liked best about the day. Then, if you wish, lie down in the grass and look up into the sky. Contemplate the clouds floating by. Observe the

branches of the tallest trees. What do you see? What will the beach be like during the other seasons of the year? Think about the beach and the surrounding area as a whole and how you feel about your experiences here.

2. Collect the *Sandy Beach Reflections* sheets to evaluate the students' experiences.

Technology Connection

Browse the following Web sites to find exciting new ideas for teaching science. Remember to use links and keywords to search even more science-related sites.

The Butterfly Web Site
http://butterflywebsite.com/

National Wildlife Federation
http://www.nwf.org/

The Science Spot
http://sciencespot.net/index.html

Earth Science Lesson Plans
http://sciencespot.net/Pages/classearth.html

Evolution Bibliography (a huge list of evolution Web sites)
http://www.calacademy.org/research/library/biodiv/biblio/evolution.htm

These Web site addresses were accurate at the time of printing; however, as these sites are updated, some of the addresses may change.

Sandy Beach Reflections

1. How does sand look when viewed from a distance?

2. When viewed up close?

3. What is the temperature of the air? The sand? The lake?

4. What color does the pH paper turn?

5. Does this mean that water is slightly acidic or slightly basic?

6. What is the weather like today?

7. What direction is the wind coming from?

8. What signs of pollution do you observe?

9. What plants do you observe?

10. What animals do you observe?

11. What animals that you might not see may also be a part of this ecosystem?

12. How do the plants and animals of the beach ecosystem live together in harmony?

13. What signs can you find of weathering, erosion, and deposition?

14. What patterns do you see in the sand and lake?

Figure 7.2

Draw what you think the shoreline would look like when viewed from an airplane.

Walk slowly along the beach. Draw your view of the shoreline.

Draw the shoreline from the point of view of a tiny sand flea or a snail.

Make a drawing or a series of sketches of the beach.

Figure 7.2   *(Continued)*

Write your thoughts about the beach trip. Use your senses to give you ideas; I see, hear, smell, feel, etc. If you wish, write a poem.

_____

_____

_____

_____

_____

_____

_____

_____

_____

_____

_____

_____

_____

_____

_____

_____

_____

_____

_____

_____

_____

_____

_____

_____

Figure 7.2 (Continued)

Lesson 2: Sandy Properties

New Science Principle: Evolutionary Biology
Grade Level: 3–8

New Science Connection

- When we pick up a handful of sand from the beach and sift it through our fingers, we are observing millions of years of geologic history. The constant wave action along the lake or ocean weathers the rocks, breaking them down into tiny grains.
- Although sand is mostly composed of quartz, other minerals are also present, accounting for the many colors observed in a sand sample. The black specks in some sand are magnetite, a magnetic, metallic mineral, originating from iron-rich, basaltic ores.
- The forces of nature, including wind, rain, waves, glacial action, and temperature change, weather the magnetite into heavy, fine particles of sand. When these smaller, heavier particles of magnetite wash up on beaches, they stay behind in scalloped, black rows while the lighter particles of sand flow back into the lake.

Curriculum Connection

- Geology
- Minerals and rocks
- Properties of matter
- Environmental science
- Beach ecosystems

National Science Education Standards

- Content Standard A; 1–9
- Content Standard B; 1
- Content Standard D; 1, 2

Objectives (Students will . . .)

- Observe that sand is made from small bits of weathered rocks, minerals, and shells.
- Experiment with magnets and sand to discover that some weathered sand particles contain the magnetic mineral, magnetite.

Materials

- ❑ Beach sand
- ❑ Variety of weathered and different colored rocks from a beach
- ❑ Magnifying lenses
- ❑ *Sandy Properties* lab sheet (Figure 7.3)
- ❑ Ziplock bags
- ❑ Magnets (round, donut-type ones work well)
- ❑ Magnetite

Procedure

Part 1

1. Begin the lesson with a brief discussion of highlights from the beach ecosystem field trip. Ask students what they liked best about the experience. Review with them what color the beach sand seemed from a distance. Pour some sand from the front of the classroom. Ask the students what color they see?

2. Gather the students into their cooperative groups of four. Assign group roles: runners, readers, recorders, reporters.

3. Runners get out the sand, rock, and fossil samples collected at the beach and pass out the lab sheets (one per group) and magnifying lenses (one for each student).

4. Explain to the students that in their groups they will read, discuss, and answer questions 1–7 on the lab sheet. (Readers read, and recorders record the group answers.)

5. Proceed with the activity. Circulate from group to group offering assistance when needed and expressing joy and enthusiasm with each new discovery.

6. When the students have completed the activity, ask reporters to share the groups' findings. Then either proceed with Part 2 or instruct the runners to collect the lab sheets and materials. Put away for another day.

Part 2

1. Ask runners to pour their sand into two ziplock bags (one for each group of two within the larger group of four). Then have them come for magnets (one for each student).

2. Show the students how to flatten out the bags on their desks. Then have the students rub the magnets back and forth over the top of the ziplock bags. Ask the students what they observe.

3. Have the students answer the remaining questions on the lab sheet.

4. When completed, discuss with the students:
   • What happened when you rubbed a magnet over the bag of sand? (The black sand stuck to the magnet.)
   • How can you explain why this happened? (The particles of black sand, known as the mineral magnetite, are magnetic.)
   • Will all sand behave this way? (No, because sand is composed of many minerals, mainly quartz, and most of them are nonmagnetic.)
   • How does sand behave like a solid? Like a liquid? (Individual grains of sand are solid but many grains together can be poured like a liquid.)

5. Show the students a magnetite specimen and demonstrate its special magnetic properties.

Closure

Bring closure to the lesson by asking the students to explain how the grains of sand are tiny parts in a great order.

Sandy Properties

1. Use a magnifying glass to observe some sand. Describe how it looks.

   _____

2. What colors do you see? _____

   _____

3. Why are there so many colors? _____

   _____

4. What shapes, sizes, and patterns do you see? _____

   _____

5. Look carefully at the rocks. Why are they so rounded? _____

   _____

6. How are the rocks and sand different? _____

   _____

7. How are they alike? _____

   _____

8. What happens when you put a magnet in the sand? _____

   _____

9. Why does this happen? _____

   _____

10. Will all sand behave this way? Why or why not? _____

    _____

Figure 7.3

Lesson 3: A Microscopic View of Sand

New Science Principle: Evolutionary Biology
Grade Level: 3–8

New Science Connection

- Subatomic particles combine to form atoms, and atoms to form molecules and crystals. Individually, sand grains interact with only their immediate neighbors. Collectively, however, sand grains are capable of generating intricate patterns, moving from simple to complex.
- Brain neurons function in the same way, communicating only with neighboring neurons, yet giving rise to complex thought patterns. We are all so like sand, tiny specks in our huge universe, trying to create new order and meaning from the laws of self-organization and patterns surrounding us.

Curriculum Connection

- Geology
- Minerals and rocks
- Properties of matter
- Environmental science
- Beach ecosystems

National Science Education Standards

- Content Standard A; 1–9
- Content Standard B; 1
- Content Standard D; 1, 2

Objectives (Students will . . .)

- Use magnifying glasses or microscopes for a close-up look at the variety of minerals, colors, shapes, and sizes of individual grains of sand.
- Make drawings of the individual sand grains as they appear under the microscope.

Materials

- ❏ Beach sand
- ❏ Microscopes (preferably handheld) or magnifying glasses
- ❏ Microscope slides
- ❏ Sand from other parts of the state, country, or world
- ❏ A Microscopic View of Sand lab sheet (Figure 7.4)
- ❏ Colored pencils

Procedure

1. Begin the lesson by repeating the focusing activity from the beach field trip. Ask the students to close their eyes and imagine themselves back at the beach. Say the following: Feel the cool breeze blow against your cheeks and the warmth of the sunshine on your face. Listen to the waves break against the shore. Watch the gulls circle above, waiting for a

chance to dive for fish. Observe the clouds drift slowly overhead. Follow them down to the horizon, where lake and sky meet. Look along the shore for as far as you can see. Focus on the sand. Continue to focus on the sand as you bring your eyes closer to where you are standing. Bend down and pick up a handful of dry sand. Observe it closely. How does it look? Feel its texture as you pour it from hand to hand and then let it slip between your fingers. How does it feel? How does the sand change as you view it up close?

2. Organize the students into cooperative groups of two. They will assist each other with the microscope, take turns, discuss their observations, and share ideas for drawings. Pass out materials, explain the procedures for the activity, and review proper microscope usage.

3. Students will then proceed with the lesson by making sand slides to view the beach sand under the microscope, drawing their observations in the microscope circles, and completing the *I observed* ... section of the lab sheet. Circulate from group to group, offering assistance when needed. When the students have completed the activity, give them time to share their drawings and discoveries.

Extensions (Students may ...)

- Use the microscope to view sand samples from a variety of sources. If possible, get sand from other states or countries. How are all the samples alike? How are they different? What patterns can you discover? Each sand sample is a beautiful study in itself!
- Make sand pictures by drizzling white school glue in patterns over a piece of colored construction paper. Sprinkle sand over the glue to create sand paintings. Let the glue and sand dry thoroughly.
- Make plaster sand sculptures by mixing sand with plaster of Paris. Add water, pour into empty milk cartons, and let harden overnight. Use old butter knives to carve animal or abstract forms from the plaster/sand blocks.
- Explore how patterns, flowing naturally and effortlessly, arise in nature.
- For an extensive list of extension ideas, refer to Figure 7.5.

Closure

1. In cooperative groups of four, and using the round robin technique (see Chapter 10), have students share their drawings and give a mini review of their microscopic observations.

2. Discuss the variety of colors, sizes, and shapes of sand grains the students were able to find in their sand samples. What did the students find the most interesting?

3. Review that the beach as a whole, when viewed from a distance, may seem static, constant, and never changing. Sand appears a monotonous tan from afar with little or no detail. What a surprise to find that a microscopic view of sand is filled with infinite color, shape, and variety! Patterns exist within patterns, revealing worlds in miniature. Imagine what an individual grain of sand would look like if we had a microscope powerful enough to view it up that close. What if we could actually get down to the molecular or even the atomic level! What would we see?

A Microscopic View of Sand

by _____

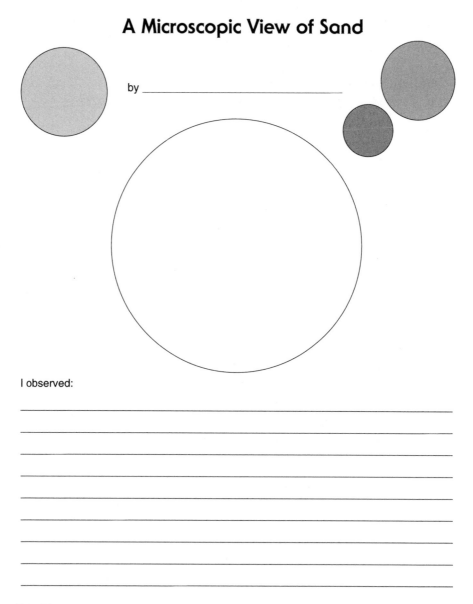

I observed:

_____

_____

_____

_____

_____

_____

_____

_____

_____

Figure 7.4

Sand Patterns and Environmental Activities Using the Multiple Intelligences

Verbal/Linguistic Intelligence

Write onomatopoeia (sound) poems about waves pounding the shore.

Write rock and fossil "shape" poems.

Make an oral presentation about a sand pattern topic.

Prepare a written report about an endangered beach life form.

Create myths to explain how rocks turn to sand, why the waves pound against the shore, and the balancing forces of nature.

Read and report on *The Sun, the Wind, and the Rain* by Lisa Westberg Peters or *The Art and Industry of Sand Castles* by Jan Adkins.

Look for other books about sand, rocks, landforms, beaches, and beach ecosystems.

Take positive environmental actions by writing letters to elected officials.

Keep a nature journal.

Make up word games, riddles, or crossword puzzles about an environmental topic.

Create a test about the beach ecosystem. Share the test with classmates.

Logical/Mathematical Intelligence

Use a three-circled Venn diagram to compare and contrast the sand, water, and air of the beach ecosystem.

Make a time line to show the geologic history of the beach.

Trace the energy flow from the microscopic algae at the bottom of a Lake Michigan food chain to the animals at the top.

Make a circle graph to illustrate the use of natural resources.

Define an environmental problem related to a beach ecosystem and brainstorm a list of possible solutions.

Conduct a survey of an environmental issue and graph the results.

Return to the beach and design your own experiment using the rocks, sand, or life found there. Follow the steps of the scientific method.

Musical/Rhythmic Intelligence

Make homemade musical instruments out of natural materials.

Compose a rhythm, rap, or song about the beach.

Read a story about a beach and add sound effects.

Find music that reminds you of sand patterns, rocks, and waves.

Listen to recordings of animal sounds. What do you think these animals are trying to communicate?

Make a list of natural rhythms that occur at the beach.

Figure 7.5   *(Continued)*

Create a musical composition with the sound of the waves as the percussion.

Compose an environmental chant and teach it to the class.

Do an interpretive dance about an environmental topic.

Make a tape of environmental sound effects.

Naturalist Intelligence

Organize a beach cleanup day.

Collect some water samples from various places along the beach shoreline. Examine them under a microscope for signs of life.

Find out about the mission of your state Department of Natural Resources.

Find out about possible careers in ecology.

Start a collection of rocks and shells.

Identify environmental problems and issues. Plan a discussion or a debate.

Make a list of things you can do to help protect the beach ecosystem.

Visual/Spatial Intelligence

Create a beach ecosystem mural.

Create murals of other ecosystems; forest, prairie, wetland, desert, etc.

Make a series of nature sketches of the beach.

Design posters related to environmental issues.

Draw beach food chains and webs to show the flow of sunlight energy.

Assemble a model to demonstrate how beaches form and change, and the effects of wave action on beaches.

Make a sand castle or a sand sculpture.

Use sandpaper to create a miniature beach scene.

Make a mobile out of materials found at the beach.

Mix several drops of food coloring with clean, dry sand. Layer the sand in jars to create interesting designs.

Illustrate your own nature story or report.

Make mind maps to explore an environmental topic.

Body/Kinesthetic Intelligence

Play a food chain, energy pyramid game.

Make up an environmental playground game or a set of exercises to do at the beach.

What would it be like to be a wave? Choreograph a wave dance.

Take a walk or jog along the lake shore.

Play a game of volleyball or softball in the sand.

Go for a swim in the lake.

Go on a birdwalk at the beach. How many varieties of birds do you see?

Act out an environmental concept.

Play beach ecosystem charades.

Figure 7.5 (Continued)

Intrapersonal Intelligence

Do activities in cooperative groups or with partners.

Interview parents and grandparents about what local parks and beaches were like when they were kids.

Share a beach story or project with a partner.

Invite another class to share in your beach discoveries.

Use the jigsaw strategy to discuss why we need to protect beach ecosystems.

Develop a group plan to preserve the local beach.

Communicate with local, state, or national officials regarding an environmental topic.

Bring in an environmental news story and share it with the class.

Become an expert on an environmental topic and share it with the class.

Take a survey or poll about an environmental topic.

Discuss your own personal feelings about the beach.

Return to the beach. Find a quiet place to think and plan.

Keep a log or journal to record drawings and/or reflections.

Think about how life would change without the lake nearby.

Lie down and look up at the sky. Imagine that you could soar above the lake like a gull. How would you feel?

Formulate a plan for environmental stewardship.

Explain how an environmental topic relates or is important to you.

Make a drawing showing yourself in some way relating to an environmental issue.

Create a series of "How Would You Feel If . . . ?" statements related to an environmental topic.

Figure 7.5   *(Continued)*

Web for Applying Evolutionary Biology

Figure 7.6

NAVIGATING THE ROAD TO
CHANGE IN SCIENCE EDUCATION

Evolutionary Biology

Too Much Order	On the Edge	Too Much Chaos
• Remain too sensitive and unable to adapt.	• Be adaptable and flexible, expecting change.	• Never stand still.
• Overemphasize steadiness, resulting in extinction.	• Teach in boundary between steadiness and oscillation.	• Throw the system into chaos with too much oscillation.
• Expect too much balance and order.	• Maintain a balanced mixture of structure and freedom.	• Offer too much freedom, resulting in a loss of balance.
• Fragment curriculum, reducing learning to rote memorization.	• Make connections with integrated curricular themes.	• Make few meaningful connections with a "cutesy," thematic approach to integration.
• Emphasize one-dimensional, disconnected topics.	• Feature multiple intelligence theory—students are smart in many ways.	• Force the unnatural use of multiple intelligence theory.
• Teach to only a few learning styles.	• Discover individuals with a global, connected view.	• Lose individuals with a global view.
• Concentrate on parts rather than the whole.	• Think nonlinearly and stay connected.	• Think nonlinearly and become disconnected.
• Think linearly and remain tightly connected.	• Think globally, act locally (balanced view).	• Think globally, act globally (too ethereal a view).
• Think locally, act locally (too narrow a view).		

Figure 7.7

8

A New Look at Self-Organization

A Metaphor for Change in Knowledge Construction

Old learning theory was based on a conception of knowledge as a thing transferred from the teacher to the student. New learning sees knowledge as something that is constructed by learners as they engage in the world.

John Cleveland (1996, p. 19)

BACKGROUND: WHAT IS SELF-ORGANIZATION?

As Stuart Kauffman (1995) stated, Darwinism is not enough. Natural selection cannot be the sole source of order arising in the world. Kauffman believes in still-undiscovered laws of self-organization that guided molecules in primordial seas to converge into self-producing cells. Jonathan Weiner (1995) averred that, like Darwin's finches, human beings fill many ecological niches, and that, as a species, people have collectively discovered how to take advantage of their highly developed ability to learn. Each generation learns from the one before it by developing a collective memory.

In sync with the latest research about brain-based learning, Margaret Wheatley and Myron Kellner-Rogers wrote that life has a natural tendency to organize into greater levels of complexity. More specifically, they stated,

> The webs of coevolution are so intimately intertwined that . . . we cannot understand the evolution of the planet separate from the evolution of the life it supports. (Wheatley & Kellner-Rogers, 1996, p. 29)

Organization happens naturally when simple relationships are created. Wheatley and Kellner-Rogers explained how the processes of discovery and creativity are continuous, using messes to organize, and intent on finding what works.

152

Opportunities lead to further possibilities as life leans toward order, identity, participation, and interdependence.

Ilya Prigogine was one of the first contemporary scientists to contend that, rather than being on a steady road to decay, living things are open, evolving systems that interact with their environment and have the potential for self-renewal (Prigogine & Stengers, 1984). Instead of breaking down, new systems emerge from their far-from-equilibrium states. Prigogine argued that even nonliving, chemical systems have the potential to create order out of chaos, to self-organize as if individual molecules are communicating with each other. The millions of bifurcation points throughout evolution contain the story of uniqueness and the capacity for continued flexibility and creativity as life's equation continues to iterate.

Prigogine maintained that life evolves in one direction only toward increasingly greater complexity (Prigogine & Stengers, 1984). Complex systems cannot be analyzed or broken into parts because the parts are constantly interfolded through continuous feedback iterations. Everything in the universe depends on everything else. Harmony, relationships, and self-organization occur when a system feeds back on itself. Viewing nature as a dynamical web, Prigogine envisioned a universe where objects are not as well defined as they are in classical or quantum physics and where the future cannot be determined because of randomness and amplification. He called this a new "uncertainty principle." He asserted that time is irreversible and that chaos is the source of structure and life (Briggs & Peat, 1989).

This natural order is similar to the way in which subatomic particles combine to form atoms, and atoms combine to form molecules and crystals. Individually, sand grains interact with only their immediate neighbors. Collectively, however, sand grains are capable of generating intricate patterns, moving from simple to complex. Brain neurons function in the same way, communicating only with neighboring neurons, yet giving rise to complex thought patterns. Perhaps more parallels exist connecting the self-organization of particles to life itself. Teachers are all like sand, tiny specks in the huge universe, trying to create new order and meaning from the laws of self-organization and the patterns surrounding them.

IMPLICATIONS OF SELF-ORGANIZATION FOR BRAIN-COMPATIBLE SCIENCE

Four implications of self-organization for science education are (1) make connections, (2) focus on thinking scientifically rather than on accumulating facts and definitions, (3) look for new forms, and (4) allow for self-organization. Related closely to brain-compatible science education, self-organization implications indicate a strong need for purposeful learning situations that capitalize on the self-organizing capacity of the human brain. Today's students face a world of increasingly complex problems. Skilled teachers train students to transfer the knowledge and skills learned at school to the real world outside the school walls.

Make Connections

How do students learn? Why aren't students mastering what they ought to be learning in school? How might teachers reconstruct knowledge for students, moving them away from their powerful misconceptions? In his book *The Unschooled Mind,*

Howard Gardner (1991) focused on the nature of learning and human understanding. He explained why students have difficulty understanding academics and offered solutions for correcting the problem. Teaching for understanding is especially challenging because of the difficulty involved with determining whether or not understanding has actually occurred. To each new learning situation, students bring strong habits of mind that can help or hinder the development of true understanding.

Gardner's colleagues at the Harvard Graduate School of Education and several Boston area teachers collaborated to investigate the nature of understanding (Perkins & Blythe, 1994). The study resulted in a teaching for understanding model, focused on the need to teach topics that link to the lives of students, allowing them to make connections between what they learn in school and their lives outside of school. The study suggested that teachers involve their students in topics that students select, topics that connect to students' interests and previous knowledge. Teachers put the learning into the context of the real world in a way that makes sense of the learning.

Several activities that illustrate students' strong need to make sense of the world around them involve basic understandings (or misunderstandings) about burning and water. The teacher can begin with a demonstration featuring a discrepant event called *The Burning Candle*. Before class, make a "candle" out of a potato by using an apple corer to cut a potato cylinder. Place the potato candle in a candle holder. Cut a small slit on top of the potato candle, and make a wick by placing a nut sliver in the slit. Light several wax candles, and tell the students to observe the candles carefully and record detailed observations. Without letting the students in on the secret, light the nut wick of the potato candle, allowing it to burn along with the wax candles. While discussing student observations, nonchalantly walk toward the potato candle. Quickly extinguish the flame (if it hasn't gone out already), take the "candle" from the holder and eat it!

As the students gasp in surprise, they are hooked into making sense of an incredulous discrepant event. Their teacher just ate a burning candle!! Invite the students to write more observations with this new piece of information. What might lead them to believe that this candle was not a normal candle? Explain how all scientific ideas are tentative and subject to change and improvement as new observations are made. Along with new observations comes the need to formulate new conclusions, as science is in a constant state of flux. Similarly, new revelations about the human brain and how students learn constantly lead to changes in education.

Continue with another activity, *The Paper Cup That Would Not Burn,* which demonstrates both science inquiry and constructivism. Begin with a discussion of students' prior knowledge about fire and burning and the properties of water. Then light a match to a small paper cup, demonstrating a concept that will be well-known to students, that fire burns paper. Next, douse the flame in a container of water to demonstrate another well-known concept, that water puts out fire. Give each pair of students a burning tea candle and a small paper cup with ¼ inch of water in the bottom. Show the students how to carefully hold the cup straight down over the flame. Challenge them to hypothesize whether the water will make any difference in the outcome. Most will think that a hole will burn in the cup, allowing the water to extinguish the flame.

The students will be amazed to discover that the paper cup will not burn as long as water is present in the bottom of the cup. Certain materials, including water, have a high specific heat capacity, giving them the ability to absorb significant amounts of heat energy. The heat energy from the flame will go into heating the water, with the cup remaining intact until all of the water has evaporated. Only then will the heat energy be transferred to the burning of the cup. At the end of the activity students can make their new knowledge even more meaningful through a discussion of how this interesting scientific phenomenon can be put to good use with the design of air conditioners, refrigerators, automobiles, and computers.

Most students find science exciting and relevant when it is taught as an active rather than a passive process. When students relate learning to their everyday lives, they feel a sense of ownership and accomplishment. Brain-compatible science involves making connections between what is known and new understandings of meaning that ideally continue long after the school day ends.

Focus on Thinking Scientifically Rather Than on Accumulating Facts and Definitions

In their *Guide to Scientific Thinking*, Richard Paul and Linda Elder (2003) concluded that teaching students to think scientifically is much more important than teaching isolated facts and definitions through mindless drills in which students fail to understand the relevance of an activity. Paul and Elder wrote that "a critical approach to learning science requires us to ponder questions, propose solutions, and think through possible experiments" (Paul & Elder, 2003, p. 45). Voicing support for the National Science Education Standards, the National Science Teachers Association asserted that "teachers, regardless of grade level, should promote inquiry-based instruction and provide classroom environments and experiences that facilitate students' learning of science" (National Science Teachers Association [NSTA], 1998, p. 32).

One of Geoffrey and Renate Caine's mind/brain principles (see Introduction) posits that the search for meaning is innate with a strong need to make sense of the world (Caine & Caine, 2006). When students think scientifically, science lessons will become deeply learned because the search for meaning is purposeful and value driven. Scientists actively investigate reality by using the scientific method, which is linear in appearance. They begin with a problem, make a hypothesis, set up an experiment by following a certain procedure, make observations, record results, and arrive at a conclusion.

The scientific method is actually a much more nonlinear process, continually feeding back in on itself as new ideas are generated. Scientists move through the steps of the scientific method, one idea feeding into the whole of the others, as they iterate their observations and new findings back into the system of the experiment (see the *Invention Bifurcations* activity at the end of Chapter 5). Derived from fundamentals of problem solving, scientific inquiry works well with brain-based learning as the brain naturally searches for meaning and connections in a learning situation.

When teaching the scientific method, teachers should present it as a way of thinking—a nonlinear process rather than as a series of steps to be followed in perfect sequence. Students must understand that when scientists go about their work to reach scientific conclusions, the process is messy, webbed, and nonlinear with much back-and-forth momentum. Richard Suchman (1968) wrote, "Inquiry is more than a method of science. Inquiry is science. It is at the center of the scientific way of life" (p. 35). Caine and Caine (2006) maintained that students' parallel-processing minds are constantly busy constructing new meaning. As teachers move into the twenty-first century, science educators must embrace new forms by looking for new ways to teach old ideas such as the scientific method.

One of the nine instructional strategies (see Introduction) identified by researchers at Mid-continent Research for Education and Learning (McREL), as a strategy to improve student achievement across all content areas and grade levels, is generating and testing hypotheses (Marzano, Pickering, & Pollock, 2001). Robert Marzano and his colleagues recommended a series of steps to provide students with a model for the experimental inquiry process (Marzano, Norford, Paynter, Pickering, & Gaddy, 2001, p. 243). The steps include observing, describing and explaining observations, making predictions, setting up experiments to test predictions, and explaining the results of experiments. Additionally, Marzano suggested the use of familiar content and graphic organizers when teaching inquiry, as well as encouraging students to explain hypotheses and conclusions while conducting experiments.

Writing about the genius of Newton, Darwin, and Einstein, Paul and Elder (2003) surmised that all three had questioning minds:

> Most people think that genius is the primary determinant of intellectual achievement. Yet three of the most distinguished thinkers had in common not inexplicable genius, but a questioning mind. Their intellectual skills and inquisitive drive embodied the essence of critical thinking. Through skilled deep and persistent questioning they redesigned our view of the physical world and the universe. (Paul & Elder, 2003, p. 26)

These three scientists were persistent, reflective, inquisitive, and passionate in their quest for finding answers to their questions and for making sense of the world.

Look for New Forms

Throughout history scientists have built collectively on the ideas of generations that came before them. Referring to ancient Egyptian, African, and Chinese cultures, which made countless contributions to the collective body of knowledge and process called science, Sir Isaac Newton once said, "If I have seen further than most men, it is because I stood on the shoulders of giants" (Newton in Carey, 1993, p. 61). Newton in turn became another giant upon whose shoulders scientists who came after him stood, and of course his theories are still relevant today. (See the linear Rube Goldberg activity, "Your Imagination Creation," Figure 8.1, and "Roller Coaster Physics," Figure 8.2.) Science is a constantly evolving discipline spanning centuries of time. Teachers should continuously watch for contemporary thinking and new forms as they arise, in science, in art, and in other fields.

Leonard Shlain (1991) proposed that the newest innovations in art encompass the earliest stages of breakthrough ideas in science that will eventually result in a paradigm shift. An example of this new way to look at reality is the change in perspective from a linear to a nonlinear point of view. In the early days of the Renaissance, artists developed stationary perspective, in which all lines of sight converge on a single viewer's eye, positioned in a fixed location. For the first time, shadow and a third dimension of depth appeared in paintings. Soon after, Copernicus wondered how the orbits of the planets would appear if viewed from the perspective of the Sun instead of from Earth (Shlain, 1991). The revolutionary ideas of Copernicus achieved for science what stationary perspective had done for art.

Later in history, Monet and Cézanne created paintings as seen from two or more points in space. Their artistic insight paralleled Einstein's theory, which proposed

(Text continues on page 161)

Your Imagination Creation

Content Focus

All energy is either potential or kinetic. Potential energy is stored energy with the potential of transforming into kinetic or active energy. When an object with potential energy, for example, a child sitting at the top of a slide, is set into motion, it acquires kinetic energy, for example, the child slides down the slide. Sitting objects, with the potential of falling, contain potential energy. At the moment that an object begins to fall or move, that potential energy is transformed into kinetic energy.

Energy can be transformed from one form to another. The potential, chemical energy stored in food can be transformed to kinetic, mechanical energy in the body. Electrical energy can be transformed to heat energy, as can be seen when an electric curling iron is plugged in and turned on. The following activity will allow you to think through a number of energy transformations as you design a complex, ridiculously energy-wasting device to do a simple task.

Procedure

1. Study some illustrations of classic "Rube Goldberg" devices. Notice how they use an exceedingly complex method, with many steps, to do a simple job such as turn a pancake or blow out a candle.

2. Decide which task you would like your device to accomplish. Here are some suggestions:

    blow out a candle
    close a door
    feed a pet
    crack an egg
    turn a pancake
    open a jar or lid
    turn on a light switch
    water a plant
    feed a pet

3. Once you have decided on your task, work backwards on paper to come up with a series of events that will culminate in performing your selected task. The object is to make the device as ridiculously energy-wasting as possible. Build as many energy transformations into your device as you can.

4. Some events that work well in these devices are:

    objects dropping onto springy surfaces
    teeter-totters and other levers and fulcrums
    trampolines
    springs
    pinwheels
    gears
    pulleys

Figure 8.1

(Continued)

       rolling objects
       animals
       helium-filled balloons

5. Draw your entire device so that it is large enough for others to see and understand clearly. Label any parts that you feel might be misunderstood. You may work alone or with a partner.

6. If you have the materials available, you may want to construct your device for real.

Be prepared to discuss the following questions:

1. Explain how your device works to accomplish the set task.

2. Describe the energy transformations that are taking place with your device.

3. What is needed to start your device? Would the device just start spontaneously? Why or why not?

Literature Connections

Steven Caney's Invention Book by Steven Caney

The Way Things Work by David Macauley

Guess Again: More Weird and Wacky Inventions by Jim Murphy

How to Be an Inventor by Harvey Weiss

The Extraordinary Invention by Bernice Myers

Inventors' Workshop by Alan J. McCormack

Figure 8.1 (Continued)

Roller Coaster Physics

You are riding on the world's largest roller coaster. As you race down the track, you are the perfect example of kinetic energy, the energy of moving objects. As you sit in your stopped car at the crest of the roller coaster's highest point, you are an example of potential energy, stored energy that can be changed into kinetic energy. Design your own roller coaster to experiment with potential and kinetic energy and Newton's three laws of motion.

Materials: foam rubber tubing, marbles, tape, ruler, pencil, wall space

Directions: On your group's wall space, tape the tubing to make a roller coaster that has valleys and loops. Remember that the only power the coaster will have is gravity and kinetic energy. Release one or more marbles at the starting end of the tubing. If the marbles don't make it to the top of a hill or get all the way through your model, revise the design.

Observations:

1. What happened on your first trial? _____

_____

_____

_____

_____

_____

_____

_____

2. What did you learn as you reworked the model? _____

_____

_____

_____

_____

_____

Figure 8.2   *(Continued)*

3. Explain why a roller coaster car doesn't need an engine to drive it. Use the terms *potential energy* and *kinetic energy* in your explanation.

_____

_____

_____

_____

_____

_____

4. Explain how Newton's laws of motion are illustrated with a roller coaster.

First Law _____

_____

_____

Second Law _____

_____

_____

Third Law _____

_____

_____

5. Draw a diagram of your roller coaster. Label the following:

- point of greatest potential energy
- point of greatest kinetic energy
- point where marbles travel the fastest
- point where marbles travel the slowest

Figure 8.2 (Continued)

that light could exist either as a wave or as a particle (Shlain, 1991). Imagine Einstein's perspective if he had actually ridden on a beam of light, as he often fantasized (Hawking, 1988). Around the same time, in the early 1900s, Picasso and Braque introduced Cubism into the artistic world:

> Objects fractured into visual fragments then were rearranged so that the viewer would not have to move through space in an allotted period of time in order to view them in sequence. Visual segments of the front, back, top, bottom, and sides of an object jump out and assault the viewer's eye simultaneously. (Shlain, 1991, p. 189)

Art and physics unite in a higher realm, which Shlain called the *universal mind*. Although their methods differ radically, artists and physicists share in their desire to investigate how interlocking pieces of reality fit together. Science eventually catches up with the images that artists portray. Interlocking pieces of reality relate to brain-compatible science as students construct their own knowledge, taking increased responsibility for their own learning. Art and science become one as the mind/brain makes holistic interconnections.

Allow for Self-Organization

Caine and Caine (2006) described the human brain as a complex, adaptive system, capable of interacting and exchanging information with the outside environment. The body, mind, and brain work together, dynamically organizing the flow of information around deeply held beliefs, meanings, and values. Like chaotic and ever-changing dynamical weather systems, the human brain has an innate ability to self-organize, to grow and evolve, and to constantly renew itself. The ability of the human brain to self-organize relates to brain-compatible science as students interact in a complex and ever-changing world.

Stephanie Pace Marshall (1995) wrote about the nonlinear, adaptive, dynamic, and pattern-seeking world of inherent order, interconnections, and potentials. Increasingly complex behaviors are created by very simple rules that govern the relationships of individuals to each other. Deep inner creativity and coherence are woven into the fabric of nature. According to Marshall, the new sciences are convincing educators to facilitate change by initiating the process of self-organization (Marshall in Hesselbein, Goldsmith, & Beckhard, 1997). Caine and Caine (1997a, p. 11) agreed that the key to educational reform is to encourage systems to self-organize and transform themselves through the open exchange of energy and information with their environment. Chaos theory and the new science principles tell teachers that if they are truly going to reinvent schools, they must look at teaching, learning, assessing, and designing curriculum from different perspectives, viewing them as dynamic, adaptive, self-organizing systems inherently designed to grow and change as they continually renew themselves.

When educators come to understand and accept a more nonlinear way of thinking about the world, changes in education are inevitable. Understanding how systems function as a whole will influence the decisions that teachers make along the way (Caine & Caine, 1997a). Caine and Caine's Perceptual Orientation 3 teachers facilitate self-organization in their schools as they build interpersonal relationships, open up curriculum and inquiry, encourage multiple inputs of information, integrate learning and behavior, and use broader cognitive horizons (Caine & Caine, 1997b, pp. 158–164).

Teachers can facilitate change by viewing their curricula, schools, and classrooms as living, open environments, capable of self-renewal and self-organization. Teachers must continually ask questions like, "What are we trying to be? What's possible now? How can the world be different because of us?" (Wheatley & Kellner-Rogers, 1996, p. 59). Teachers need to foster tinkering and discovery, working with what is available and encouraging new forms to structure themselves. What works today may not work tomorrow. With the world constantly changing, teachers must keep reinventing themselves by allowing self-organization to occur.

APPLICATION FOR BRAIN-COMPATIBLE SCIENCE

The following brain-compatible lesson plan, *Jabberwocky: Webs and Transformations*, introduces the new science principle of self-organization into an activity centered around the imaginary animal world of Lewis Carroll. Human brains naturally look for meaning in the nonsensical words of Carroll's "Jabberwocky" poem. Additionally, the Jabberwocky activity integrates science with literature and language arts. Following the lesson plan is a web to incite more creative ideas (Figure 8.7) and a chart to navigate the road to change in the brain-compatible classroom (Figure 8.8).

Lesson: Jabberwocky—Webs and Transformations

New Science Principle: Self-Organization
Grade Level: 3–8

New Science Connection

- Organization happens naturally when simple relationships are created.
- The human brain is a complex, adaptive system, capable of interacting and exchanging information with the outside environment.
- The brain has an innate ability to self-organize, to grow and evolve, and to constantly renew itself.
- Human brains naturally look for meaning in the nonsensical words of the "Jabberwocky" poem.

Curriculum Connection

- Environmental science
- Food chains and webs
- Ecosystems
- Endangered plants and animals
- Poetry
- Parts of speech

National Science Education Standards

- Content Standard A; 1–9
- Content Standard C; 4, 5
- Content Standard F; 3

Objectives (Students will . . .)

- Transform the first verse of the "Jabberwocky" poem by placing real words in place of the nonsense ones.
- Represent plants or animals from the Jabberwock's tulgey wood and the adjoining sundial plot to build a classroom food web with yarn.
- Investigate what happens to a food web if even one plant or animal species becomes extinct or is harmed in any way.
- Explore the brain's natural ability to self-organize as it interacts and exchanges information with the outside environment.

Materials

- ❏ Copies of the "Jabberwocky" poem (Figure 8.3)
- ❏ Copies of the first stanza worksheet of the "Jabberwocky" poem (Figure 8.4)
- ❏ Copies of the first stanza possible translations of the "Jabberwocky" poem (Figure 8.5)
- ❏ Copies of a Venn diagram (Figure 8.6)
- ❏ Tagboard signs with names of Jabberwocky animals and plants (Jabberwock, tove, borogove, rath, Jubjub bird, Bandersnatch, Tumtum tree, additional nonsensical plants and animals created by students—one for each)
- ❏ Large ball of thick, brightly colored yarn

Preactivity Discussion

Day One

1. Read and discuss Lewis Carroll's poem "Jabberwocky" (see Figure 8.3). For a beautifully illustrated picture-book version, read *Jabberwocky* (Base, 1987).

2. Discuss what the first and last verse of the poem mean. Ask students what kind of language the poem uses. What do the nonsense words mean to the students?

Day Two

1. Review food chains and food webs. Ask students what the difference is between the two and for examples of both.

2. Ask students what eats what in the "Jabberwocky" poem. Also ask them to explain additional ways that the plants and animals in the Jabberwocky ecosystem depend on each other.

Procedure

Day One

1. Have students read the poem again. This time tell them to look carefully for clues to unlock the meaning of the nonsensical words in the verse and to look for nonsense words that act as nouns, verbs, adjectives, adverbs, and prepositions.

(Text continues on page 168)

"Jabberwocky"

by Lewis Carroll

'Twas brillig and the slithy toves
Did gyre and gimble in the wabe:
All mimsy were the borogoves,
And the mome raths outgrabe,

"Beware the Jabberwock, my son!
The jaws that bite, the claws that catch!
Beware the Jubjub bird, and shun
The frumious Bandersnatch!"

He took his vorpal sword in hand:
Long time the manxome foe he sought—
So rested he by the Tumtum tree,
And stood awhile in thought.

And, as in uffish thought he stood,
The Jabberwock, with eyes of flame,
Came whiffling through the tulgey wood,
And burbled as it came.

One, two! One, two! And through and through
The vorpal blade went snicker-snack!
He left it dead, and with its head
He went galumphing back.

"And hast thou slain the Jabberwock?
Come to my arms, my beamish boy!
O frabjous days! Callooh! Callay!"
He chortled in his joy.

'Twas brillig and the slithy toves
Did gyre and gimble in the wabe:
All mimsy were the borogoves,
And the mome raths outgrabe.

Figure 8.3

'Twas brillig and the slithy toves

_____

_____

_____

_____

Did gyre and gimble in the wabe:

_____

_____

_____

_____

All mimsy were the borogoves,

_____

_____

_____

_____

And the mome raths outgrabe.

_____

_____

_____

_____

Figure 8.4

Possible Translations

'Twas brillig and the slithy toves

'Twas sunny and the shiny seashells

'Twas midnight and the snowy owls

'Twas morning and the plunky frogs

Did gyre and gimble in the wabe:

Did glisten and gleam in the waves:

Did stare and listen from their tree:

Did hop and jump in the pond:

All mimsy were the borogoves,

All playful were the dolphins,

All hungry were the foxes,

All frisky were the fish,

And the mome raths outgrabe.

And the coral reef swayed.

And the little mice shivered.

And the dragon flies darted.

Figure 8.5

Venn Diagram

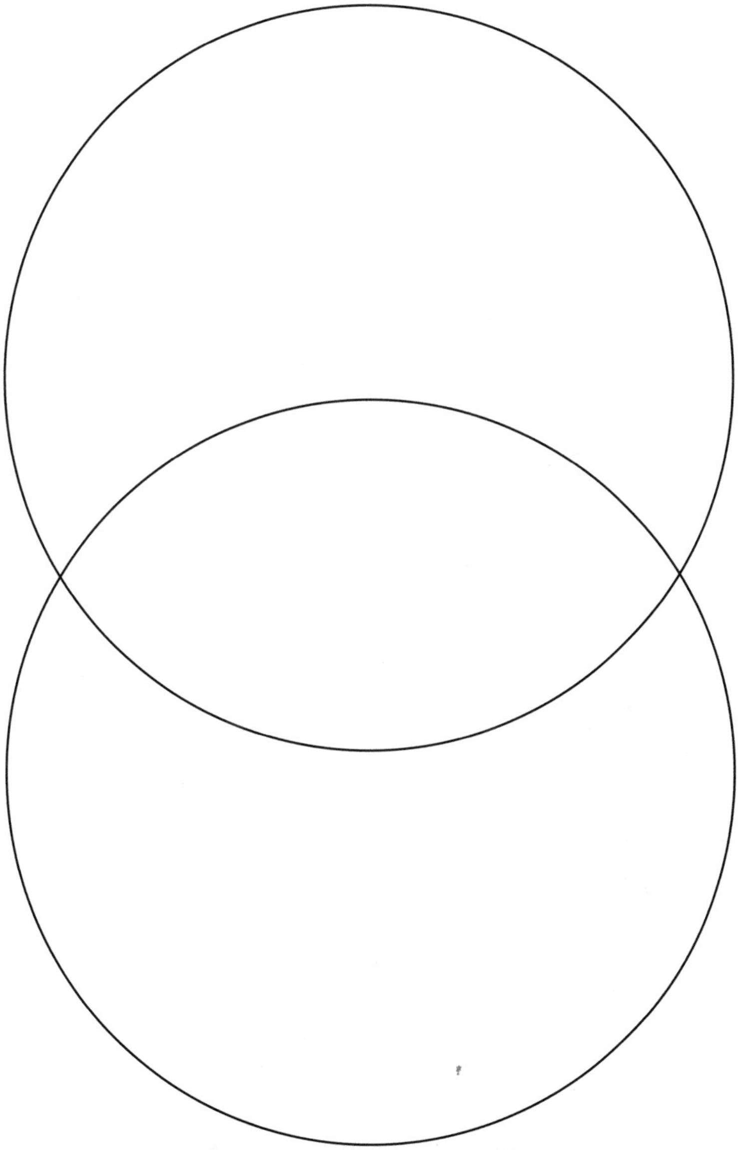

Figure 8.6

2. Pass out copies of Figure 8.4. After guiding the students through several examples (see Figure 8.5), ask the students to transform the first verse of the "Jabberwocky" poem using real words in place of the nonsense ones.

Day Two

1. Put students in small groups of three or four. Ask them to make up some nonsensical animals and plants that could also live in the Jabberwock's tulgey woods and the adjoining sundial plot.

2. Have the students brainstorm to create as many Jabberwocky food chains as they can. Have them record the food chains on paper.

3. Have the students form a large circle and sit down on the floor. Give each student a Jabberwocky plant or animal sign. Make sure that the signs can be easily read.

4. Beginning with the student representing the toves, ask the students, "What animal would eat a tove?" The students may suggest an animal higher up in the food chain, such as a Jubjub bird or a Bandersnatch.

5. Hand the end of a ball of yarn to the tove. Connect the tove to the Bandersnatch. Then connect the Bandersnatch to an animal that eats it, and so on. Connect animals to plants, back and forth, to either something that it eats or that eats it. As you move around the middle of the circle connecting your students with yarn, ask them to keep the yarn still and to hold it loosely and close to the floor.

6. Continue connecting students with the ball of yarn until all of the students are connected into a large food web. You may need to connect some of the plants and animals more than once. There is no one right way for this activity. It will organize itself!

Closure

Day One

Suddenly the words in the Jabberwocky verse have meaning! Students' brains find order in the chaotic nonsense as they relate the nonsensical words in the verse to animals that are a part of their own life experience. Students find that what they thought was gibberish actually reads very much like English. Their brains look for patterns and find them in the natural flow of the English language. Their brains self-organize, creating meaning out of the nonsensical language in the poem.

Day Two

When all students are connected with the yarn at least once, tell them to close their eyes and to keep the yarn absolutely still. Ask the student representing the Jabberwock to gently tug on the yarn. As other students feel a tug, they should tug as well, until the entire web feels the effect of the Jabberwock's fateful death. Have the students open their eyes to what happens when one component of a food web is affected. Because of the interconnectedness of the system, all the others are affected in turn. Everything in the Jabberwocky ecosystem is interconnected, as is everything in all of the Earth's ecosystems. An ecosystem may be as tiny as a single drop of water or as large as the planet Earth.

Questions and Extensions

Day One

At the close of the activity, pose these questions to students to elicit a discussion, or have students reflect on these questions in journals.

1. What kind of mood was Lewis Carroll trying to create with the first and last verse of his "Jabberwocky" poem?
2. Why are the first and last verses of the poem the same? Perhaps Carroll was setting the stage for the gruesome action in the "Jabberwocky" poem by providing a tranquil beginning and ending verse. The little creatures in the sundial plot near the Jabberwock's woods were busy doing their thing before, during, and after the battle between the boy and the Jabberwock. The toves, borogoves, and raths carry on with their little animal activities much in the same way that squirrels, rabbits, and groundhogs live their lives in parks and fields.

Day Two

At the close of the activity, pose these questions to students to elicit a discussion, or have students reflect on these questions in journals.

- What happens when one organism in a food web becomes threatened or endangered?
- How might pollution harm an organism?
- What food web examples exist in your own yard?
- What kinds of pollution can damage a pond? Forest? Lake? Garden? Your own backyard?
- Was the boy right to slay the Jabberwock? Explain why you agree or disagree.
- What would you recommend if the Jabberwock were the last of its kind on Earth?

Integrate the multiple intelligences with the following activities:

- Have students construct a pictorial timeline summarizing the events in the poem.
- Give students a Venn diagram (see Figure 8.6) to compare and contrast a borogove and a tove, a Bandersnatch, and the Jabberwock. How are they alike, and how are they different?
- Tell students to write the lyrics and music to a song that one of the Jabberwocky characters would sing if it became a rock star.
- Let students pretend they are news reporters and write articles summarizing the events in the Jabberwocky story.
- Have students create a bulletin board depicting the Jabberwocky ecosystem including the plants and animals that live there.
- Let students invent their own nonsense words, define the words, and use them to create an original story or poem.
- Repeat the activity, substituting real animals and plants from various ecosystems: ocean, desert, woods, prairie, pond, lake, and the like.

Technology Connection

Browse the following Web sites to find exciting new ideas for teaching science. Remember to use links and keywords to search even more science-related sites.

Education Oasis (link to Jabberwocky lessons)
   http://www.educationoasis.com/index.htm

Jabberwocky.Com
   http://www.jabberwocky.com/

Jabberwocky Variations
http://www76.pair.com/keithlim/jabberwocky/

Amusement Park Physics
http://www.learner.org/exhibits/parkphysics/

Amusement Park Physics #2
http://curie.uncg.edu/~mturner/title.html

The Science Spot: Physics Lessons
http://sciencespot.net/Pages/classphys.html

How to Make a Roller Coaster Work
http://www.fearofphysics.com/Roller/roller.html

These Web site addresses were accurate at the time of printing; however, as these sites are updated, some of the addresses may change.

Web for Applying Self-Organization

Figure 8.7

NAVIGATING THE ROAD TO CHANGE IN SCIENCE EDUCATION

Self-Organization

Too Much Order	On the Edge	Too Much Chaos
• Teach topics in the order they appear in the textbook.	• Teach topics more connected to the lives of students.	• Teach trendy topics that go with the flow of the moment.
• Keep all learning separated into content areas.	• Put learning into the context of the real world.	• Provide little direction or real context.
• Focus too much on making logical connections.	• Search for meaning and connections through scientific inquiry.	• Do not bother to make any logical connections.
• Learn linearly and sequentially in a step-by-step process.	• Learn both linearly and nonlinearly.	• Spontaneously generate nonlinear and nonsequential curricula.
• Focus on accumulating facts and definitions.	• Focus on thinking scientifically, internalizing facts and definitions in a meaningful way.	• Focus on experimenting without linking observations to conclusions.
• View curricula, schools, and classrooms as closed systems.	• Look at schools as living, open systems, capable of self-renewal and self organization.	• Look at schools as open systems following one educational fad after another.
• Transfer knowledge from teacher to student—students are a blank slate.	• Remember that knowledge is "constructed" by teachers and learners as they engage together in the world.	• Gain knowledge haphazardly at best, with little help from the teacher.

Figure 8.8

9

Dissipative Structures

A Metaphor to Emphasize the Significance of Community and Values

Constructivism is not only an open-ended form of learning; it is essentially about reality, connectivity, and the search for purpose. Growing evidence suggests that a constructivist form of learning matches the brain's natural learning patterns. Constructivist learning dictates that learning arrangements must move beyond what occurs in a classroom. It requires a whole new understanding of the learning community—and that includes everyone, not just teachers.

John Abbott & Terence Ryan (1999, p. 69)

BACKGROUND: WHAT ARE DISSIPATIVE STRUCTURES?

Ilya Prigogine saw self-organizing structures emerging everywhere in the individual and collective behavior of slime molds, termite activity, and bees in a hive. "He [called these] instances of disequilibrium and self-organization *dissipative structures*" (Briggs & Peat, 1989, p. 138) because to evolve and maintain their shape, they must use up energy and matter. They must dissipate their energy before they recreate themselves into new forms of organization (Wheatley, 1994). Open to the environment, dissipative systems take in matter, energy, and information from the outside. They produce entropy or waste and feed it back into the surrounding environment.

The name *dissipative structure* expresses a paradox central to Prigogine's vision. Dissipation suggests chaos and falling apart; structure is its opposite. Dissipative structures are systems capable of maintaining their identity only by remaining continually open to the flux and flow of their environment. (Briggs & Peat, 1989, p. 139)

Darwin's finches in the Galapagos, a beach ecosystem, and the complexities of the human brain are examples of dissipative structures (see Chapter 7).

Many chemical clock reactions exhibit the properties of dissipative structures. In outward growing circular waves, a chemical clock reaction is a combination of chemicals that grows like a cellular life-form. As energy is continually supplied to the system, the chemical reaction begins to oscillate between two different states in a uniform manner. Clocklike fluctuations appear regularly between blue and red molecules, which iterate back into the production of more red and blue molecules, and then generate into spiraling patterns of self-organization.

Margaret Wheatley (1994) wrote that self-organizing dynamics exist in all open systems, unifying science across many disciplines.

The two forces that we have always placed in opposition to one another—freedom and order—turn out to be partners in generating viable, well-ordered, autonomous systems. (p. 95)

The world of dissipative structures is rich in knowledge of how the world works, of how order is sustained by growth and change. (p. 99)

Margaret Wheatley and Myron Kellner-Rogers (1996) further elaborated on the principle of self-organization. They stated that growth comes out of disorder and disequilibrium, not out of order and balance. Without change, life cannot explore new possibilities, yet if stable systems do not welcome explorations, "they become rigid and die" (p. 33). In classical thermodynamics, equilibrium occurs when a system has exhausted its capacity for change, when it can produce nothing more. As its energy is completely transformed to different kinds of energy, never to be retrieved, the system evolves toward entropy, the state of inert uniformity and death.

Wheatley (1994) described organizations that tap into the property of self-organizing or self-renewing systems. Known as adaptive organizations, they avoid rigid or permanent structures and instead develop a capacity to respond with great flexibility to external and internal change. Expertise, tasks, teams, and projects emerge in response to a need. When the need changes, so does the organizational structure. Wheatley discussed how most organizations function with machine imagery and an emphasis on parts permeating the system. Responsibilities are organized into functions, people into roles, and knowledge into disciplines and subjects.

Until recently we really believed that we could study the parts, no matter how many of them there were, to arrive at knowledge of the whole. We have reduced and described and separated things into cause and effect, and drawn the world in lines and boxes. (Wheatley, 1994, p. 99)

Instead, teachers must take in the whole of things, focusing on the unifying processes of freedom and possibility. Teachers need to "trust that new thoughts and ideas can self-organize in the environment of our minds and our organizations. And we would do well to take clouds more seriously" (Wheatley, 1994, p. 99).

IMPLICATIONS OF DISSIPATIVE STRUCTURES FOR BRAIN-COMPATIBLE SCIENCE

Four implications of dissipative structures for science education are (1) stay open to the environment, (2) affirm the power of community in learning, (3) commit to a compassionate concern for morality and humanity, and (4) sustain order through growth and change. These implications stress the importance of understanding science as a process for producing knowledge. Because process depends on making careful observations and developing theories to support those observations, openness to the environment and constant change in knowledge are inevitable. Then, by challenging prevailing theories, new observations lead to the testing, improving, and occasional discarding of theories. "Scientists assume that even if there is no way to secure complete and absolute truth, increasingly accurate approximations can be made to account for the world and how it works" (Rutherford & Ahlgren, 1989, p. 4).

Stay Open to the Environment

In *Science for All Americans,* F. James Rutherford and Andrew Ahlgren wrote about how scientists share beliefs and attitudes about their work. Scientists presume that things and events in the universe occur in consistent patterns that are comprehensible through careful study. They believe that people can discover patterns in all of nature by using their intelligence and instruments to extend the senses. Science assumes that the universe is a single system operating under basic rules where an understanding of one part of the universe will generate understanding of other parts (Rutherford & Ahlgren, 1989). Wheatley (1994) argued that greater autonomy arises in an organization when the organization, remaining open to its surroundings, behaves like a dissipative structure.

> We tend to think that isolation and clear boundaries are the best way to maintain individuality. But in the world of self-organizing structures, we learn that useful boundaries develop through openness to the environment. As the process of exchange continues between system and environment, the system, paradoxically, develops greater freedom from the demands of the environment. (Wheatley, 1994, p. 93)

Scientists maintain their identity by remaining open to their environment.

Research conducted by Marion Diamond showed how brain structures are modified by the environment. The brain can actually grow new connections through environmental stimulation. Like organizations, the brain has an amazing ability to constantly change its structure and function in response to external experiences (Diamond & Hopson, 1998).

Paralleling Diamond's research, another of the Caines' mind/body principles (see Introduction) explained how the brain is a complex adaptive system, capable of interacting and exchanging information with its environment (Caine & Caine, 2006). "The functions of the brain are holistic, interdependent, and complex" (Caine & Caine, 1997a, p. 87), allowing the brain to self-organize. Brains in isolation do not learn. Designed to deal with the confusion of the world, and behaving like dissipative structures, human brains must remain open to the environment, continuously processing vast quantities of information nonlinearly rather than in a logical, step-by-step fashion (Caine & Caine, 2006).

Affirm the Power of Community in Learning

As education moves toward greater involvement with the community and business world, private funding, auctions, PTA money-raising events, school-business partnerships, grants and fellowships, and programs linking elementary and high school science teachers with local colleges and universities are on the rise. More direct community and business involvement draws attention to the importance of developing science literacy in students. The responsibility of educating young people will eventually spread out into the environment, beyond the walls of schools and into communities where it belongs. This flow of energy between schools and communities creates a dissipative structure that will help to initiate changes in science education.

John Abbott and Terence Ryan explained how the constructivist approach facilitates learning as students progress from curiosity about the world to new knowledge. Discussing how constructivism is the dynamic interaction between the environment and a student's brain, Abbott and Ryan advocated a movement away from traditional formal education to a much more interactive, community-centered education.

Instead of thinking of the brain as a computer, researchers now see it as a far more flexible, self-adjusting entity—a living, unique, ever-changing organism that grows and reshapes itself in response to challenge, with elements that wither if not used (Abbott & Ryan, 1999, pp. 66–67).

Calling for active learning, constructivism connects students in meaningful relationships with their world. Partnerships between the home, the school, and the community are compatible with educators' growing perceptions of the human brain.

In her principles for the new story of learning, Stephanie Pace Marshall affirmed the power of relationships and community in learning. One of her principles concludes with "Engaged learning requires an intergenerational community learning together" (Marshall, 1999, p. 3). Educators can connect to the community in many ways. Teachers can identify people who may want to share their talents, collections, or expertise. They can develop a list of parents and community members to serve as mentors for students. Teachers can organize a schoolwide or districtwide science exploratorium where students and their families gather to participate in hands-on science activities. To encourage active at home participation in science, teachers can develop take-home science activity kits for students to enjoy with their families. They can initiate a program where students share science activities with senior citizens.

Teachers can apply for grant money at the local, state, and national level, as well as from businesses and private corporations. They can look to the community for additional resources and innovations. They can search for ways to provide constant input to enable students' brains to detect patterns and to extract meaning from learning situations that engage their constructivist minds. Caine and Caine (1997a) suggested that when a (a school) begins to interact more freely and unpredictably with its environment (the community), a state of disequilibrium arises and that out of the disequilibrium self-organization emerges.

Commit to a Compassionate Concern for Morality and Humanity

In the introduction to *A New Mind for the New Millennium* by Robert Kiely and Anthony DiSanto, Stephanie Pace Marshall wrote about her strong belief that the fundamental purpose of education is to create young people who are able to think deeply about essential questions of humanity (Marshall in Kiely & DiSanto, 1999). Marshall's vision of a new paradigm is one that draws out the innate goodness and genius from every student. She stated that educators are responsible for creating vibrant, dynamic learning communities that honor children through the nurturing of their humanity, their imaginations, and their spirits. She hoped that a new educational paradigm would enable students to respond to essential questions about life, empowering them with a sense of how they belong to the world and to each another.

Marshall asserted that we must rediscover a concern for morality and humanity, which the current learning paradigm has allowed us to relinquish. She hoped to regain an acquisition of wisdom, a deep commitment to the ecological future of the world, and a greater emphasis on issues of consequence, including a concern for human and community prosperity. Believing in the power of constructivism, Marshall encouraged deep learning designed around essential questions and relationships. These attributes are a portion of Marshall's vision for a new educational paradigm, "all of which offer us the possibility to invite the creation of a new global mind, a mind capable of imagining and creating a compassionate and sustainable world that works for everyone" (Marshall in Kiely & DiSanto, 1999, p. 3).

In his book *Beyond Discipline*, Alfie Kohn (1996) discussed the need for classrooms that promote a sense of community where strong values such as trust, fairness, responsibility, and kindness are encouraged. In value-driven schools, students feel safe to learn and grow both physically and emotionally. Kohn reported a high correlation between schools featuring a strong sense of community, students liking school, and students finding relevance in learning. Students in these schools are more concerned about each other and better at resolving conflicts.

One of the strategies that Kohn suggested to build a value-driven, caring school community is to provide opportunities for class and schoolwide activities. A science fair where students celebrate science without competition and an Earth Day Exploratorium, where students participate in a series of environmental activities led by teachers, administrators, and parents, can accomplish much in improved relationships between the school and the community.

Another easy-to-implement and popular strategy is a "science buddy" program where older students are paired with younger students to conduct safe and simple science experiments. This strategy works especially well when teachers pair fourth, fifth, or sixth graders with kindergarten, first, and second graders. Sink-float activities and experiments with magnets, light, sound, and electrical energy offer a win-win situation for all involved—even the teachers. Encouraged to develop caring friendships across grade levels, students share in engaging science learning activities that have relevance, ensure connectiveness, and bring a sense of joy to the learning situation.

Wheatley (1994) asserted that a clear core of values and vision, when kept in motion through continued dialogue, may lead to order and rebirth. Howard Gardner so eloquently stated,

The task of the new millennium is not merely to hone our various intelligences and use them properly. We must figure out how intelligence and morality can work together to create a world in which a great variety of people will want to live. (Gardner, 1999, p. 4)

When teachers commit to a compassionate concern for morality and humanity, they are successful in generating brain-compatible science with a holistic view of discovering the basic underlying truths of the universe, one of which is a genuine concern for all of humanity.

Sustain Order Through Growth and Change

As teachers prepare to teach science differently, they need an updated set of teaching tools. The old chalk and blackboards do not work anymore; neither do the worksheets and textbooks and multiple-choice tests that teachers have used and abused and grown so accustomed to. Teachers may need to toss their dusty charts and pointer sticks, unless they think of some novel ways to use them. Perhaps students can measure out and draw life-size whales and dinosaurs on the school playground with yardsticks and chalk, use the chart paper to make Venn diagrams comparing the Earth and Moon, or display colorful butterfly and coral reef posters on the magnetic chalkboards. And the pointer stick? Teachers will think of something (Figure 9.1).

Equipped with a new set of tools, teachers are ready for growth and change and a new kind of order. Mirrors, microscopes, and rainbow glasses guide students to see the world differently. Tuning forks and a tape of whale calls lead students to hear the sounds and dance to the rhythms of change. Teachers can use crystals for touching, prisms for pondering, and polarizing filters and kaleidoscopes for reflecting. Teachers can also use trade books, Web sites, and CD-ROMs along with the best from their science texts. They can construct a planetarium by taping together two huge pieces of black plastic. They can make a grid to plot and poke holes for constellations in the winter sky. They can inflate the planetarium with a fan and sit inside with their students. With space odyssey music playing in the background, teachers and students can share constellation myths while watching the "stars" come out, revealing a much more natural and holistic way to teach and to learn.

Wheatley (1994)wrote that a world based on machine images is a world filled with boundaries. Stephanie Pace Marshall concurred by surmising that educators have moved "from a linear language to a living language, from machine-based metaphors to ecology-based metaphors, and from rigid structures to mutable environments" (Marshall in Hesselbein, Goldsmith, & Beckhard, 1997, p. 182). Changes in the language science teachers use promote growth as new metaphors replace the old with revitalized energy and meaning. Figures 9.2 and 9.3 compare the old (-ing verbs for Newtonian schools) with the new (-ing verbs for future schools) as scientists and educators search constantly for new, improved theories to replace the old. Dancing, singing, celebrating, embracing, pondering, dreaming, meandering, weaving: The words are familiar. Only the way teachers interpret them has changed.

Teachers need to reinvent definitions as they enter into the new science education paradigm. They must box up take-home science kits rather than boxing up students into tight little overscheduled containers of stifling learning situations. Instead of cutting and pasting, teachers can try blending and bifurcating. Teachers need to energize, revitalize, reorganize, and harmonize. They must try not to memorize, moralize, scrutinize, and standardize. Teachers need to muse and empower,

(Text continues on page 183)

Science Teacher Paraphernalia

OLD NEWTONIAN WAY	NEW CHAOS-INSPIRED WAY
Dusty old textbooks	Candles
Science worksheets	Flower pots
Multiple-choice tests	Seeds
True-false quizzes	Mirrors and prisms
Vocabulary lists	Kaleidoscope
Ditto masters	3-D glasses
Ditto fluid	Rainbow glasses
Typewriter	Polarizing filters and mica
Carbon paper	New age music
Blackboard pointer	3-D / Acid-base markers
Blackboard	Food coloring
Flannel board	Microscope
Chalk	Computer disks
Chalkboard eraser	Bubble solution
Pens and pencils	Baking soda and vinegar
File folders	Goggle glasses
Lined paper	Crystals
Rubber eraser (there's only one right answer)	Pattern books
	Bright posters
Slide rule	Science trade books
Dissecting tools	Open-ended lessons
Periodic chart	Feathers
Puzzles	Balloons
Classification manuals	Dream catcher
Glossary	Grow butterflies, then let them go
Protractor	New language inspired by
Compass	Lewis Carroll's *Jabberwocky*
Ruler	Mylar
Yardstick	Slinky
Scale	Water
Newtonian demonstrator	Tornado tubes
Pulleys	Fractal pictures
Levers	Good science catalogs
Mounted butterfly collection	Animals observed in natural setting
Specimens preserved in formaldehyde	Web sites
Old machine-imagery language	Scientific method—nonlinear
Scientific method—linear	LOTS of paper towels!

Many could go either way, depending upon how they are used.

Figure 9.1

-ing Verbs for Newtonian Schools

programming	providing	matching	factoring
evaluating	balancing	recalling	fueling
confronting	equalizing	counting	vectoring
producing	reasoning	identifying	marching
deciding	analyzing	classifying	setting
debating	preventing	sequencing	working
researching	reciting	restating	recording
comparing	lecturing	labeling	ignoring
contrasting	controlling	distinguishing	designating
computing	instructing	separating	meeting
examining	rating	discriminating	conferencing
interrupting	ranking	excluding	dictating
consulting	directing	regulating	cause-effecting
proposing	overseeing	measuring	automating
organizing	tracking	weighing	inspecting
justifying	testing	arguing	forcing
originating	reporting	criticizing	forging
selecting	ordering	producing	pointing
appraising	commanding	accounting	lining
supervising	telling	precisioning	straightening
assessing	requiring	constraining	outlining
disciplining	denying	dominating	infomating
choosing	mandating	mistrusting	polishing
concluding	relating	shrinking	refining
prioritizing	solving	resisting	scrutinizing
scheduling	perfecting	projecting	waiting
struggling	figuring	administering	paralleling
monitoring	unraveling	threatening	note-taking
reprimanding	deciphering	authoritating	standardizing
addressing	dominating	fighting	steering
moralizing	checking	interfering	heading
preaching	boxing	ruling	managing
memorizing	fearing	executing	governing
mechanizing	dissecting	turn-taking	superintending
hypothesizing	investigating	warping	administrating
experimenting	timing	correcting	leveling
readjusting	structuring	grading	rebuilding
grouping	budgeting	marking	decision-making
building	causing	filing	naming
self-managing	affecting	cutting	listing
segregating	pasting		

Depending on how they are used, many of these words are appropriate for a chaos-inspired educational paradigm.

Figure 9.2

-ing Verbs for Future Schools

transcending	cycling	discerning	welcoming
valuing	branching	blending	dialoguing
meditating	reabsorbing	empathizing	owning
unifying	interacting	involving	resting
intuiting	caring	localizing	musing
liberating	sharing	designing	pondering
sensing	contributing	decentralizing	mulling
integrating	mediating	leading	clarifying
conceptualizing	mentoring	observing	bookmarking
mysticizing	guiding	initiating	finding
loving	coaching	mainstreaming	extending
freeing	inviting	diversifying	suggesting
feeling	disagreeing	persevering	nudging
listening	cooperating	enriching	receiving
trusting	respecting	relaxing	promising
expressing	wondering	focusing	allowing
accepting	empowering	immersing	imagining
thriving	supporting	engaging	meandering
centering	believing	inventing	dreaming
discovering	inspiring	planning	arranging
developing	life-affirming	hoping	doing
varying	evolving	joining	adapting
revitalizing	changing	responding	weaving
gaining	rhyming	acting	mending
connecting	energizing	praying	advising
reorganizing	creating	enabling	fostering
problem-solving	recycling	enlightening	risking
patterning	sustaining	composing	informing
reframing	renewing	including	accommodating
surfing (the Net)	conserving	swaying	uniting
clustering	preserving	moving	melding
orchestrating	reusing	growing	correlating
webbing	nurturing	reassuring	relating
exploring	saving	spiritualizing	affiliating
infusing	harmonizing	opening	journaling
processing	playing	gathering	layering
communicating	singing	exchanging	congregating
networking	dancing	helping	bifurcating
brainstorming	celebrating	linking	thinking
collaborating	embracing	projecting	being
facilitating	envisioning	discussing	pausing
flowing	globalizing	conversing	contemplating
tinkering	reaching	attracting	cerebrating

Figure 9.3

We can energize our science curricula . . .

We have the potential to move from this:	To this:
I can't.	Let's go!
It's too messy.	The students love it!
I don't have the right equipment.	I think we can do it!
It takes too much time.	Let's work as a team!
There's so much else to do.	Let me help you find some magnets!
I don't have the background.	Come on in and see what we're doing!
It's too hard.	The kids figured it out!
The kids will act up.	We only spilled one cup of bubble solution!
What about the content?	I had terrific cleanup helpers!
Where are the vocabulary words?	That worked great!
I don't have a sink.	Now I understand!
I hated science when I was a kid.	What a great rubric!
It's too noisy.	Can we do this during recess?
I'll lose control.	My students had a great idea!
The students can't.	Maybe this will work!
No one will help me.	Yeah, it did!
I'm all burned out.	Science is really fun!
I'm all out of energy.	I feel energized!

Figure 9.4

collaborate and flow. The Newtonian verbs excluding, threatening, commanding, and dominating never belonged in the classroom. Teachers must rethink their definitions of directing, evaluating, supervising, and scheduling. Above all else, teachers must stop making excuses for why they can't energize their science teaching and figure out things that they can do to encourage brain-compatible learning environments for their students (Figure 9.4).

APPLICATION FOR BRAIN-COMPATIBLE SCIENCE

The following brain-compatible lesson plan, *Endangered Species Boxes,* introduces the new science principle of dissipative structures into an environmental science research activity. Remaining continually open to the outside world, the human brain processes great quantities of information in a constant quest to create meaningful knowledge. Likewise, living things are consistently open to the changes in the environment surrounding them where they struggle for survival in a frequently hostile world. Following the lesson plan is a web to incite more creative ideas (Figure 9.7) and a chart to navigate the road to change in the brain-compatible classroom (Figure 9.8).

Lesson: Endangered Species Boxes

New Science Principle: Dissipative Structures
Grade Level: 3–8

New Science Connection

- Dissipative structures are systems capable of maintaining their identity only by remaining continually open to the environment.
- Dissipative structures take in energy from the outside, produce entropy or waste, and feed it back into the surrounding environment.
- Darwin's finches, beach ecosystems, and the complexities of the human brain are examples of dissipative structures.
- Extinct, endangered, and threatened animals and plants have lost, or are in the process of losing, their openness to their environment.
- Self-organizing dynamics exist in all open systems.
- Free to grow and evolve, life-forms remaining open to the environment stand a greater chance of surviving in the modern, changing world.
- Life-forms that close themselves off from an outside energy source have less chance of survival.

Curriculum Connection

- Endangered species
- Ecosystems
- Biomes
- Food webs and chains
- Environmental science
- Animal kingdom

National Science Education Standards

- Content Standard C; 1–5
- Content Standard F; 2, 3

Objectives (Students will . . .)

- Research a threatened, endangered, or extinct species using selected Internet sites to access and download information.
- Create a small box decorated outside with pictures and text to illustrate the animal and inside with a diorama or with things that represent the animal.
- Investigate how dissipative structures and life-forms that remain continually open to their environment are far more likely to survive than life-forms that close themselves off from an outside energy source.

Materials

- ❏ Endangered species list (Figure 9.5)
- ❏ Computer with Internet access and World Wide Web software
- ❏ Computer printer
- ❏ Endangered animal resources
- ❏ Shoe boxes or other small boxes (one for each student or group of students)
- ❏ Paper
- ❏ Crayons, markers, colored pencils
- ❏ Glue
- ❏ Small objects of students' choice

Preactivity Discussion

Prior to the activity, discuss the following questions with students:

1. What are some of the many things that animals give to us? In what ways are we dependent on animals?

2. What are some of the things that we give back to animals? In what ways are they dependent on us?

3. Name some animals that you know are endangered.

4. Why are many animals endangered?

5. What responsibility do we have for the animals on the Earth?

Procedure

1. Ask students to choose an endangered animal that they are interested in (see Figure 9.5). Have students use a variety of reference books and Internet sources to research the species.

2. Have students create an endangered species box by decorating the sides and top of a shoe box with pictures, sentences, and short paragraphs to illustrate the chosen animal. Ideas for the sides of the box include the following:
   - Write the name of the animal in fancy writing on the top or one side of the box.
   - Draw the animal (entire body view).
   - Draw the animal (close-up of face only).

- Draw the animal doing various things in its habitat (e.g., eating, running, climbing, swimming, flying, grazing in a herd).
- Draw the mother with her babies or an individual baby.
- Write about the animal's natural habitat.
- Make a map showing where in the world the animal lives.
- Write the story of why the animal is endangered.
- Write about how the animal can be helped.
- Write interesting facts about the animal.
- Write riddles about the endangered animal.
- Write about your responsibility to all the animals on the Earth.
- Write questions and answers about the animal.
- Write about how you feel about this endangered animal.
- Write a poem or a short story about the animal.
- Pretend you are the animal, and write a letter to yourself.
- Pretend you are the animal, and write a letter to humanity.
- Write a diary of your day as the animal.

3. Let students choose something to represent the animal to place inside the box (or outside, if the item is too large). Encourage students to be creative and original and to trust in their own ideas! Some starter ideas include the following:
- A picture or photograph of the animal
- A little stuffed toy animal or puppet
- A clay or soap model of the animal
- A book or article about the animal
- Something the animal eats
- Something to represent the animal's habitat
- Something that symbolizes the animal (e.g., a coin, flag, or stamp)
- A tape of the animal's sound (e.g., whale or bird calls, a tiger's roar)
- A song featuring the animal
- A map showing where the animal lives
- A diorama of the animal in its habitat
- A short report, paragraph, poem, or story
- A letter to a senator or representative expressing your thoughts about endangered animals
- A letter that the animal would write to you

Closure

- Let students present their endangered animal boxes to the rest of the class, perhaps in a cooperative learning, round robin format (see Chapter 10). Students could also share their boxes with science buddies or with senior citizens at a nearby nursing home.
- Ask the students to close their eyes and think about their animal. What does it look like? Have students picture it in its habitat. What does the sky look like? Is there water nearby? Woods? Rain forest? Desert? Field? Shrubs and flowers? What is the animal doing? Tell students to picture the animal eating, moving about with its babies, and in danger. How does it feel? How will it react? What is around the animal? How will it interact with others of its species? Have students imagine the smells and sounds of the natural surroundings. Tell students to pretend to touch some of the natural surroundings. What are the textures? Have students imagine touching the animal. Do students feel comfortable with the animal nearby or are they afraid? Have students think about how the habitat will change if the animal

becomes extinct. Tell them to think about their responsibility to their endangered animal and to every other living thing in the world. Have students think about what they can do to save these animals from extinction.

Questions and Extensions

At the close of the activity, pose these questions to students to elicit a discussion, or have students reflect on these questions in journals.

1. Conduct an endangered species interview. What questions would you ask your animal?

2. Read *Brother Eagle, Sister Sky* (Jeffers, 1992) (Figure 9.6).

3. Join hands to form a large circle. Place a large candle in the middle of the circle. Play an inspiring piece of music. Go around the circle students in turn boldly stating the names of their endangered animals and how their animals are important to the global ecosystem.

Evaluation

See Rubric for Endangered Species Box, Figure 5.6.

Technology Connection

Browse the following Web sites to find exciting new ideas for teaching science. Remember to use links and keywords to search even more science-related sites.

Especies Fact Sheets
http://www.kidsplanet.org/factsheets/map.html

Sea World
http://www.seaworld.org/

Endangered Species
http://www.worldwildlife.org/endangered/index.cfm?searchen=google

School World's Endangered Species Project
http://www.schoolworld.asn.au/species/species.html

Water Conservation Resource for Educators
http://www.bellinghamma.org/waterdpw/teacherswater.htm

These Web site addresses were accurate at the time of printing; however, as these sites are updated, some of the addresses may change.

Endangered Species

Listed here are some of the endangered or threatened species that you may choose for your endangered species box:

Elephant	Grizzly Bear
Tiger	Humpback Whale
Spotted Leopard	Manatee
Jaguar	Bald Eagle
Asiatic Lion	Brown Pelican
Ocelot	Trumpeter Swan
Canada Lynx	Great Egret
Zebra	Peregrine Falcon
Gorilla	California Condor
Rhinoceros	Whooping Crane
Kangaroo	Galapagos Penguin
Koala Bear	Ivory-billed Woodpecker
Panda	Yellow-throated Warbler
Red Wolf	Barn Owl
Timber Wolf	Osprey
Mandrill (a Baboon)	Green Sea Turtle
Aye-Aye (a Monkey)	Loggerhead Sea Turtle
Hyena	Bighorn Sheep
Ferret	Steller Sea Lion
Pine Marten	Wild Mustang
Yak	Gila Monster
Gray Bat	Loon
Polar Bear	Northern Spotted Owl
Mountain Lion	Seal (Harp and Monk)

Figure 9.5

Brother Eagle, Sister Sky

A Message From Chief Seattle

OBJECTIVES (Students will . . .)

1. Read and discuss the book, *Brother Eagle, Sister Sky.*

2. Utilize critical thinking skills to compare Chief Seattle's words with their own thoughts about the sacredness of the Earth.

3. Contemplate additional literature, looking for connections and understandings of the Earth.

PROCEDURE

1. Read *Brother Eagle, Sister Sky* (paintings by Susan Jeffers, Scholastic Books, 1992) out loud to the students.

2. Discuss the following questions, first in cooperative groups, and then as a class:

   - Do you think someone could "buy the sky"? If so, how?
   - How does Chief Seattle explain that we are all interconnected?
   - Why did Chief Seattle's people believe that each part of the Earth is sacred?
   - What are your feelings about the beautiful artwork in this book?
   - What do Chief Seattle's words mean to you?
   - What will happen to the Earth if we fail to listen to Seattle's message?

ADDITIONAL LITERATURE CONNECTIONS

Under Your Feet by Joanne Ryder

Sky Tree by Thomas Locker

The Pebble in My Pocket: A History of Our Earth by Meredith Hooper

Prehistoric Journey: A History of Life on Earth by Kirk R. Johnson and Richard K. Stucky

The Weather Sky by Bruce McMillan

Everybody Needs a Rock by Byrd Baylor

The Magic School Bus Inside the Earth by Joanna Cole

Figure 9.6

Web for Dissipative Structures

Figure 9.7

NAVIGATING THE ROAD TO CHANGE IN SCIENCE EDUCATION

Dissipative Structures

Too Much Order	On the Edge	Too Much Chaos
• Promote schools that are closed to the outside environment and isolated with clear boundaries.	• Promote schools with flexible boundaries that are open to the outside environment.	• Promote schools that are open to the environment with no constraints or boundaries.
• Carefully monitor the flow of information.	• Provide constant, current, and relevant information.	• Provide copious and confusing amounts of information.
• Remain isolated from the community and business world.	• Initiate involvement with the community and business world.	• Allow the community and business world to take over schools.
• Continue using the same old tools.	• Use old tools along with new ones in novel ways.	• Throw out the old educational tools in favor of all new and shiny tools.
• Keep all the old machine-age language.	• Use a combination of old language, reinterpreted and defined, along with new language.	• Adopt a totally new chaos-inspired language.
• Adhere to a strict, inflexible moral code.	• Integrate morality with respect for humanity.	• Place no emphasis on humanity or morality.
• Feature outdated values and narrow vision.	• Feature a clear core of values and vision.	• Fail to provide values and clear vision.

Figure 9.8

10

Quantum Mechanics

A Metaphor for Change in the Power of Relationships, Energy, and Paradox

We must learn to embrace complexity in human organizations. We must seek patterns of order beneath the surface chaos and search for structures and patterns of interaction that release and amplify the energies within the system.

Robert Garmston & Bruce Wellman (1995, p. 10)

BACKGROUND: WHAT ARE QUANTUM MECHANICS?

The theory of quantum mechanics, underlying nearly all of modern science, describes the behavior of atomic particles and other small-scale effects. Quantum theory was first proposed in 1900 by German physicist Max Planck to explain how light, X-rays, and other waves are emitted by a hot body (Hawking, 1988). Planck suggested that radiation is emitted not in a continuous stream but in the form of discrete units or quanta. By using quantum mechanics to construct a theoretical framework for describing the fundamental properties of matter and the forces at work in the universe, physicists hope to explain the origin and evolution of the universe.

The uncertainty principle, formulated for quantum mechanics by Werner Heisenberg, states the impossibility of knowing with total accuracy both the position and the momentum of any subatomic particle (Hawking, 1988). The uncertainty principle established the need for probability in the description of particle behavior because of the lack of precision at the atomic level. Unlike the deterministic precision and predictability of the Newtonian Age, where everything was precisely measured and understood, quantum mechanics introduced an element of unpredictability and randomness into the scientific world.

Stephen Hawking argued that even if a unified theory of the universe did exist, scientists would still be unable to predict events accurately. Nothing in the universe exists alone. Everything at the atomic level is in constant motion and totally interconnected. In the quantum world, matter loses its *thingness* by appearing as localized points in space or as waves of energy, depending on how it is measured. Although scientists continue to search for answers, they must learn to live with the uncertainty of not knowing.

Physicists can measure particle position or study energy momentum, but they can never measure both at the same time. The total identity of matter, containing the potential for both particles and waves, is known as an energy bundle or wave packet. Leonard Shlain (1991) quoted Heisenberg, who said,

> The common division of the world into subject and object, inner world and outer world, body and soul, is no longer adequate. . . . Natural science does not simply describe and explain nature; it is part of the interplay between nature and ourselves. (p. 23)

In making a choice between the two, the scientist becomes a part of the system (Garmston & Wellman, 1995).

Shlain (1991) explored how Albert Einstein's theory of relativity changed the notion of objective external reality, or thingness. There can be no absolute time or space because the force of gravity has the effect of "curving" both. What is real for one viewer may be an illusion for another. There is no one favored point of view. Space and time, which in Newton's day had been objective, precise, and measurable, are now viewed as subjective, indefinite, and obscure.

In the early twentieth century, when physicists first began questioning the laws of the universe, many paradoxes emerged. Relationships became more important than things. If . . . then, cause-and-effect ways of thinking were replaced by both . . . and ways of thinking. Time was thought of as being reversible. Systems were viewed holistically instead of as a sum of their parts.

Reality could no longer be precisely measured. Space was suddenly full of invisible fields, unseen structures, and infinite connections.

> A quantum universe is enacted only in an environment rich in relationships. Nothing happens in the quantum world without something encountering something else. Nothing is independent of the relationships that occur. . . . This is a world of process, not a world of things. (Wheatley, 1994, p. 68)

Invisible energy fields became the intangible substance of the universe, as real as particles in the new quantum world. Yet, paradoxically, the fields were nonmaterial.

IMPLICATIONS OF QUANTUM MECHANICS FOR BRAIN-COMPATIBLE SCIENCE

Four implications of quantum mechanics for science education are (1) develop and nurture relationships, (2) learn to accept uncertainty, (3) focus on energy not things, and (4) welcome the tension of paradox. Advocating cooperative learning to ensure quantum interconnectedness, the quantum mechanics implications stress the importance of relationships to foster energy and growth. Like the quantum world, scientific pursuits contain an element of uncertainty featuring paradox as a necessary part of the process.

Develop and Nurture Relationships

Teachers reach bifurcation points (see Chapter 5) in their careers when decisions must be made. Never knowing what may spur new growth, teachers attend conferences and conventions to develop relationships and to stay connected with other science educators. The National Science Teachers Association (NSTA) and local associations for teachers such as the Wisconsin Society of Science Teachers (WSST) offer numerous networking and professional development opportunities for science educators.

Similarly, teachers converse with colleagues within their own schools and districts. Garmston and Wellman (1998) wrote of the benefits resulting when school faculties develop the skills of dialogue and discussion. They asserted that "developing a staff's capabilities for talking together may be the most significant investment faculties can make for student learning" (Garmston & Wellman, 1998, p. 33). Continuing staff development and further education provide bifurcation points throughout teachers' professional careers. Cooperation, collaboration, teamwork, networking, and the ability to solve problems together are essential skills that teachers need to model for their students.

The importance of teaching students to work together cooperatively and collaboratively is more apparent today than ever before. Another of Geoffrey and Renate Caine's (2006) mind/brain principles (see Introduction) states that the brain is a social brain. Concluding that teachers cannot ignore the influence of relationships on learning, the Caines advocate cooperative learning as a means of engaging the human brain in meaningful learning experiences. Cooperative learning is a proven strategy for reaching all students (Fogarty, 1997a; Gregory & Chapman, 2002; Jensen, 1998; Kohn, 1996; Marzano, Norford, Paynter, Pickering, & Gaddy, 2001; National Science Standards, 1996).

Robert Slavin (1989–90) reviewed the research and found that cooperative methods, incorporating group goals, individual accountability, and group processing accelerate student learning. Students gain in self-esteem, have improved attendance, like school better, and spend more time on task. Small, heterogeneous groups of students work effectively together to successfully complete a task for the combined good of all. Slavin and his colleagues have developed a cooperative team learning approach that has proven to be very effective in improving student achievement and relationships among students (Slavin, 1994). This cooperative team approach helps students learn important concepts or review material before a test.

Many cooperative learning strategies work well in science classrooms. Students can "turn toward their neighbors" to discuss, explain, or summarize a portion of a lesson. The *jigsaw* strategy puts students in groups of three or four, with each student reading and studying a portion of the science text or a relevant article. Then the group reconvenes, and each student teaches his or her piece to the others in the group. *Focus trios* asks students, before a lesson or an experiment, to summarize as a group what they already know about a subject and to come up with questions that they would like answers to. After the lesson, the trios answer questions, discuss new information learned, and pose additional questions. With the *round robin* strategy, students in groups of three or four take turns sharing projects or their views on a science topic. Students can partner up to complete *A Microscopic View of Pond/Creek Water* (Figure 10.1).

Name _____

A Microscopic View of Pond/Creek Water

Focus Question: *In a complete sentence, predict what organisms you will see when viewing pond/creek water under a microscope?*

_____

_____

_____

Procedure
1. Use a tweezers and a toothpick to pull a small amount of algae from the pond or creek sample (no more than what would fit inside the letter o). Place the algae in the center of a clean microscope slide.
2. Use a dropper to draw several milliliters of water from the bottom of the sample cup.
3. Squeeze two or three drops of the pond/creek sample on the algae and cover gently with a cover slip.
4. View under the microscope, first at the low power (x4), next at the medium power (x10), and finally at the highest power (x40). Remember to use only the fine adjustment on the high power objective.
5. Use colored pencils to make three labeled drawings of your observations, one for each of the power objectives. Each drawing should include at least one species of algae and one or more additional organisms of your choice, e.g., protozoa, duckweed, scud, insect larva, snail, etc. Label the drawings with as much detail as possible.
6. Use the identification materials to identify the organisms.
7. In two or more complete sentences, describe the appearance, behavior, and movements of the organisms.

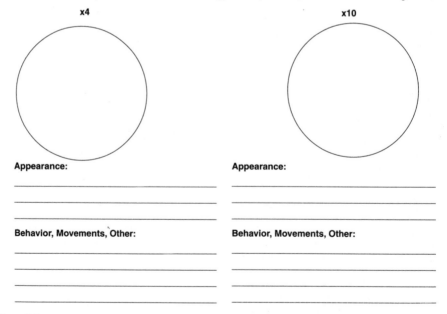

x4

x10

Appearance:

_____

_____

_____

Appearance:

_____

_____

_____

Behavior, Movements, Other:

_____

_____

_____

_____

Behavior, Movements, Other:

_____

_____

_____

_____

Figure 10.1

x40

Pond / Creek Food Web

Appearance:

_____

_____

_____

Behavior, Movements, Other:

_____

_____

_____

1. What biome does this water sample represent?

_____

2. What additional living things may also be a part of this ecosystem?

_____

_____

3. Did you like this lab? Explain why or why not.

_____

_____

_____

_____

_____

_____

_____

Rubric for "A Microscopic View"					
Focus Question	0	1	2	3	4
Microscopic View # 1	0	2	4	6	8
Microscopic View # 2	0	2	4	6	8
Microscopic View # 3	0	2	4	6	8
Concluding Questions	0	2	4	6	8
Food Web	0	2	4	6	8

Total points _____ **Percentage Grade** _____

Scoring Key

4 / 8 points - correct, complete, detailed, in color, over and beyond

3 / 6 points - partially correct, complete, detailed, nicely done

2 / 4 points - mostly correct, partially complete, lacks some detail

1 / 2 points - incorrect or incomplete, needs assistance

0 points - no attempt

Figure 10.1

(Continued)

As the world becomes increasingly troubled and problem-ridden, teachers must improve their ability to live and work cooperatively. In *Science for All Americans*, F. James Rutherford and Andrew Ahlgren (1989) shared this view:

> The collaborative nature of scientific and technological work should be strongly reinforced by frequent group activity in the classroom. Scientists and engineers work mostly in groups and less often as isolated investigators. Similarly, students should gain experience sharing responsibility for learning with each other. (p. 189)

Cooperative learning strategies encourage and teach students to work with others, a necessary skill for harmonious living, both in and out of school. The ability to work together in cooperative teams is a prerequisite for living successfully in the twenty-first century.

An example of incorporating cooperative learning into a science lab is an activity in which students simulate food gathering with four different kinds of insect mouths to discover how insects are adapted for eating certain types of food. Students sit in groups of four with their desks clustered together. The teacher builds in individual accountability, where each student is responsible for his or her own contribution, by assigning each to a specific insect mouth part and group role. Positive interdependence, which teaches students to collectively care about the group process, is accomplished as students share materials, fill out one group lab sheet, and depend on each other to perform in their assigned roles of runner, reader, recorder, and reporter (Figure 10.2). Students discuss their "eating" experiences and come to a group consensus as to which "mouth" is best adapted to each "food type." To conclude the activity, the group processes how productively they worked together. (For a more detailed view of group roles, see Figure 10.3.)

Focusing on the importance of relationships, information, and vision in organizations, Wheatley (1994) concluded, "The more we feel part of the organization, the more work gets done" (p. 144). She averred that teachers should stop teaching facts and focus instead on relationships to generate new understandings, setting the stage for exciting new growth and learning.

> None of us exists independent of our relationships with others. Different settings and people evoke some qualities from us and leave others dormant. In

Science Group Roles

Runner: Gets and returns materials

Reader: Reads directions for activity

Recorder: Records group answers

Reporter: Reports results to class

Cleanup: Everyone pitches in and helps

Figure 10.2

each of these relationships, we are different, new in some way. (Wheatley, 1994, p. 34)

As teachers develop and nurture relationships with staff, parents, and students, interconnected webs grow, encompassing teaching with renewed energy and meaning. In a universally connected quantum world, relationships between individuals generate naturally.

Which is more important, the system or the individual? Wheatley (1994) argued that in a quantum world teachers do not have to choose. What is critical is the relationship between the two.

There are no familiar ways to think about the levels of interconnectedness that seem to characterize the quantum universe. Instead of a lonely space, with isolated particles moving about, space appears filled with connections. (Wheatley, 1994, pp. 41–42)

Particles and brain neurons do not seem to exist independently of their relationships with each other. Neither do people. People need each other. Cooperative learning groups promote brain-compatible science by encouraging shared vision and collective brain power to help solve the open-ended, complex problems of the real world.

Learn to Accept Uncertainty

For some insight into the indecision plaguing the modern world, teachers have only to read the latest issues of science journals such as *Scientific American*. Current scientific research deals with everything from the nebulous nature of cellular biology and the unpredictability of volcanoes and earthquakes to the ambiguities of string theory, black holes, and distant galaxies. The perplexing and still undetermined question of whether there is life on Mars or the possibility of a buried ocean filled with strange creatures on Jupiter's icy moon will remain unresolved until more data can be gathered (Powell, 1997). Because teachers are still so new at exploring the vast universe, they have no choice but to exist in the vague obscurity of their unsteady and changing surroundings.

The unpredictable nature of the quantum world suggests that in education teachers may wish to let up on the precision. Teachers need not straighten, file, and analyze things to perfection, nor must they justify, inspect, and dissect. Why label things so precisely? Teachers place such an emphasis on time with their endless schedules, bells, whistles, and meetings. Teachers grade and check, rate and rank, weigh and track. Teachers are forever correcting, deciphering, and figuring. And the endless reporting and grading is wearing teachers down.

An acceptance of uncertainty allows teachers to wonder and flow, diversify and globalize. Inspired and freed, teachers can web and cycle, welcoming and immersing themselves and their schools in change. If some aspects remain cloudy, teachers can greet the instability as a part of the process. Accepting uncertainty relates to brain-compatible science because the body of scientific knowledge is constantly changing. Presuming that there is no absolute truth, scientists accept uncertainty as a natural component of their research (Rutherford & Ahlgren, 1989).

Cooperative Group Roles

Recorder/Communicator

- records all important data and observations

- makes sure all group members participate in the data collection and discussion of the activity

- communicates with the teacher only after working to clarify or answer questions within the group

- summarizes findings and reports to the class

- collects group work and gives it to the teacher

Materials/Noise Level Manager

- obtains needed materials for the group and returns them when the activity is complete

- watches for group safety

- coordinates the cleanup

- makes sure that ALL the materials are returned

- keeps the group noise level down

Reader/Coordinator

- reads directions so that the group can understand them

- directs the procedure

- divides up the task, with input from the group

- reminds group members of their responsibilities

- checks the activity results

Tracker/Coach

- makes sure each group member understands the directions

- checks that each step is complete before going on to the next

- reminds group members to stay on task

- uses words of encouragement to ensure that all group members have equal opportunity for involvement in the activity

- keeps track of time

Figure 10.3

Focus on Energy, Not Things

In the quantum world, the electron has two identities. It can exist as a particle or as a wave. If teachers observe an electron as a particle, it behaves as a particle; if teachers observe it as a wave, it exhibits properties of a wave. Neither a particle nor a wave, an electron is both and is understood only in its relationship to other electrons. Quantum theory has definite implications for education and how teachers view each other and students. Teachers must explore how their perceptions of people and events shape their reality, maintaining high expectations from all their students. Students behave the way they are perceived. "In quantum schools, leaders pay attention to the flow and interchange of energy. Energy, not things, becomes the avenue to attainment" (Garmston & Wellman, 1995, p. 8). In the future, teachers may take for granted that human energy fields exist. Supporting self-renewal and high performance, educators may harvest and use these invisible fields to reorganize and reinvent schools and to make them more adaptive.

Organisms on the Earth exist to grow and to maintain themselves. Science teachers need to create brain-compatible environments that allow energy to organize itself. Loren Eiseley (1978) wrote about the star thrower, who every morning walks the beaches of Costabel searching for starfish cast upon the sand during low tide. Knowing that the starfish will surely die as sand plugs the tiny breathing pores in their thousands of tube feet, the thrower picks the starfish up, one by one, and flings them back into the sea in a desperate effort to save them. Eiseley (1978) wrote,

> In the sweet rain-swept morning, that great many-hued rainbow still lurked and wavered tentatively beyond him. Silently I sought and picked up a still-living star, spinning it far out into the waves. I spoke once briefly. "I understand," I said. "Call me another thrower." Only then I allowed myself to think, He is not alone any longer. After us there will be others. (pp. 183–184)

Teachers are all star throwers, throwing their students back to the creative edge where energy and life are focused. "We [are all a] part of the rainbow—an unexplained projection into the natural" guiding, leading, and rescuing (Eiseley, 1978, p. 184). As Eiseley contended, the teacher's task is not to be taken lightly.

Focused on the energy of life, as he joins the star thrower on the beach of Costabel, Eiseley (1978) explained how he becomes a part of some unknown dimension of existence:

> I picked and flung another star. Perhaps far out on the rim of space a genuine star was similarly seized and flung. I could feel the movement in my body. It was like a sowing—the sowing of life on an infinitely gigantic scale. . . . Small and dark against the receding rainbow, the star thrower stooped and flung once more. I never looked again. The task we had assumed was too immense for gazing. (pp. 184–185)

Great paradoxes exist in the world. "Continuity and stability are as characteristic of science as change is, and confidence is as prevalent as tentativeness" (Rutherford & Ahlgren, 1989, p. 4). The world is not an either/or place but a both/and place. New order and meaning emerge out of chaos, simplicity out of complexity, freedom out of stability. Teachers search for structure and security in a nonlinear world. Focused on energy, brain-compatible science teachers understand and accept both the power and the limitations of paradox.

Welcome the Tension of Paradox

Several of the mind/brain principles (see Introduction) proposed by Caine and Caine (2006) suggest paradox. The human brain is capable of simultaneously perceiving parts and wholes. Learning involves both focused and peripheral perception as well as conscious and unconscious processes. A global, all-inclusive approach is just as important as one paying attention to specifics and details. Teachers need the right balance between all factors, and these change from day to day and year to year. All of the Caine and Caine mind/brain principles work together concurrently to define each unique learning situation. The complexity of this interaction makes changes inevitable in the teaching and learning process.

Hawking (1988) asked how people can expect to predict future events exactly when they cannot even precisely measure the present state of the universe. Teachers can only look at the world from their own point of view. Hawking wrote, "What we call real is just an idea that we invent to help us describe what we think the universe is like" (p. 139). He continues on to explain the futility of trying to choose between real or imaginary time. Teachers simply must determine which is the more useful description.

A controversial paradox exists regarding the importance of the individual versus the system. Quantum mechanics shows that both are important. Although children are alike in many ways, they are also incomparably precious as they tend diligently to their unique set of brain neurons and individual learning styles (Caine & Caine, 2006). Teachers seek to reach all students by offering variety and choices and by expressing their unquestionable love and great faith in students' potential. Sensitive dependence constantly reminds teachers of the supreme importance of each and every child. Yet at the same time, teachers do not exist in isolation from one another. They are a part of their schools, their communities, and the world—like tiny grains of sand on the larger universal beach of change.

The tide ebbs and flows. Along with Eiseley's star thrower, teachers continue rescuing their students, one by one, leading them to discover their inherent potential. A teacher himself, Eiseley (1971) averred that teachers are saviors of souls as they go about their daily task of harvesting lives from the living seas of their classrooms. Eiseley discussed how teachers forever seek the balance between custom, tradition, and conformity and the freedom and creativity of the human spirit. Teachers are placed in a paradoxical position, expected to be both guardians of stability and exponents of societal change.

Teachers somehow need to find a balance between stability and personal discovery, perhaps at the boundary between order and chaos. Too much order results in loss of energy and death. Too much chaos results in confusing tangents that never end. Stability and change are not opposites. Dynamical systems exhibit both in their cycling progression through time. "From this level of understanding, creative responses emerge and significant change becomes possible" (Wheatley, 1994, p. 115). Teachers can only hope to reach all their students with a vision of what science education has the potential for becoming. Welcoming the tension of paradox may sustain teachers in their quest for brain-compatible science.

APPLICATION FOR BRAIN-COMPATIBLE SCIENCE

The following brain-compatible lesson plan, *Quantum Alternatives,* introduces the new science principle of quantum mechanics into an activity with light and color. Exploring the quantum mechanics premise that light exists both as a particle and as a wave, depending on how it is viewed, students learn about paradox firsthand as they observe light from a variety of perspectives. Unpredictability and randomness are a necessary component of the quantum universe. Following the lesson plan is a web to incite more creative ideas (Figure 10.4) and a chart to navigate the road to change in the brain-compatible classroom (Figure 10.5).

Lesson: Quantum Alternatives

New Science Principle: Quantum Mechanics

Grade Level: 3–8

New Science Connection

- Appearing colorless, sunlight is actually a continuous spectrum containing all wavelengths or frequencies of visible light.
- Prisms and diffraction gratings separate white light into a spectrum of colors. (The rays in the violet end of the visible spectrum, corresponding to the shorter wavelengths, are more sharply refracted or bent by a prism than are the longer wavelengths in the red end of the spectrum.)
- Since the earliest of times, scientists have sought to explain the mysteries of light; Sir Isaac Newton, Thomas Young, James Clerk Maxwell, Max Planck, and Albert Einstein are just a few of the many masterminds who agreed and disagreed about whether light is a particle or a wave.
- In the early twentieth century, when physicists first began questioning the laws of the universe, many paradoxes emerged; unlike the deterministic precision and predictability of the Newtonian Age, quantum mechanics introduced an element of unpredictability and randomness into the scientific world.

Curriculum Connection

- Physics
- Astronomy
- Quantum mechanics
- Light energy (spectrum, prisms, diffraction, refraction, reflection)
- Rainbows
- Wave behavior

National Science Education Standards

- Content Standard A; 1–9
- Content Standard B; 3

- Content Standard D; 3
- Content Standard G; 1, 2

Objectives (Students will . . .)

- Describe the colors of the spectrum made by a prism.
- Analyze different light sources with diffraction gratings to discover that although a light source appears one color, it really comprises a number of colors.
- View a variety of light sources through a bird feather for still another rainbow perspective.
- Explore the quantum mechanics premise that light exists both as a particle and as a wave depending on how it is viewed.

Materials

- ❏ Prism
- ❏ Overhead projector or other light source
- ❏ Diffraction grating plastic cut into 2-inch squares
- ❏ Small bird feathers (Quail feathers work perfectly.)
- ❏ Lightbulb and holder
- ❏ Candle and holder
- ❏ String of multicolored Christmas lights
- ❏ Matches

Optional:

- Spectroscope
- Bubbles
- Drinking straw

Preactivity Discussion

Turn out the lights in the classroom. Hold a prism in the beam of light from an overhead projector so that the light strikes one of the three sides. Slowly rotate the prism until a pattern of colors appears on the wall. Ask students the following questions:

1. What color is the light before it passes through the prism? (white)

2. What colors appear on the wall? (red, orange, yellow, green, blue, violet)

3. How does a prism separate white light into rainbow colors? (White light is refracted as it enters and leaves a prism. The amount of refraction depends on the wavelength of the light, with shorter wavelengths bending more than longer wavelengths. Violet light with the shortest wavelengths bends more than red light with the longest wavelengths. Refracted slightly more or less than violet and red light, each of the other rainbow colors leaves the prism at a slightly different angle.)

Procedure

1. Pass out a small square of diffraction grating plastic to each student.

2. Ask students to look through the diffraction grating at a variety of different light sources, such as lightbulb, candle, multicolored Christmas lights, the Sun (indirectly, of course), fluorescent ceiling lights.

3. Have students look at the same light sources through the tip of a bird feather. (A lit candle flame in a darkened room works best.)

4. Invite students to slowly rotate the bird feather for a revolving view, move closer to the light for another view, and move away from the light for still another perspective.

Closure

Explain to the students how a diffraction grating acts like a prism, separating light into its constituent wavelengths and rainbow colors. A diffraction grating consists of a surface ruled with thousands of parallel slits, each slit only several light wavelengths wide. With tiny slits between their barbs, bird feathers also possess the ability to separate white light into the rainbow colors. A bird feather is nature's diffraction grating. Viewing light through a bird feather offers an alternative and creative view of the world. The white light from the candle diffracts into rainbows of color as it passes through the narrow slits of the bird feather. Continuous spectrums of light and color, rainbows are eternally promising, symbolic of the quantum connectedness of the universe.

Questions and Extensions

At the close of the activity, pose these questions to students to elicit a discussion, or have students reflect on these questions in journals.

1. What color is closest to the light source? (Violet light, bending the most, is the closest to the light source.)

2. What color is farthest from the light source? (Red light, bending the least, is the farthest from the light source.)

3. How does the diffraction grating view compare to the feather view? How are the views alike? How are they different?

4. Compare a continuous spectrum with a banded spectrum by viewing white sunlight and fluorescent light through a spectroscope to experience how astronomers learn about lit objects in space. (The spectroscope separates starlight into its colors. Spectrum colors differ slightly, providing information about the chemical composition of planets and stars, as well as the temperature, pressure, magnetic field, and condition of the gases in the star. Spectrums allow astronomers to learn if the distance between Earth and a star is increasing or decreasing. The study of spectrums is one of the most useful tools that astronomers have for learning about the universe.)

5. To understand light further, blow some bubbles on a blank overhead transparency. Using an overhead projector, project the image for all to see. (Just as white light separates into different colors when it passes through a prism, white light also separates into colors when it bounces off a soap bubble. Made of many layers of differing thickness, the soap film reflects white light to produce rainbow colors. The thickest soapy layers reflect red light and the thinnest layers reflect violet light. The colors change as the thickness of the soap bubble changes.)

Technology Connection

Browse the following Web sites to find exciting new ideas for teaching science. Remember to use links and keywords to search even more science-related sites.

NASA Homepage
http://www.nasa.gov/home/

NASA for Kids
http://kids.msfc.nasa.gov/

Spaceweather
http://www.spaceweather.com/

The Nine Planets
http://www.nineplanets.org/

The Art and Science of Teaching with Technology
http://www.teach-nology.com/

Enchanted Learning Biomes and Habitats
http://www.enchantedlearning.com/biomes/

Biomes of the World
http://mbgnet.mobot.org/sets/

These Web site addresses were accurate at the time of printing; however, as these sites are updated, some of the addresses may change.

Web for Applying Quantum Mechanics

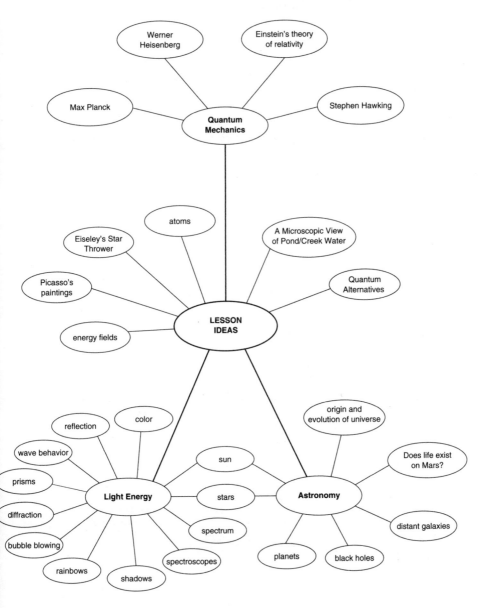

NAVIGATING THE ROAD TO CHANGE IN SCIENCE EDUCATION

Quantum Mechanics

Too Much Order	On the Edge	Too Much Chaos
• Promote that individuals remain unconnected.	• Nurture relationships with staff, parents, and students to generate new understandings.	• Exist independently of relationships with others.
• Students learn alone with competition.	• Use cooperative and collaborative learning strategies.	• Loosely organize students into groups with no parameters or direction.
• Consider the individual more important than the system.	• Consider the individual and system equally important.	• Consider the system more important than the individual.
• Believe that space is lonely with isolated particles.	• Believe that space is filled with connections.	• Create confusion with too many connections.
• Provide no networking opportunities.	• Provide networking opportunities, believing that they are vital to growth.	• Place too much emphasis on networking and team building.
• Overly control and stabilize.	• Learn to understand and deal with uncertainty.	• Exist in a state of constant uncertainty and confusion.
• Straighten, file, and analyze things to perfection.	• Need not straighten, file, and analyze things to perfection.	• Let things pile up and become totally disorganized.
• Focus only on things.	• Focus on both energy and things.	• Focus only on energy, never on things.
• Emphasize: complexity, stability, structure, and real time.	• Emphasize paradox: complexity and simplicity, stability and freedom, structure and security, real and imaginary time.	• Emphasize: simplicity, freedom, security, and imaginary time.

Figure 10.5

SECTION 3

Chaos Theory and New Science Principles Summary

A NEW APPROACH TO SCIENCE EDUCATION

Fractal shapes abound at the beach, in the sand and the rocks, in the water and the waves, in trees on the shore, and in feathers of gulls as they swoop down to the lake searching for fish. The simple truths in the sand and water reveal greater complexities as teachers search for repeating patterns in the clouds, and view the beach from differing perspectives. Teachers construct sand castles of new meaning from the old while discovering the interacting systems of sand, water, air, and the diversity of life in the beach ecosystem. Life's natural tendency to organize surrounds teachers with creativity and fractal simplicity.

One grain of sand hits another, which hits another, as they iterate dynamically in an ongoing, cycling process. Imagine teachers tracing out the phase portrait of a single grain of sand, going back in time to its origin, and following it forever into the future. Was it once a dark basaltic rock carried by a continental glacier? Or perhaps a part of a crinoid or a brachiopod from an ancient sea? Someday, layered by wind and water, the same sand will accumulate and change back into sedimentary rock. Connected designs repeat with unexpected regularity as long as the right information continues to feed into the system. Each tiny detail of sand shows sensitive dependence on initial conditions of the other grains close by as they collectively form into larger patterns, communicating with an energy all their own.

A certain similarity in systems exists in the world, a security blanket of orderliness. The stars appear in the sky according to the star charts. The sand blows around at the beach forming ripple designs. The waves break down the rocks to form new sand. Yet beneath the seeming order of every system, lies the strange attractor pulling this way, then that. If teachers trust in the inherent order, set invisible boundaries with freedom to expand, offer greater freedom and flexibility, and believe in the power of guiding principles and values, a new shape will emerge, tracing out a phase portrait within the phase space of the beach ecosystem. Teachers understand the mystery when they observe the flocking behavior of birds overhead.

Teachers resist bifurcation and period doubling because they dislike storms and transitions into turbulence. Too much disorder disorients teachers, leaving them confused and apprehensive. Avoiding the inevitable, teachers hide from the unpredictable ways of the universe. To find true order, teachers look deeply within the systems around them. Recognizing more than one right way by providing choices, and seeking out turmoil, and surprise, their reward comes with the joy of revitalization and renewal. Teachers expect the order to reemerge from beneath the turbulence. While waiting, teachers resolve to loosen up and have some fun, giving over some of the control as they discover new relationships and webs of meaning in the Sun, the sky, the sand, and in each of their students.

Teachers find new niches by remaining flexible and adaptable as they face each new day anticipating and expecting change. Creativity and new life center on the boundary between steadiness and oscillation. Order itself is not rigid, but a dynamic energy swirling around teachers.

"Relational holism and self-organization work in tandem to give us the living universe. Two dynamic processes, fed by information, combine to create an ordered world. The result is evolution, the organization of information into new forms. Life goes on, richer, more creative than before." (Wheatley, 1994, p. 119).

Chaos theory and new science principles contain countless implications for teaching, learning, assessing, and designing science curriculum. Compatible with the human brain and learning theories, these principles advocate many of the same ideas that scientists pursue—differing perspectives, interacting systems, creative energy, and new life. Simple truths reveal greater complexities as interconnected designs repeat with unexpected regularity. Life's natural tendency to organize becomes an ongoing, cycling process. Looking deeply within systems, scientists search for repeating patterns as they discover new science knowledge. Brain-compatible science teachers help their students to do the same as they encourage webs of understanding through relationships and exchange with the surrounding environment.

Implications for Teaching

Evolutionary biology implies that teachers balance their outlook for the science education of the future. True energy lies on the edge, at the boundary between steadiness and oscillation. Too much steadiness results in extinction. Too much oscillation throws the system into chaos. To be truly brain compatible, science teaching, learning, assessing, and curriculum designing need to be somewhere in the middle. Viewing science education from a variety of perspectives for a balanced outlook, teachers construct new meanings from old, using higher-level thinking skills. The tunnel vision view, ignoring previous learning, is not the answer. Nor is the answer an overly romanticized and idealistic view, leading to pointless wandering on useless tangents, with no structure, organization, or planning. Fractals show teachers how to simplify their teaching by working with life's natural tendency to organize and searching for meaning in patterns. To raise the level of understanding, help students to confront their misunderstandings and connect instructional objectives to experiences in real life.

Sensitive dependence on initial conditions leads teachers to pay attention to details, realizing that small may lead to big. Seeking a balance between too little and too much stimulation, teachers engage the peripheral perception of their learners with stimulating classrooms. They must not ignore small things, having mediocre expectations from one group of students and high expectations from another. Brain-compatible science teachers must provide strong female and minority role models and work to overcome their tendency toward male-dominated, exclusive, single-culture-oriented classrooms and curricula.

Teachers learn from strange attractors, phase space, and phase portraits to provide a positive learning environment for students where productive habits of mind are encouraged, the impact of emotions are considered, and relationships are valued. Encouraging participation by all in their classrooms, to enhance learning and self-esteem, and to increase their students' chances for success, teachers need to offer a nurturing and accepting phase space for all students, regardless of gender, ethnicity, or special needs. For science teaching to be truly brain compatible, teachers must approach all students and situations with sensitivity and understanding, providing equally for divergence and bifurcations of new knowledge.

Brain-compatible teachers need to be both prepared and flexible with an understanding of dissipative structures giving them incite into how to use their old teaching tools along with the new in novel ways. Fully equipped with a large repertoire of teaching skills and strategies, teachers can redefine Newtonian language to reassess the noise level and freedom of movement in their classrooms. Expanding their phase space, with guiding principles and values serving as the strange attractor, perhaps teachers no longer need to insist on quiet and perfect adherence to the rules at all times. Brain-compatible teachers must take a few risks, not changing for the sake of change, but willing to seek out surprises and unpredictable events, discovering life's bifurcations with a new sense of flexibility. Strange attractors stress the importance of providing a brain-compatible learning environment.

The chaos principles of turbulence and bifurcation imply a need for excitement, novelty, the freedom to play and experiment. The turbulent clutter, mess, and noise become part of the process in a brain-compatible science classroom. By limiting lecture, teachers can guide groups of students in scientific inquiry and discussion, sharing the responsibility for the learning. Brain-compatible teachers ask for student input on the design and control of some activities; while other activities are teacher-planned. Teachers must carefully select and adapt curriculum, setting up flexibly structured classrooms, with many things happening at the same time. Teachers need to avoid an overstimulating, agitating, school-is-a-party attitude, although they must smile and laugh frequently, while guiding student learning from the sidelines. Brain-compatible teachers understand that they must expect turbulence as a necessary part of the curriculum and instructional process.

Iteration can help teachers to cultivate a reflective attitude in students rather than moving too quickly and efficiently from subject to subject, or wandering off on useless tangents with pointless exploration. Brain-compatible teachers frequently use graphic organizers to show relationships including how things are alike and how they are different. Self-organization encourages all teachers to help students use the knowledge learned at school in new, real-life situations to ensure brain compatibility.

Implications for Learning

The new science principle of quantum mechanics shows teachers how to use cooperative and collaborative learning strategies, in which students dialogue and share science topics within the context of their everyday lives. Teachers need to group students in clusters of three or four to encourage and promote teamwork rather than learning alone through competition. In brain-compatible science classrooms, teachers use interactive strategies to facilitate student learning, encouraging exploration and discovery. Teachers need to avoid irrelevant, disconnected, or trendy topics that go with the flow of the moment with no real direction or context; with poorly organized cooperative and collaborative ventures, knowledge is gained haphazardly at best.

Students learn actively rather than passively as recipients of information provided by the teacher. Teachers must create knowledge through the relationship between the knower and the known realizing that the outcome may not always be known in advance. Teachers need to provide bifurcation and period-doubling, brain-based instruction for individual learning styles, incorporating Howard Gardner's (1983) multiple intelligences theory. Higher-level questioning strategies, promoting creative, divergent, and critical thinking lead to brain-compatible, real-life, problem-solving scenarios where there is no one right answer. Instead, many solutions exist for the same problem, unlike puzzle learning and worksheets where all answers are the same.

Brain-compatible teachers must shift the emphasis from how they teach to how students learn. Parallels exist linking fractal theory to brain-compatible science education. Teachers need only to look at the many natural patterns surrounding them to understand the innate ability of the human brain to make connections by constructing new meaning from the old. Self-organization indicates a strong need for purposeful learning situations that capitalize on the learning process, making use of the latest brain-based research.

Teachers forcing the unnatural use of Gardner's multiple intelligences theory or offering too many choices may cause confusion and lack of focus for learners. Teachers who take an overly global view may lose students' interest and concentration. Nor should teachers favor only a few learning styles, concentrating on the parts rather than the whole, with one-dimensional and irrelevant topics. Evolutionary biology implies that thinking may be nonlinear and connected at the same time in a way that is consistent with discovering and saving individuals. Similar to Loren Eiseley's starfish on the beach at Costabel (see Chapter 10), brain-based science teachers are inclusive rather than exclusive.

In designing a more flexible phase space for students, and encouraging more holistic phase portraits, teachers rethink the "box" paradigm in favor of a larger learning community, where everyone learns and grows together. Confining students to desks in rows in classrooms in buildings and using only whole-group activities with low-level questioning and teaching strategies are no longer the only ways to teach. Students need the freedom to learn within a much larger realm both in and beyond the walls of the school, with the beach or garden used for more than just a short field-trip experience. Students need input into the design of classroom rules and opportunities to share ideas about learning as they move more freely about the classroom.

Brain-compatible science teachers encourage students to learn creatively on the border between order and chaos as they grow naturally through everyday experiences. Students learn science effectively when they actively participate in relevant activities embedded in their lives both in and out of school. The learning process continually iterates back on itself creating a depth of understanding, fostering energy and revitalization.

Bifurcation and period doubling imply that rather than using reward and punishment as motivation or eliminating all stress and anxiety from the learning situation, brain-compatible teachers must provide a joyful classroom atmosphere involving low threat and high challenge. Teachers need to consider student attitudes and perceptions about learning, designing lessons to shape positive attitudes (Marzano, 1992), and paying attention to the flow and interchange of energy. In a brain-compatible science classroom, learning skills evolve constantly. Students learn science effectively when their brains and entire physiology are totally immersed in the learning activity (Caine & Caine, 2006). Encouraging internal, intrinsic motivation, a certain amount of turbulence in the educational process engenders creativity and revitalization as new understandings generate from the old.

Implications for Assessing

When teachers discover bifurcations in their brain-compatible teaching and learning strategies, they also need to find different ways of looking at assessment in science education. The shift to a new paradigm in assessment is difficult as teachers cling to their old measures, relying on traditional, more subjective forms of assessment, whole group assessment, and traditional end-of-chapter tests. Pencil-and-paper, short-answer, and multiple-choice tests based on simple recall of information are no longer adequate and, even more important, do not work as an effective assessment tool for many students.

Brain-compatible teachers need a combination of assessment methods, including traditional tests, as well as performance assessment, rubrics, and portfolios—that is, varying assessment methods to match specific learning experiences. More varied, authentic, and embedded assessment helps teachers focus on their students' use of knowledge and complex reasoning rather than on recall of low-level information. Brain compatibility is all about many bifurcations in teaching, learning, assessing, and designing curriculum.

Implications for Designing Curricula

Evolutionary biology shows teachers how to be adaptable and flexible, anticipating and expecting change in their science curricula and classrooms. Thinking locally and acting locally is too narrow a view; thinking globally and acting globally, too ethereal a view. For a balanced outlook, brain-compatible science teachers must think globally and act locally. Interdisciplinary, integrated, holistic curricular themes help students make connections and generate thought patterns. Teachers need to work collaboratively with other teachers and staff members to more fully integrate science into other areas of the curriculum. Science belongs with math, literature, language arts, social studies, technology, environmental education, art, and music.

Brain-compatible teachers learn from the chaos theory principle of iteration to generate science curriculum content from science processes. Content and process interconnect. Teachers should not consider one without the other. A single-text, knowledge-based curriculum constricts and inhibits. To encourage brain cells to generate new knowledge, teachers must teach fewer topics in depth rather than a disjointed overview of too many teacher-selected topics, resulting in a fragmented curriculum. Brain-compatible science teachers need to thoughtfully infuse technology into the science curriculum, viewing information as energy flowing through the educational process and trusting in the strange attractor inherent within this nonlinear, multidimensional age of information.

The principles of self-organization and dissipative structures show teachers that curriculum is a continuously evolving process rather than a thing. Similar to the human brain, schools are living, open systems, capable of self-renewal and self-organization. Schools should not be closed to the outside environment, isolated within strict boundaries, nor should they be totally open, following one educational trend after another. Brain-compatible science curricula must develop flexible boundaries with a strong vision and a clear core of values. Greater involvement with the community and business world encourages partnerships and teamwork, fostering a sense of shared responsibility. Science curricula must involve real-life problems and situations where the whole world becomes the curriculum, offering truly interactive and challenging experiences. Open to change in prevailing scientific theories, brain-compatible science teachers can provide students with a global perspective never before possible.

A FINAL GLIMPSE OF CHAOS

Quantum mechanics offers implications for science teaching, learning, curriculum, and assessment, as well as for teacher education of the future. Ongoing professional development opportunities for teachers must emphasize relationships with staff, parents, and students to ensure that individuals remain connected. The world is not a lonely space with isolated particles. Brain-compatible teachers do not exist independently of their relationships with others. The individual is not more important than the system, nor is the system more important than the individual. Space is filled with connections, and networking is vital to growth as educators. Teachers need to understand and deal with uncertainty, welcome instability as a part of the process, and focus on both energy and things, not on either/or. The human brain and the scientific world include both.

Some argue philosophically against chaos theory as an agent of change in their modern-day schools (Maxcy, 1995). Believing that individuals will become lost in an ethereal, global view, Maxcy wrote that chaos theory, based on mathematical theories, has no place in social institutions such as schools. Although these pragmatic arguments, from an intellectual standpoint, are certainly mind expanding, they go beyond the purpose of this book, which is to offer a metaphor for change and a glimpse of where science education may be headed. This book focuses on constructing meanings with students in the fuzzy region of the brain-compatible science classroom—where the innovative action is and where the true creativity of teaching lies.

In "Connoisseur of Chaos," Wallace Stevens said, "A violent order is disorder . . . A great disorder is an order. These two things are one" (Briggs & Peat, 1989). Complexity and simplicity, stability and freedom, structure and security, real and imaginary time, the individual in a global universe—these are the paradoxes of the modern world. Science teachers must prepare with a more global, inclusive, and brain-compatible perspective, one remaining open to constant growth and renewal.

For a final glimpse of what chaos theory may offer science education of the future, teachers can light a candle. They can look at the glowing flame through the tip of a bird feather for a creative way of viewing the world. The white light from the candle diffracts into rainbows of color as it passes through the narrow slits of the bird feather. Continuous spectrums of light and color, the rainbows teachers see are eternally promising, symbolic of the connected nature of their universe. Teachers then need to slowly rotate the feather for a revolving view and move away from the flame for still another perspective.

"Is science magic?" the students ask.

"No," the teacher replies, "Magic is science!"

Teachers need to reflect on the beauty of children and the magical promises they bring to the world. Each and every child is truly chaos transcending. For their sake, teachers are compelled to change.

Glossary

bifurcation. A continual branching process in which large swirls break into smaller swirls and into still smaller swirls. A bifurcation, or forking, occurs in a system when a single happening is amplified so greatly by iteration that the system takes off in a whole new direction.

brain compatible. Teaching and learning processes that parallel or complement the way the brain/mind makes meaning and remembers.

butterfly effect. Small changes in a system lead to big changes later on. Components that do not appear related may interact and influence one another. For example, the beating of a butterfly's wings in Beijing could lead to a major storm in New York.

chaos. Order without predictability or persistent instability. Using simple, nonlinear equations, one may arrive at very complex and unpredictable results.

chaos theory. Significant mathematical development of the twentieth century. Randomness and unpredictability are essential to chaos theory, which describes the way systems change over time.

Darwinian evolution. A steady, ongoing evolution spanning centuries of time, where living things evolve through the process of natural selection by competing intensely with each other for survival.

dissipative structure. Systems capable of maintaining their identity only by remaining continually open to the flux and flow of their environment. Many chemical reactions exhibit the properties of dissipative structures; examples include the collective behavior of slime molds, termite activity, and bees in a hive.

dynamical systems. The study of processes in motion; an evolving, self-organizing network creating order out of chaos. Examples include the motion of stars and galaxies, weather systems, chemical changes, pendulum motion, the rise and fall of populations, and the human brain and schools undergoing change.

evolutionary biology. Species carve out individual niches as they interact with the whole environment and with each other. Species become so interwoven with their surroundings that they regulate their own population, as do the finches on the Galapagos Islands. Unlike Darwinian evolution, changes may occur within extremely short time periods.

fractals. Computer-generated shapes that repeat themselves on a smaller and smaller, self-similar scale, creating patterns within patterns. Natural patterns include ferns, clouds, feathers, trees, blood vessels, broccoli, rocks, rivers, and galaxies.

holistic. Looking at a system as a whole rather than as a sum of its parts. Connection and relationships become more meaningful; everything is related to everything else nonlinearly.

iterate. Output from a previous operation becomes the input for the next operation as a mathematical process is repeated, continuously reabsorbing and enfolding what has come before. Examples include changing weather systems, the replacement of cells in human bodies, and the learning process.

linear. Cause and effect are functionally related as one proceeds in a step-by-step order, sequentially and very predictably. Linear relationships may exist on a graph in a straight line and may be put back together or solved. For example, Newton's third law of motion states that for every action there is an equal and opposite reaction.

Newtonian physics. Sir Isaac Newton's deterministic view of the universe is ordered, linear, and predictable as is the mechanical pendulum motion of a clock. Like a giant machine, the world was governed by simple cause-and-effect relationships. Matter and energy were thought of as separate entities.

nonlinear. Cause and effect are not functionally related as one proceeds in a nonsequential and random order. Nonlinear systems generally are insolvable and, if taken apart, cannot be put back together. Outcomes are unpredictable as the rules change constantly. Examples include animal populations and weather systems.

period doubling. A common factor in the way order breaks down into chaos. First, there are 2 possibilities, then 4, 8, 16, and so on.

phase portrait. A computer-generated picture or shape formed by the strange attractor, within phase space, as a system changes over time. Examples include the Lorenz attractor, coupled pendulums, and the chaotic flow of fluids.

phase space. Provides a way of turning numbers into pictures, abstracting every bit of essential information from a system of moving parts, mechanical or fluid, and making a flexible road map to all its possibilities. The strange attractor both defines and stays within the boundaries of phase space.

quantum mechanics. The theory that radiant energy is transmitted in the form of discrete units. Bundles of energy (quantum) in motion (mechanics) is the discipline dealing with the behavior of all atomic particles. For example, light energy may behave like a wave or a particle, depending on how the light is measured.

self-organization. An open system that constantly interacts with its environment and cannot be understood in isolation. A self-organizing system is always a part of a larger system or environment that it exchanges matter, energy, and information with. Examples include the evolution of the stars and the genetic code, containing within itself the past, present, and future of all living things.

sensitive dependence on initial conditions. Small, rounded-off errors in computation may become greatly magnified when they are iterated, quickly growing out of proportion as they move through a system. Small things may have great implications.

strange attractor. Randomness with an underlying order; the shape that indecision traces. A turbulent system is contained within the defined space of the strange attractor.

system. An entity composed of interconnected parts. May be as large as the universe or as small as an atom; all are complex and nonlinear.

turbulence. Breaks up orderly systems; occurs in nature in air currents, fast-flowing streams, tornadoes, tidal waves, and hot lava flowing from volcanoes. Arises when all the pieces in a system are interconnected, with each piece depending on every other piece and the resulting feedback.

universal theory. Discovered in 1975 by physicist Mitchell Feigenbaum; states that certain equations behave similarly when going through the transition from order to chaos. Unrelated transitions, such as the boiling of water and the magnetizing of metals, follow the same rules.

References

Abbott, J., & Ryan, T. (1999) Constructing knowledge, reconstructing schooling. *Educational Leadership, 57*(3), 66–69.

American Association for the Advancement of Science (AAAS) Project 2061. (1993). *Benchmarks for science literacy.* New York: Oxford University Press.

American Association for the Advancement of Science (AAAS) Project 2061. (2001a). *Atlas of science literacy.* New York: Oxford University Press.

American Association for the Advancement of Science (AAAS) Project 2061. (2001b). *Designs for science literacy.* New York: Oxford University Press.

American Association of University Women (AAUW). (1992). *How schools short-change girls.* Washington, DC: The American Association of University Women Educational Foundation.

Anderson, O., & Stewart, J. (1997). A neurocognitive perspective on current learning theory and science instructional strategies. *Science Education, 81*(1), 67–90.

Atwater, M. (1995). The cross-curricular classroom. *Science Scope, 18*(2), 42–45.

Barr, R., & Parrett, W. (2003). *Saving our students, saving our schools.* Thousand Oaks, CA: Corwin Press.

Base, G. (1987). *Jabberwocky.* New York: Harry N. Abrams.

Briggs, J., & Peat, F. (1989). *Turbulent mirror.* New York: Harper & Row.

Caine, G., & Caine, R. (1997a). *Education on the edge of possibility.* Alexandria, VA: Association for Supervision and Curriculum Development.

Caine, G., & Caine, R. (1997b). *Unleashing the power of perceptual change: The potential of brain-based teaching.* Alexandria, VA: Association for Supervision and Curriculum Development.

Caine, G., & Caine, R. (2006). *Making connections: Teaching & the human brain* (3rd ed.). Thousand Oaks, CA: Corwin Press.

Carey, S. J. (1993). *Science for all cultures.* Arlington, VA: National Science Teachers Association (NSTA).

Carson, R. (1961). *The sea around us.* New York: New American Library.

Cleveland, J. (1996). *Dancing on the edge of chaos.* R. Jan LeCroy Center for Educational Telecommunications, Dallas County Community College District. PBS Adult Learning Service.

Crockett, C. (2004). What do kids know and misunderstand about science? *Educational Leadership, 61*(5), 34–37.

Darwin, C. (1964). *On the origin of species* (E. Mayr, Ed.) (facsimile of 1st ed.). Cambridge, MA: Harvard University Press. (Original work published 1859)

Demi. (1997). *One grain of rice: A mathematical folktale.* New York: Scholastic Press.

Devaney, R. L. (1992). *A first course in chaotic dynamical systems.* Reading, MA: Addison-Wesley.

Diamond, M., & Hopson, J. (1998). *Magic trees of the mind.* New York: Dutton Books, Penguin-Putnum.

217

Eiseley, L. (1971). *The night country.* New York: Scribner.

Eiseley, L. (1978). *The star thrower.* New York: Harvest/HBJ.

Erwin, J. C. (2003). Giving students what they need. *Educational Leadership, 61*(1), 19–23.

Fogarty, R. (1991). Ten ways to integrate curriculum. *Educational Leadership, 49*(2), 61–65.

Fogarty, R. (1997a). *Brain-compatible classrooms.* Thousand Oaks, CA: Corwin Press.

Fogarty, R. (1997b). *Problem-based learning & other curriculum models for the multiple intelligences classroom.* Thousand Oaks, CA: Corwin Press.

Fogarty, R., & Stoehr, J. (1995). *Integrating curricula with multiple intelligences.* Thousand Oaks, CA: Corwin Press.

Freeman, D. (1998, Fall). Science education: How curriculum and instruction are evolving. *ASCD Curriculum Update,* 1–3, 6, 8.

Gardner, H. (1983). *Frames of mind.* New York: BasicBooks.

Gardner, H. (1991). *The unschooled mind.* New York: BasicBooks.

Gardner, H. (1995). Reflections on multiple intelligences: Myths and messages. *Phi Delta Kappan, 77*(3), 202–209.

Gardner, H. (1999). *Intelligences reframed: Multiple intelligences for the 21st century.* New York: BasicBooks.

Garmston, R., & Wellman, B. (1995). Adaptive schools in a quantum universe. *Educational Leadership, 52*(7), 7–12.

Garmston, R., & Wellman, B. (1998). Teacher talk that makes a difference. *Educational Leadership, 55*(7), 30–34.

Gender gaps remain in science education, says report. (2000/2001, December/January). *National Science Teachers Association Newsletter,* p. 24.

Gleick, J. (1987). *Chaos: Making a new science.* New York: Penguin Books.

Grant, R., & Grant, P. (1989). Natural selection in a population of Darwin's finches. *American Naturalist, 133,* 377–393.

Gregory, G., & Chapman, C. (2002). *Differentiated instructional strategies.* Thousand Oaks, CA: Corwin Press.

Gunter, M. A., Estes, T. H., & Schwab, J. (1995). *Instruction: A models approach.* Boston: Allyn & Bacon.

Hall, N. (1991). *Exploring chaos.* New York: W. W. Norton.

Hampton, E., & Gallegos, C. (1994). Science for all students. *Science Scope, 17*(6), 5–6, 8.

Hawking, S. (1988). *A brief history of time.* Toronto: Bantam Books.

Hesselbein, F., Goldsmith, M., & Beckhard, R. (1997). *The organization of the future.* San Francisco: Jossey-Bass.

Holloway, J. (2000). How does the brain learn science? *Educational Leadership, 58*(3), 85–86.

James, J. (1995). Negotiating the grand canyon of change. *The School Administrator, 52*(1), 22–29.

Jeffers, S. (1992). *Brother eagle, sister sky.* New York: Scholastic.

Jensen, E. (1998). *Teaching with the brain in mind.* Alexandria, VA: Association for Supervision and Curriculum Development.

Jensen, E. (2000a). *Brain-based learning.* Thousand Oaks, CA: Corwin Press.

Jensen, E. (2000b). Brain-based learning: A reality check. *Educational Leadership, 57*(7), 76–80.

Jensen, E. (2000c). Moving with the brain in mind. *Educational Leadership, 58*(3), 34–37.

Jukes, I., & McCain, T. (2000). *Windows on the future: Education in the age of technology.* Thousand Oaks, CA: Corwin Press.

Kauffman, S. (1995). *At home in the universe: The search for the laws of self-organization & complexity.* New York: Oxford University Press.

Kiely, R., & DiSanto, A. (1999). *A new mind for the new millennium.* The Illinois Mathematics and Science Academy and the 21st Century Learning Initiative at the State of the World Forum, October 3, 1999.

King-Friedrichs, J., & Browne, D. (2001). Learning to remember. *The Science Teacher, 68*(8), 44–46.

Kohn, A. (1996). *Beyond discipline*. Alexandria, VA: Association for Supervision and Curriculum Development.

Kotar, M., Guenter, C. E., Metzger, D., & Overholt, J. L. (1998). Curriculum integration: A teacher education model. *Science and Children, 35*(5), 40–43.

Libbrecht, K. (2003). *The snowflake winter's secret beauty*. Stillwater, MN: Voyageur Press.

Lowery, L. (1996a, Spring). Changing the metaphor. *FOSS Newsletter*.

Lowery, L. (1996b, ·Spring). Benchmarks and standards: An historical perspective. *FOSS Newsletter*.

Lowery, L. (Ed.). (1997). *NSTA pathways to the science standards: Elementary school edition*. Arlington, VA: National Science Teachers Association.

Lowery, L. (1998). How new science curriculums reflect brain research. *Educational Leadership, 56*(3), 26–30.

Mandelbrot, B. (1983). *The fractal geometry of nature*. New York: W.H. Freeman.

Mangan, R., & Mangan, M. (1998). *Sand patterns*. Milwaukee, WI: New Science Productions.

Marshall, S. P. (1995). The vision, meaning, & language of educational transformation. *The School Administrator, 52*(1), 8–15.

Marshall, S. P. (1999). Principles for the new story of learning. *New Horizons Online Journal 5*(3): Retrieved October 15, 2005, from www.newhorizons.org/future/marshall.htm

Marzano, R. (1992). *A different kind of classroom: Teaching with dimensions of learning*. Alexandria, VA: Association for Supervision and Curriculum Development.

Marzano, R. (2003). *Classroom management that works*. Alexandria, VA: Association for Supervision and Curriculum Development.

Marzano, R., & Marzano, J. (2003). The key to classroom management. *Educational Leadership, 61*(1), 6–13.

Marzano, R., Norford, J., Paynter, D., Pickering, D., & Gaddy, B. (2001). A handbook for *classroom instruction that works*. Alexandria, VA: Association for Supervision and Curriculum Development.

Marzano, R., Pickering, D., & Pollock, J. (2001). *Classroom instruction that works*. Alexandria, VA: Association for Supervision and Curriculum Development.

Maxcy, S. J. (1995). *Democracy, chaos & the new school order*. Thousand Oaks, CA: Corwin Press.

May, R. (1976). Simple mathematical models with very complicated dynamics. *Nature, 26*(1), 459–467.

Morrison, P., & Morrison, R. (1987). *A ring of truth*. New York: Random House.

National Council for the Social Studies. (1992). Curriculum guidelines for multicultural education. *Social Education, 56*(5), 274–294.

National Research Council. (1996). *National science education standards*. Washington, DC: National Academy Press.

National Science Teachers Association. (1998). The national science education standards: A vision for the improvement of science teaching and learning. *Science and Children, 35*(8), 32–34.

O'Connor, K. (2002). *How to grade for learning*. Thousand Oaks, CA: Corwin Press.

Paul, R., & Elder, L. (2003). *A miniature guide to scientific thinking*. Dillon Beach, CA: The Foundation for Critical Thinking.

Peitgen, H. O. & Richter, P. H. (1986). *The beauty of fractals*. Heidelberg, Germany: Springer-Verlag.

Perkins, D., & Blythe, T. (1994). Putting understanding up front. *Educational Leadership, 52*(5), 4–7.

Pinkerton, K. (1994). Using brain-based techniques in high school science. *Teaching and Change, 2*(1), 44–61.

Powell, C. (1997). The greening of Europa. *Scientific American, 276*(4), 28–29.

Prigogine, I., & Stengers, I. (1984). *Order out of chaos. Man's new dialogue with nature*. Toronto: Bantam Books.

Rakow, S., & Vasquez J. (1998). Integrated instruction: A trio of strategies. *Science and Children, 35*(6), 18–22.

Rutherford, F., & Ahlgren, A. (1989). *Science for All Americans: American Association for the Advancement of Science Project 2061.* New York: Oxford University Press.

Sadker, D. (1999). Gender equity: Still knocking at the classroom door. *Educational Leadership, 56*(7), 22–26.

Sadker, M., & Sadker, D. (1994). *Failing at fairness: How our schools cheat girls.* New York: Touchstone Press.

Sadker, M., Sadker, D., Fox, L., & Salata, M. (1993–1994, Winter). Gender equity in the classroom. *The College Board Review, 170,* 14–21.

Shepardson, D. P., & Britsch S. J. (1997). Children's science journals: Tools for teaching, learning, and assessing. *Science and Children, 34*(5), 12–17.

Shlain, L. (1991). *Art & physics.* New York: William Morrow.

Slavin, R. (1989–90). Research on cooperative learning: Consensus & controversy. *Educational Leadership, 47*(4), 52–54.

Slavin, R. (1994). *Using student team learning.* Baltimore: Johns Hopkins Team Learning Project.

Sneider, C. 1. (1989). *Earth, moon & stars.* Lawrence Hall of Science, University of California, Berkley: Great Explorations in Math and Science (GEMS).

Sprenger, M. (1999). *Learning and memory: The brain in action.* Alexandria, VA: Association for Supervision and Curriculum Development.

Steinberger, E. (1995). Margaret Wheatley on leadership for change. *The School Administrator, 52*(1), 16–20.

Stepans, J. (1996). *Targeting students' science misconceptions.* Riverview, FL: Idea Factory.

Suchman, R. (1968). *Developing inquiry in earth science.* Chicago: Science Research Associates.

Sylwester, R. (1994). How emotions affect learning. *Educational Leadership, 52*(2), 60–65.

Thinking and learning. (1993). *Journal of Staff Development, 14*(4), 78–80.

Weiner, J. (1995). *The beak of the finch.* New York: Vintage Books.

Weiss, I., & Pasley, J. (2004). What is high-quality instruction? *Educational Leadership, 61*(5), 24–28.

Wheatley, M. (1994). *Leadership & the new science: Learning about organizations from an orderly universe.* San Francisco, CA: Berrett-Koehler.

Wheatley, M., & Kellner-Rogers, M. (1996). *A simpler way.* San Francisco: Berrett-Koehler.

Willis, S. (1995, Summer). Reinventing science education: Reformers promote hands-on, inquiry-based learning. *ASCD Curriculum Update,* 1–8.

Zemelman, S., Daniels, H., & Hyde, A. (2005). Best practice in science. In S. Zemelman, H. Daniels, & A. Hyde (Eds.), *Best practice: New standards for teaching and learning in America's schools.* Portsmouth, NH: Heinemann.

Index

AAAS. *See* American Association for the Advancement of Science
Abbott, John, 173, 176
Ahlgren, Andrew, vi, xvii, 175, 196
American Association for the Advancement of Science (AAAS), xvii
Atlas of Science Literacy (AAAS), xvii

Baker transformation iteration, 25, 35, 38
Benchmarks for Science Literacy (AAAS), xvii–xviii
Beyond Disciple (Kohn), 177
Bifurcations and period doubling
  activity logs, reflection pages assessments, 94–96*figs.*
  activity-oriented lessons and memory learning, 98
  application web regarding, 105*fig.*
  background and definitions regarding, 77–78
  bifurcation, defined, 214
  brain-compatible classroom changes, 106*fig.*
  choices in assessing, 87–88, 89–97*figs.*
  choices in curriculum, 88
  choices in learning, 80
  choices in teaching methods, 79–80, 81*fig.*
  With a Cluck Cluck Here lesson plan, 82*fig.*, 83–86*fig.*
  conceptual change learning model, conflict resolution, 98
  emotional expression by students, 99
  goal-setting by student, 87
  implications for science education, xxi, 208, 209, 210, 211
  informal checklists, 90*fig.*
  Invention Bifurcations lesson plan, 100–102, 103–104*figs.*
  joyful classroom atmosphere, 99
  multiple intelligences, pluralistic view of the mind, 80, 82*fig.*, 83–86*fig.*

nonlinguistic representations and learning, 98
period doubling, defined, 215
portfolio assessment, 87, 89*fig.*
rubric assessments, 91–93*figs.*
safe learning environment, 99
spatial *vs.* reward and punishment memory systems, 88, 98
student self-assessment, 97*fig.*
surprises and accompanying joy, 98
web sites regarding, 102
Brain-based learning
  brain-based science, defined, vii
  essential classroom strategies, xix
  mind/brain principles of, xviii–xix
  in science education, vii–ix, xx
Brain-Based Learning (Jensen), xvix
Brain Compatible Classrooms (Fogarty), 62
Brain compatible, defined, 214
Briggs, John, 24, 108
Brother Eagle, Sister Sky (Chief Seattle), 188*fig.*
Butterfly effect, in chaos theory, 44, 53, 214
  See also Sensitive dependence on initial conditions

Caine, Geoffrey, xiv, xv, xviii, 52
  adaptation and change, 128
  bifurcation points in school reform, 78
  brain as a social brain, cooperative learning, 193
  brain changes through environment interaction, 175–176
  brain uniqueness and similarities, 80, 200
  brains search for meaning, 62
  community involvement in learning, 176
  conscious and unconscious learning processes, 7
  educational change process as strange attractor, 66
  emergence and self-organization, 77, 155

emotions are critical to patterning, 66
  enriched educational environments, 49
  focused attention and peripheral perception, 45, 155
  integrated, holistic curricular themes, 131
  joyful classroom atmosphere, 99
  learning at developmental stages, 79
  learning opportunities search, 26
  meaning search through patterning, 11
  mind and body engagement, 28, 78–79, 108, 113, 123, 161
  mind/brain principles, 1
  self-organization and transformation process, 161–162
  spatial *vs.* reward and punishment memory systems, 88, 98
  student parallel-processing minds, 155
  teacher control by letting go, 113
  teaching and learning perceptual orientations, 12, 108
Caine, Renate Nummela, xiv, xv, xviii, 52
  adaptation and change, 128
  bifurcation points in school reform, 78
  brain as a social brain, cooperative learning, 193
  brain changes through environment interaction, 175–176
  brain uniqueness and similarities, 80, 200
  brains search for meaning, 62
  community involvement in learning, 176
  conscious and unconscious learning processes, 7
  educational change process as strange attractor, 66
  emergence and self-organization, 77, 155

emotions are critical to
patterning, 66
enriched educational
environments, 49
focused attention and peripheral
perception, 45, 155
integrated, holistic curricular
themes, 131
joyful classroom atmosphere, 99
learning at developmental
stages, 79
learning opportunities search, 26
meaning search through
patterning, 11
mind and body engagement, 28,
78–79, 108, 113, 123, 161
mind/brain principles, 1
self-organization and
transformation process,
161–162
spatial *vs.* reward and
punishment memory
systems, 88, 98
student parallel-processing
minds, 155
teacher control by letting go, 113
teaching and learning perceptual
orientations, 12, 108
Chaos theory
bifurcations and period doubling
and, 77–78
butterfly effect concept in, 44, 53
definitions regarding, 1, 214
dissipative structures and,
173–174
implications for assessing, 211
implications for curricula design,
211–212
implications for learning, 210–211
implications for science
education, xv, xxii, 212–213
implications for teaching,
208–209
Lorenz attractor concept, 44, 108
and the new sciences, xv–xvi
order metaphors emerging from
chaos, vii, xv, xvi
randomness and unpredictability
in, xv
strange attractor, defined, 60
summary regarding, 212–213
See also Bifurcations and period
doubling; Fractals; Iteration;
Sensitive dependence on
initial conditions; Strange
attractors, phase space, and
phase portraits; Turbulence
Chapman, Carolyn, 32
Classroom Instruction That Works
(Marzano, Pickering, and
Pollock), xix
Classroom management.
See Turbulence
Cleveland, John, 129, 152, 208

Community and values, 177
See also Dissipative structures
Community-centered education,
176, 210
Constructivism, 173
community-centered education
and, 176
See also Dissipative structures;
Fractals
Crockett, Cynthia, 10

Darwin, Charles, 156
evolution and natural selection
concepts of, 126, 127, 152
Galapagos Island finch
population, 125–126, 174
Darwinian evolution,
defined, 214
Demi, 77
Diamond, Marion, 175
DiSanto, Anthony, 177
Discipline. *See* Turbulence
Dissipative structures, 123, 186
application web regarding,
189*fig.*
background and definitions
regarding, 173–174, 214
brain-compatible classroom
changes, 178, 182*fig.*, 183,
190*fig.*
chaos theory and, 173–174, 181*fig.*
community involvement in
learning, 176, 177
constructivism and, 173, 176
curricula energized, 182*fig.*
Endangered Species Boxes lesson
plan, 183–186, 187–188*figs.*
implications for science
education, xxii, 209, 212
morality and humanity
commitment, 177–178
Newtonian physics verbs,
180*fig.*, 183
Newtonian physics *vs.* chaos
theory, 179*fig.*
order sustained through
growth and change,
179–182*figs.*, 183
self-organization and, 173
stay open to the environment,
175–176
web sites regarding, 186
Dynamical systems, defined, 214

Earth, Moon, Sun, and stars
relationships lesson, 10–11
Education on the Edge of Possibility
(Caine and Caine), xv
"Eggsperiment," 26,
27*fig.*, 28
Einstein, Albert, xiv, 156, 192
Eiseley, Loren, 128, 199, 210
Elder, Linda, 155
Erwin, Jonathan, 113

Evolutionary biology, 123
adaptation and change, 128
application web regarding,
150*fig.*
background regarding, 125–127
brain-compatible classroom
changes, 151*fig.*
curriculum integration for
holistic view, 131–132
Darwin's theories and,
126–127
defined, 214
Galapagos Island finch
population, 125–126, 174
implications for science
education, xxii, 208–209, 210
implications for science
education, curricula
design, 211
Microscopic View of Sand lesson
plan, 144–145, 146*fig.*
multiple intelligences, *Sand
Patterns* curriculum, 132,
147–149*fig.*
Sandy Beach lesson plan, 133–137,
138–140*fig.*
Sandy Properties lesson plan,
141–142, 143*fig.*
self-organization and, 127
sensitive dependence on initial
conditions concept, 126
teach in the boundary between
steadiness and oscillation,
128–129, 130*fig.*
think global, act local,
132–133, 211
web sites regarding, 137

Feedback, 24, 35, 38
See also Iteration
Feigenbaum, Mitchell, 25, 28, 78
Focus trios cooperative teaching
strategy, 193
Fogarty, Robin, 62
Fractals
application web regarding,
22*fig.*
background and definitions
regarding, 3–6
brain-compatible classroom
changes, 23*fig.*
Changing Perspectives lesson plan,
13–22, 14*fig.*, 17–23*figs.*
computer "windows" and, 34
defined, 214
examples of, 8–9*figs.*
implications for science
education, xxi, 207, 210
Koch snowflake, 4, 5*fig.*
measurement concepts, 4
new meaning constructed from
old, 7, 10–11
repeating patters and different
perspectives, 11–12

simple to complex paradoxes, 4, 6
simple truths reveal greater complexities, 6–7
web sites regarding, 16
Freeman, Dan, 109

Gallegos, Charles, 49–50
Gardner, Howard, 10, 26
  morality focus of, 177–178
  multiple intelligences, pluralistic view of the mind, 80, 82*fig.*, 83–86*fig.*, 131–132, 210
  nature of student understanding, 154
Garmston, R., 191
Gender equity and diversity, 49–51
  See also Sensitive dependence on initial conditions
Glasser, William, 113
Gleick, James, xv, xvi, 25–26, 44
  turbulence, 107
  "Rube Goldberg" devices activities, 156, 157–158*fig.*
Grant, Peter, 125, 126, 127
Grant, Rosemary, 125, 126
Gregory, Gayle, 32
Guide to Scientific Thinking (Paul and Elder), 155

Habits of mind. *See* Strange attractors, phase space, and phase portraits
Halloway, John, xx
Hampton, Elaine, 49–50
Hawking, Stephen, 192, 200
Heisenberg, Werner, 191, 192
Holistic, defined, 215

Information management. *See* Iteration
Internet. *See* Web sites
Iteration
  application web regarding, 41*fig.*
  background and definitions regarding, 24–25
  baker transformation concept, 25, 35, 38
  brain-compatible classroom changes, 42*fig.*
  Color Lab, 28, 29–31*fig.*
  connected, concentrated curriculum, 35
  dynamic process and flexibility emphasis, 25–28, 27*fig.*
  "Eggsperiment," 26, 27*fig.*, 28
  Feigenbaum number concept, 25
  grain of sand example, 207
  graphic organizers technique, 32, 33*fig.*, 34

implications for science education, xxi, 209
implications for science education, curricula design, 211–212
information systems, 34–35
iterate, defined, 215
Magma Mix Activity Log, 40*fig.*
Magma Mix lesson plan, 35–39
phase space, strange attractors, phase portrait and, 61–62
reflective attitudes focus, 26
science process skills, 26, 27*fig.*, 28
similarities and differences in systems focus, 28–34, 32*fig.*, 33*fig.*
Venn diagram technique, 33*fig.*, 34, 132, 167*fig.*
web sites regarding, 39

Jensen, Eric, xvix, 34, 35
  body needs and learning, 114
  emotions role in learning, 66
  enriched environments, 49, 66
  movement, energizers in learning situations, 114
  music in learning, 114
  non-threatening learning environments, 99
Jigsaw cooperative teaching strategy, 193
Jukes, Ian, 67–68

Kauffman, Stuart, 126–127, 152
Kellner-Rogers, Myron, 4, 6, 60, 98
  freedom to play and experiment, 109
  self-organization focus of, 152, 174
Kiely, Robert, 177
Knowledge construction. *See* Self-organization
Koch, Helge von, 4
Koch curve, 4, 6*fig.*
Koch snowflake, 4, 5*fig.*, 14*fig.*
  lesson plan regarding, 13–16, 17–23*figs.*
Kohn, Alfie, 99, 107, 113, 177

Learning environments. *See* Strange attractors, phase space, and phase portraits
Lesson plans
  Changing Perspectives (fractals), 13–22, 14*fig.*, 17–23*figs.*
  A Closer Look at Crystals (sensitive dependence on initial conditions), 53–56
  With a Cluck Cluck Here (bifurcations and period doubling), 82*fig.*, 83–86*fig.*

Dancing Raisins (strange attractors, phase space, and phase portraits), 69, 70–71, 72*fig.*, 73
Endangered Species Boxes (dissipative structures), 183–186, 187–188*figs.*
Invention Bifurcations, 100–102, 103–104*figs.*, 103*fig.*
Jabberwocky (self-organization), 162–163, 164–167*figs.*, 168–170
Magical Milk Colors (turbulence), 107–108, 114, 116–118, 119*fig.*
Magma Mix (iteration), 35–39
A Microscopic View of Pond/Creek Water (quantum mechanics), 194–195*figs.*
Microscopic View of Sand (evolutionary biology), 144–145, 146*fig.*
Nature Patterns (sensitive dependence on initial conditions), 45, 46–48*fig.*
Quantum Alternatives (quantum mechanics), 201–204
Sandy Beach (evolutionary biology), 133–137, 138–140*fig.*
Sandy Properties (evolutionary biology), 141–142, 143*fig.*
Lightening lesson, 10
Linear, defined, 215
Lorenz, Edward, 44
Lorenz attractor, 44, 61, 61*fig.*, 108
Lowery, Lawrence, xvi, xx, 24, 28

Mandelbrot, Benoit, 3–4, 24, 77
Mandelbrot set, 25
Mangan, Margaret, xii
Marshall, Stephanie Pace, xv
  community-centered education and, 176
  integrated, holistic curricular themes, 131
  learning motivators, 113
  meaning constructed through personal inquiry and pattern formation, 7
  morality and humanity focus, 177
  from Newtonian physics to brain-compatible science, 178
  self-organization process to facilitate change, 161
Marzano, Jana, 69
Marzano, Robert
  assessment, 87
  classroom management variables, 68–69
  experimental inquiry process, 156
  positive attitudes and perceptions affect learning, 66
  productive habits of mind, 66

student-teacher relationship
importance, 69
using knowledge meaningfully, 7
May, Robert, 78, 128
McCain, Tec, 67–68
McREL. *See* Mid-continent Research
for Education and Learning
Mid-continent Research for
Education and Learning
(McREL), xvix, 32, 45, 87,
98, 156
Morrison, P., 125
Morrison, R., 125
Multicultural issues in science
education, 51–52
Multiple intelligences
pluralistic view of the mind, 80,
82*fig.*, 83–86*fig.*, 131–132, 210
Sand Patterns curriculum,
132, 147–149*fig.*

National Council for the
Social Studies, 50
National Research Council, xvii,
xviii, 49, 109
*National Science Education Standards
Project* (National Research
Council), xvii, xviii,
49, 109
National Science Teachers
Association (NSTA), 50, 155
A New Mind for the New Millenium
(Kiely and DiSanto), 177
New science principles
chaos theory and, xv–xvi
implications for assessing, 211
implications for curricula design,
211–212
implications for learning,
210–211
implications for science
education, xxii, 123
implications for teaching,
208–209
See also Dissipative structures;
Evolutionary biology;
Quantum mechanics; Self-
organization
Newton, Sir Isaac, xiv, 26, 156
See also Newtonian physics
Newtonian physics, vii, xiv, xv, xvi,
159–160*fig.*, 171*fig.*
defined, 215
vs. quantum mechanics,
191, 192
Nonlinear, defined, 215
NSTA. *See* National Science
Teachers Association
*NSTA Pathways to the Science
Standards* (Lowery), 28

O'Connor, Ken, 87
One Grain of Rice (Demi), 77

Paradoxes
simplicity to complexity and, 4, 6
Patterns. *See* Fractals
Paul, Richard, 155
Peat, F. David, 24, 108
Period doubling
defined, 215
See also Bifurcations and
period doubling
Perspectives. *See* Fractals
Phase space, phase portraits
defined, 215–216
See also Strange attractors, phase
space, and phase portraits
Pinkerton, K., xx
Planck, Max, 191
Prigogine, Ilya, 78, 153, 173
Project 2061, xvii–xviii

Quantum mechanics, xiv, 123
accepting uncertainty, 197
application web
regarding, 205*fig.*
background and definitions
regarding, 191–192
brain-compatible classroom
changes, 206*fig.*
cooperative group roles, 198*fig.*
cooperative learning by teachers
and students, 193,
194–195*fig*, 196, 196*fig*,
198*fig.*
defined, 215
develop and nurture
relationships, 193, 196,
196*fig.*, 198*fig.*
focus on energy, not things,
199–200
implications for science
education, xxii, 210
importance of individual *vs.*
system paradox, 200
*A Microscopic View of Pond/Creek
Water* lesson plan,
194–195*figs.*
Quantum Alternatives lesson plan,
201–204
real *vs.* imaginary time
paradox, 200
science group roles, 196*fig.*
space and time variables, 192
uncertainty principle and, 191
vs. Newtonian physics, 191
web sites regarding,
203–204
welcome the tension of
paradox, 200

Relativity, theory of, xiv
Round robin cooperative teaching
strategy, 193
"Rube Goldberg" devices
activities, 156

Ruelle, David, 61–62
Rutherford, F. James, vi,
xvii, 175, 196
Ryan, Terrence, 173, 176

Sadker, David, 50, 51
*Saving Our Students, Saving Our
Schools* (Barr and Parrett), 52
Science education
brain-based learning theory,
vii–ix, xviii–xx
change in metaphors, xv
chaos theory and the new
sciences, vii, xv–xvi
*National Science Education
Standards
Project*, xviii
new science principles
applications to, 123
old *vs.* new science, xiv
process-oriented science
curriculum shift,
ix, xviii
Project 2061, xvii–xviii
purpose of, vi
reform in, vii, xvi–vii
today's problems, vi
See also Bifurcations and period
doubling; Chaos theory;
Dissipative structures;
Evolutionary biology;
Fractals; Iteration; Quantum
mechanics; Self-
organization; Sensitive
dependence on initial
conditions; Strange
attractors, phase space, and
phase portraits; Turbulence
Science for All Americans
(Rutherford and Ahlgren),
vi, xvii, 175, 196
Science for All Cultures
(Carey), 50
Seattle, Chief, 188*fig.*
Self-organization, 123
allowing for, 161–162
application web regarding,
171*fig.*
art history and scientific
discovery, 156, 161
background regarding, 152–153
brain-compatible classroom
changes, 172*fig.*
brain-compatible education
changes, 172*fig.*
The Burning Candle example, 154
community-centered education
and, 176, 210
defined, 215
dissipative structures and,
173, 174
generating and testing
hypotheses, 156

implications for science education, xxii, 208, 210
implications for science education, curricula design, 212
inquiry-based instruction technique, 155
Jabberwocky lesson plan, 162–163, 164–167*figs.*, 168–170
linear to nonlinear perspective change, 156
look for new forms, 156, 161
make connections, 153–155
natural selection and, 126–127
The Paper Cup That Would Not Burn example, 154–155
"Roller Coaster Physics" activity, 156, 159–160*fig.*
scientific method and, 155
scientific thinking *vs.* facts and definitions accumulation, 155–156
web sites regarding, 169–170
"Your Imagination Creation" activity, 156, 157–158*fig.*
Selye, Hans, 98
Sensitive dependence on initial conditions, 66
application web regarding, 58*fig.*
attention to details, 45, 46–48*fig.*, 49
background and definitions regarding, 44
brain-compatible classroom changes, 59*fig.*
butterfly effect concept, 44, 53
A Closer Look at Crystals lesson plan, 53–56
critical thinking skills development, 45, 49
cues, questions, and advance organizers techniques, 45
defined, 215
gender equity and diversity, 49–51
impact of changing demographics, 51–53
implications for science education, xxi, 209
Nature Patterns lesson plan, 45, 46–48*fig.*
sensitivity to unique dynamics, 49–51
snowflake example, 44, 57*fig.*
student diversity and accessibility, 49–50
teacher decisions' impact, 49
web sites regarding, 56
Shlain, Leonard, 98, 156
Slavin, Robert, 193
Static electricity lessons, 7, 10
Steinberger, Elizabeth, 109
Stephans, Joseph, 98
Stevens, Wallace, 212
Strange attractors, phase space, and phase portraits

application web regarding, 75*fig.*
background and definitions regarding, 60–62
brain-compatible classroom changes, 76*fig.*
classroom management variables, 68–69
Dancing Raisins lesson plan, 69, 70–71, 72*fig.*, 73
educational change process as strange attractor, 66
emotions role in learning, 66
freedom and flexibility importance, 67–68
guiding principles and values importance, 68–69
implications for science education, xxi, 207–208, 209
learning, brain, and memory relationship, 62
Lorenz attractor concept, 44, 61, 61*fig.*, 108
phase portraits, 66–67, 208
phase portraits, defined, 215
phase space, 61, 66–67, 208
phase space, defined, 215
productive habits of mind, 66
set invisible boundaries with expansion freedom, 66–67
strange attractors, defined, 215–216
student-teacher relationship importance, 69
teachers as strange attractors, 66
Toying With Toys lab as strange attractor, 63–65*fig.*
trust in the inherent order, 62, 66
web sites regarding, 74
Suchman, Richard, 155
Sylwester, Robert, 99
System, defined, 216

Theory of relativity, xiv
Title IX of the Education Amendments Act of 1972, 51
Turbulence
application web regarding, 120*fig.*
background and definitions regarding, 107–108
body needs and learning, 114
brain-compatible classroom changes, 121*fig.*
defined, 216
discipline, 113–114
expect the order to reemerge, 108–109
freedom to play and experiment, 109
implications for science education, xxi
intrinsic *vs.* extrinsic motivation, 113
let go of the control to keep it, 113–114

loosen up and have some fun, 109, 110–112*fig.*, 113
Magical Milk Colors lesson plan, 107–108, 114, 116–118, 119*fig.*
movement, energizers in learning situations, 114, 115*fig.*
order emerging from chaos, 108
social and ethical development of students, 107
student lack of motivation, 113
web sites regarding, 118

Universal theory, defined, 216
Unleashing the Power of Perceptual Change (Caine and Caine), xv
The Unschooled Mind (Gardner), 153–154

Venn diagram, 33*fig.*, 34, 132, 167*fig.*

Web sites
bifurcation and period doubling, 102
endangered species, 186
evolutionary biology, 137
fractals, 16
iterations, 39
quantum mechanics, 204
sensitive dependence on initial conditions, 39
strange attractors, phase space, and phase portraits, 74
turbulence, 118
Weiner, Jonathan, 126–127, 152
Wellman, B., 191
Wheatley, Margaret, 4, 5, 6, 60
adaptive organizations, 174
creative energy creating classroom order, 109
dissipative structures and, 174, 175
freedom to play and experiment, 109
information and evolution, 34–35
machine images boundaries, 178
morality, humanity, compassion focus of, 177
nurturing relationships, 196–197
principles and values of teachers importance, 69
self-organization focus of, 152, 174, 175
surprises and accompanying joy, 98
tension of paradoxes, 200
think global, act local concept, 132–133
trust in the inherent order, 62
world of process, not of things, 192
Windows on the Future: Education in the Age of Technology (Jukes and McCain), 67–68